cabinet
181 Wyckoff Street
Brooklyn NY 11217 USA
tel + 1 718 222 8434
fax + 1 718 222 3700
email info@cabinetmagazine.org
www.cabinetmagazine.org

Summer 2005, issue 18

Printed in Belgium by the patient perfectionists at Die Keure

Cabinet (USPS # 020-348, ISSN 1531-1430) is a quarterly magazine published by Immaterial Incorporated, 181 Wyckoff Street, Brooklyn, NY 11217. Periodicals Postage paid at Brooklyn, NY and additional mailing offices.

Postmaster:
Please send address changes to Cabinet, 181 Wyckoff Street, Brooklyn, NY 11217

Individual subscriptions
1 year (4 issues): US $28, Canada $34, Western Europe $36, Other $50
2 years (8 issues): US $52, Canada $64, Western Europe $68, Other $95

Please either send a check in US dollars made out to "Cabinet," or mail, fax, or email us your Visa/MC/AmEx/Discover information. Subscriptions also available online at www.cabinetmagazine.org or through Paypal (paypal@cabinetmagazine.org). For back issues, see the last page of this issue.

Institutional subscriptions
Institutions can subscribe through EBSCO or Swets, or through our website.

Advertising
Email advertising@cabinetmagazine.org or call + 1 718 222 8434.

Distribution
Email Laura Howard at laura@cabinetmagazine.org or call 718 636 9100 x107

Cabinet is available in the US and Canada through Big Top Newsstand Services, a division of the IPA. Big Top distributes via Ingram, IPD, Tower, Armadillo News, Small Changes, Last Gasp, Emma Marian, Cowley, Kent News, Media Solutions, The News Group, Newsways, Primary Sources, Total Circulation, Ubiquity, Newbury Comics, Disticor, Newsways, and Don Olson Distribution.
Call + 1 415 643 0161, fax + 1 415 643 2983, or email info@BigTopPubs.com.

Cabinet is available in Europe and elsewhere through Central Books, London.
Email: orders@centralbooks.com

Cabinet is available worldwide as a book (with ISBN) through D.A.P./ Distributed Art Publishers. Tel: + 1 212 627 1999, Email: dap@dapinc.com

Submissions
See www.cabinetmagazine.org or email submissions@cabinetmagazine.org.

Cabinet is a non-profit 501 (c) (3) magazine published by Immaterial Incorporated. Contributions to Cabinet are fully tax-deductible. Our survival is dependent on such contributions; please consider supporting us at whatever level you can. Donations of $25 or more will be acknowledged in the next possible issue. Donations above $250 will be acknowledged for four issues. Checks should be made out to "Cabinet." Please mark the envelope, "Rub your eyes before opening."

Cabinet wishes to thank the following visionary foundations and individuals for their support of our activities during 2005. Additionally, we will forever be indebted to the extraordinary contribution of the Flora Family Foundation from 1999 to 2004; without their generous support, this publication would not exist. Thanks also to the Andy Warhol Foundation for the Visual Arts for their two-year grant in 2003-2004. We would also like to acknowledge David Walentas/Two Trees for their generous donation of an office in DUMBO, Brooklyn. All contact information remains unchanged.

$15,000
The Greenwall Foundation
The National Endowment for the Art

$10,000 - $14,999
Stina & Herant Katchadourian
The Peter Norton Family Foundation
The American Center Foundation

$5,000 - $9,999
The New York State Council on the Arts
Helen & Peter Bing
The Frankel Foundation

$3,000 or under
The New York City Department of Cultural Affairs
Steven Rand

$2,500
The Fifth Floor Foundation

$2,000 or under
Nick Debs
Terry Winters

$1,000 or under
Janine Antoni
The Milton and Sally Avery Arts Foundation
Walter Sculley
Debra Singer

$500 or under
The Dowd/Freundlich Calvert Giving Fund, Julia Meltzer

$250 or under
Monroe Denton, Sarah Feinstein, Friends of Jesse Kaufman

$100 or under
M.A. Armstrong, Caroline Berley, Katherine Carl, Elizabeth Casale, Walter Cotten, Jane Daye, Ellynne Dec, Spencer Finch, Emily Larned, Effie Phillips Martinez, Maureen McQuillan, Ariel Swartley

Erratum:
In an interview for "Psychocivilization and its Discontents," (Cabinet #2, Spring 2001), a profile of Dr. José Delgado, authors Magnus Bärtås and Fredrik Ekman cited a widely circulated quote purportedly drawn from Delagdo's congressional testimony on 24 February 1974. However, a Cabinet reader recently brought it to our attention that Delgado did not in fact testify before Congress on that date. The quote in question was actually a compilation of statements from Delgado's various publications, which were accurately cited in an article by Dr. Peter R. Breggins, "The Return of Lobotomy and Psychosurgery." It was this article that was presented to Congress on 24 February 1972 (not 1974 as stated in the article). We regret the error.

Cover: The coronation of Morten Holmefjord, Viceroy of Fusa. Photo Knut Egil Wang
Page 3: *Falls of Eternal Despair*, 1895, artist unknown. Preaching diagram accompanying a sermon by Methodist pastor Martin Wells Knapp published in 1901.
Back cover: Seal of the Kingdom of Fusa. Photo Ryann Cooley.

COLUMNS

MAIN

FICTIONAL STATES

AND

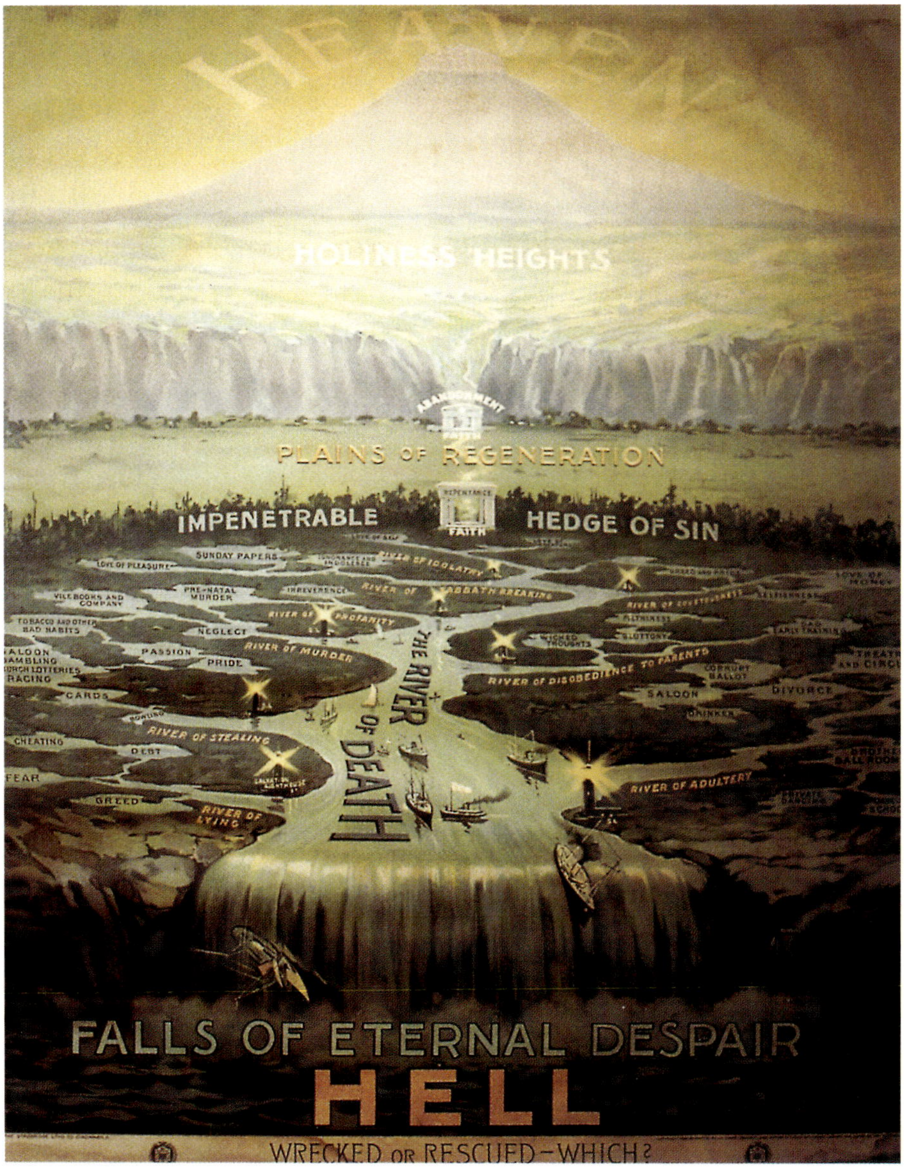
HOLINESS HEIGHTS
PLAINS OF REGENERATION
IMPENETRABLE
HEDGE OF SIN
FAITH
SUNDAY PAPERS
LOVE OF PLEASURE
RIVER OF IDOLATRY
VILE BOOKS AND COMPANY
PRE-NATAL MURDER
IRREVERENCE
RIVER OF SABBATH BREAKING
RIVER OF PROFANITY
TOBACCO AND OTHER BAD HABITS
NEGLECT
PASSION
PRIDE
RIVER OF MURDER
RACING
CARDS
RIVER OF STEALING
CHEATING
DEBT
FEAR
GREED
RIVER OF LYING
THE RIVER OF DEATH
WICKED THOUGHTS
GLUTTONY
RIVER OF DISOBEDIENCE TO PARENTS
CORRUPT BALLOT
SALOON
DIVORCE
DRINKER
RIVER OF ADULTERY
FALLS OF ETERNAL DESPAIR
HELL
WRECKED OR RESCUED—WHICH?

Sasha Archibald is an associate editor of *Cabinet*.

John Bear, an educational author, has researched diploma mills for thirty years. He regularly gives expert witness testimony in diploma mill trials. He is co-author, with Allen Ezell, of *Degree Mills: The Billion-Dollar Industry That Has Sold Over a Million Fake Diplomas* (Prometheus Books, 2005).

Robert Blackson is the curator of the Reg Vardy Gallery at the University of Sunderland, UK. In 2004 he curated "We Could Have Invited Everyone," an exhibition researching the formation of independent principalities, micronations, and secret societies.

William Bryk, a columnist for *The New York Sun*, lives in Manhattan.

Sasha Chavchavadze is an artist working on "The Museum of Matches," an interdisciplinary project including installations and a book. She had a recent solo exhibit at the Kentler International Drawing Space in Brooklyn.

Mark Dery is a cultural critic. The author of *Escape Velocity: Cyberculture at the End of the Century* (Grove press, 1997) and *The Pyrotechnic Insanitarium: American Culture on the Brink* (Grove press, 1999), he is at work on "Don Henley Must Die," a series of essays on the cultural psyche of Southern California, specifically the badlands and borderlands of San Diego, where he grew up. He teaches at New York University in the Department of Journalism. He can be reached at <markdery@optonline.net>

Allen Ezell worked for the FBI for thirty-five years (he is now retired). He founded and headed the agency's "DipScam" diploma mill task force.

Charles Green is Associate Professor of Contemporary Art at the University of Melbourne and Adjunct Senior Curator of 21st Century Art at the National Gallery of Victoria. His books include *The Third Hand: Artist Collaborations from Conceptualism to Postmodernism* (University of Minnesota Press, 2001). He is an artist and since 1989 has worked in collaboration with Lyndell Brown. He is a contributing editor of *Cabinet*.

Invertebrate is a group formed in 2000 who come together in pursuit of common aims and often in a published format. Most recently they have produced "THEM!" – a new movie script where 10 leading fictional mad scientists are forced into communication with one another, published by the Medical Research Council, 2004.

Craig Kalpakjian is an artist based in New York. See <www.kalpakjian.com>

David Levi Strauss is the author of *Between the Eyes: Essays on Photography & Politics*, with an introduction by John Berger (Aperture, 2003), *The Fighting Is a Dance, Too*, on the works of Leon Golub and Nancy Spero (Roth Horowitz, 2000), *Between Dog & Wolf: Essays on Art & Politics* (Autonomedia, 1999), and *Broken Wings: The Legacy of Landmines* (Greenville Museum of Art, 1997). He received a Guggenheim fellowship for 2003-04 to write his next book on how and why we believe photographic images.

Brian McMullen encourages *Cabinet*'s shier potential Enemies to come forward without further hesitation. For details, see the back cover of the previous issue.

Glexis Novoa is an artist based in Miami.

George Pendle has written for the *Times* (London), *The Sunday Times*, *The Financial Times*, and *frieze*. His first book, *Strange Angel: The Otherworldly Life of Rocket Scientist John Whiteside Parsons*, was published by Harcourt in February 2005.

Elizabeth Pilliod is an art historian and writer living in Princeton, NJ. She is the author of *Pontormo, Bronzino, Allori: A Genealogy of Florentine Art* (Yale University Press, 2001) and is finishing a book on Pontormo's *Diary* for the University of Chicago Press.

Patrick Pound is a Melbourne-based artist. He is represented by GRANTPIRRIE Gallery in Sydney, Hamish McKay Gallery in Wellington, New Zealand, and Anna Bibby Gallery in Auckland, New Zealand, with whom he has an exhibition in August.

Bonnie and Roger Riga are philatelists who specialize in "cinderella" stamps. Before forming their business, Rigastamps, in 1982, both had collected stamps since childhood. They sell items online at: <http://pricelist.rigastamps.com> and provide a free reference resource at: <http://www.cinderellas.info>.

Lynne Roberts-Goodwin is a Sydney- based photographic artist. Her work has been the subject of solo exhibitions and associated publications in New York, Los Angeles, London, Paris, the United Arab Emirates, and Melbourne, and her latest Australia Council-funded project, "Disappearing Act," about the Frankincense Trail was shown in April 2005 at Sherman Galleries, Sydney.

Tal Schori is the manager of Storefront for Art and Architecture and a former editorial assistant at *Cabinet*. He lives in Brooklyn.

Cecilia Sjöholm is Associate Professor in Comparative Literature and teaches at the program of Aestetics at Södertörn University College, Sweden. Her books include *The Antigone Complex: Ethics and the Invention of Feminine Desire* (Stanford University Press, 2004) and *Kristeva and the Political* (Routledge, forthcoming).

Frances Stark is an artist and writer based in Los Angeles.

Michael Taussig is the author of numerous books, including *Shamanism, Colonialism, and the Wild Man: A Study in Terror and Healing* (University of Chicago Press, 1987), *The Nervous System* (Routledge, 1992), *Mimesis and Alterity: A Particular History of the Senses* (Routledge, 1993), *Defacement: Public Secrecy and the Labor of the Negative* (Stanford University Press, 1999), *Law in a Lawless Land* (The New Press, 2003), and *My Cocaine Museum* (University of Chicago Press, 2004). He is a professor of anthropology at Columbia University.

Christopher Turner is an editor at *Cabinet* and is currently writing a book, *Adventures in the Orgasmatron: How the Sexual Revolution Came to America* to be published by Farrar, Straus and Giroux.

Jonathan Ward is a record collector and writer living in Echo Park, Los Angeles. His previous examinations of undiscovered music appear online at Perfect Sound Forever (http://www.perfectsoundforever.com), and at bobvido.com, an ongoing project documenting a forgotten outsider musician.

Christine Wertheim is a faculty member of the School of Critical Studies at the California Institute of the Arts where she teaches writing, literature, and critical theory. Her most recent articles on art and aesthetics have appeared in *X-tra* and *Art Seminar*, an anthology forthcoming from Routledge. In 2004, she organized "Séance," a two-day conference at REDCAT on the conditions of language and narrative in contemporary writing. She is co-director of the Institute For Figuring.

Peter Lamborn Wilson is the author of many books, including *"Shower of Stars" Dream & Book: The Initiatic Dream in Sufism and Taoism* (Autonomedia, 1996), *Escape from the Nineteenth Century* (Autonomedia, 1998), and *Ploughing the Clouds: The Search for Irish Soma* (City Lights, 1999).

Tony Wood is an editor at *New Left Review*.

Shea Zellweger is the former Chairman of the Psychology Department at Mount Union College in Alliance, Ohio. His long-standing Logic Alphabet Project began with offhand insights in 1953, and developed into a fully-fledged notation in 1961-1962. It has evolved into patents in the United States, Canada, and Japan.

"Ingestion" is a column that explores cuisine, aesthetics, and philosophy. / Inventory" is an occasional column that features and sometimes examines a list, register, or catalogue. / "Colors" is a column in which a guest writer responds to a specific color assigned by the editors of *Cabinet*. / "Black Pyramid" is a new occasional column featuring Peter Lamborn Wilson on the poetics of esoterica.

INGESTION / PONTORMO'S *DIARY*

ELIZABETH PILLIOD

Pontormo's *Diary* is an intimate autograph manuscript of twenty-three pages, in which the artist records aspects of his daily existence from January 1554 to October 1556, just a few months before his death. Discovered at the beginning of the last century in the National Library at Florence, the diary likely survived due to the diminutive drawings in its margins. After listing what he ate, occasionally Pontormo would add, "and I began the figure that looks like this," drawing a line from the text to a tiny sketch of a contorted human figure. These sketches provide valuable information about Pontormo's final commission, the frescoes in the choir of San Lorenzo. The paintings, visionary and disturbing, were destroyed during an eighteenth-century remodeling of the church. It is against this backdrop that Pontormo's *Diary* was first interpreted.

Pontormo's detailed but terse account of food eaten, symptoms of illness, the weather, encounters with friends and other artists, and, most famously, his bowel movements, is unlike any other artist's diary. He also describes hiding from friends who came to call. Most remarkable are his comments about his own psychological states: he mentions feeling depressed, hopeless, irritated, and, when his young assistant Naldini stays out all night, desperately lonely. The *Diary* depicts an artist who was obsessed with his diet, body, and emotions, a melancholic who preferred solitude to social interaction. Moreover, the weirdness of Pontormo's last paintings was the product of this psyche. Thus the artist's own words, written in his own hand, matched an early twentieth-century idea that psychological imbalance is a precondition of creativity and genius. Pontormo's character was fixed, and he has, with few exceptions, been imagined a disturbed but gifted man ever since.

But perhaps there's another way to read the *Diary*. What if we were to compare it to other sixteenth-century reports on weather and everyday events in Florence; cookbooks, health guides, and dietary treatises, to name only a few of the published sources with which Pontormo would have been familiar? It seems that, rather than revealing his deviance from sixteenth-century norms, the *Diary* instead demonstrates that he was embedded in the popular culture of his time. For instance, a new interpretation (my own, in fact, gleaned over a decade's close study of contemporaneous writings) shows that Pontormo followed the notions of the Renaissance philosopher Marsilio Ficino in trying to manage his melancholy specifically to optimize his artistic inspiration. This suggests that Pontormo thought of painting as a lofty charge, one that could best be met by putting the body into a state most sensitive to divine intervention. It is this pursuit that is traced, in prose by turns prosaic, painful, and lively, in Pontormo's *Diary*.

The following excerpt from folios 75 and 76 of the original diary manuscript covers a period from early January to mid-October of 1554.

On the 7th of January 1554, on Sunday evening, I fell down and struck my shoulder and arm, and was in pain.

And I stayed at Bronzino's[1] house six days; then, went back home. I felt bad until Mardi Gras, which was on the 6th of February 1554.

On the 11th of March 1554, on Sunday morning, I ate lunch with Bronzino—chicken and veal—and felt well (it is true that I was in bed when he came for me at home. It was quite late and upon getting up I felt swollen and full. It was a very beautiful day). In the evening I ate a bit of roasted dry meat which made me thirsty.

Monday evening I ate a cabbage and an omelet.

Tuesday evening I ate one half of the head of a kid and soup.

Wednesday evening I had the other half, fried, and a pretty big helping of zibibbo grapes, and 5 quattrini of bread, and capers in salad.

Thursday morning I felt a dizziness that lasted all day; and even after [it passed] I still felt bad and my head was weak.

Thursday evening, a soup of good mutton and salad of goat's beard.

Friday evening, salad of goat's beard and two eggs in an omelet.

Saturday, fasted. Sunday evening, which was the evening of Palm Sunday, I ate a little boiled mutton and salad, and had to eat three quattrini of bread.

Monday evening after dinner I felt very lively and agreeable. I ate a salad of lettuce, a thin soup of good mutton and 4 quattrini of bread.

Tuesday evening I ate a salad of lettuce and an omelet.

Holy Wednesday: evening, 2 quattrini of almonds, and an omelet and some walnuts. And I did the figure that is above the head [of another figure].[2]

The Duchess came to San Lorenzo; the Duke came, too.

Thursday evening, a salad of lettuce and some caviar, and one egg.

Friday evening an omelet with fava beans, and a bit of caviar and 4 quattrini of bread.

Saturday I ate two eggs.

Sunday, which was Easter morning and the Feast of the Annunciation, I went to eat lunch with Bronzino. And I ate dinner there, too.

Monday evening I ate a salad that was of borage and a half-lemon, and 2 eggs in an omelet.

Tuesday evening I was all hoarse and ate a rosemary bread and an omelet and a salad and some dry figs.

Wednesday, fasted.

Thursday evening, a rosemary bread, an omelet of one egg and a salad and 4 quattrini of bread, in all.

Friday evening, salad, pea soup, and an omelet and 5 quattrini of bread.

Saturday, butter, salad, sugar, and an omelet.

On the 1st of April, Sunday, I ate lunch with Bronzino. And in the evening I did not eat dinner.

Monday evening I ate boiled bread with butter and an omelet and 2 ounces of torte.

Tuesday.

Wednesday.

Thursday.

Friday.

Saturday I went to the tavern: salad and omelet, and cheese, and I felt good.

Sunday I ate lunch and dinner with Bronzino.

Monday, a small boiled kidney of good lamb.

Tuesday 2 fried eggs and a salad.

Wednesday.

Thursday evening 4 quattrini of bread, a salad of the boiled lamb that was badly cooked.

On the 13th—Friday evening I ate cooked radicchio, 4 quattrini of bread and an omelet.

Saturday evening.

Sunday evening I ate boiled lamb meat and cooked salad and cheese.

Wednesday, the 23rd of May, I ate some meat.

Thursday, which was Corpus Domini, I ate lunch with Bronzino. I had some Greek wine, meat and fish. And in the evening an ounce of torte with not much meat, and with little appetite.

On the 2nd of June, Saturday evening, I got the chair, which costs 16 lire.

On the 9th of June 1554, Marco Moro began to prepare the walls and fill in the cracks in San Lorenzo.

On the 18th, the evening of the Feast of St. Luke, I began to sleep downstairs with the new mattress.

On the 19th of October I felt ill, that is, with a cold, and I could not clear my throat and with great effort—it took several evenings—that hard thing came out of my throat, like I had had other times. I don't know if this was because the weather had been beautiful for a while and I still ate well.

And on the same day I began to take care of myself a little and 30 ounces of bread lasted me 3 days, that is, 10 ounces at each meal, that is, one time a day; and I drank little. Before this, on the 16th of the same month, I bottled 6 barrels of Radda wine.

1 Abbreviated by Pontormo as "Bro." Agnolo Bronzino (1503-72) was Pontormo's premier pupil and court artist to the Medici.

2 A tiny drawing of a figure appears at this point in the margin.

Translation by Elizabeth Pilliod. With the exception of occasional dashes and the parentheses in the third paragraph, all punctuation has been added by the translator for clarity. Punctuation rules were not consistently applied in handwritten manuscripts in Renaissance Italy. Please note that the translation has remained faithful to the original manuscript in using letters and Arabic numerals interchangeably to indicate numbers.

Special thanks to Karl Larsson and Andreas Mangione whose book "Extract of Pontormo's *Diary*" first brought the sparse poetry of the diary to our attention.

opposite: Pontormo, *Supper at Emmaus* (detail), 1525.

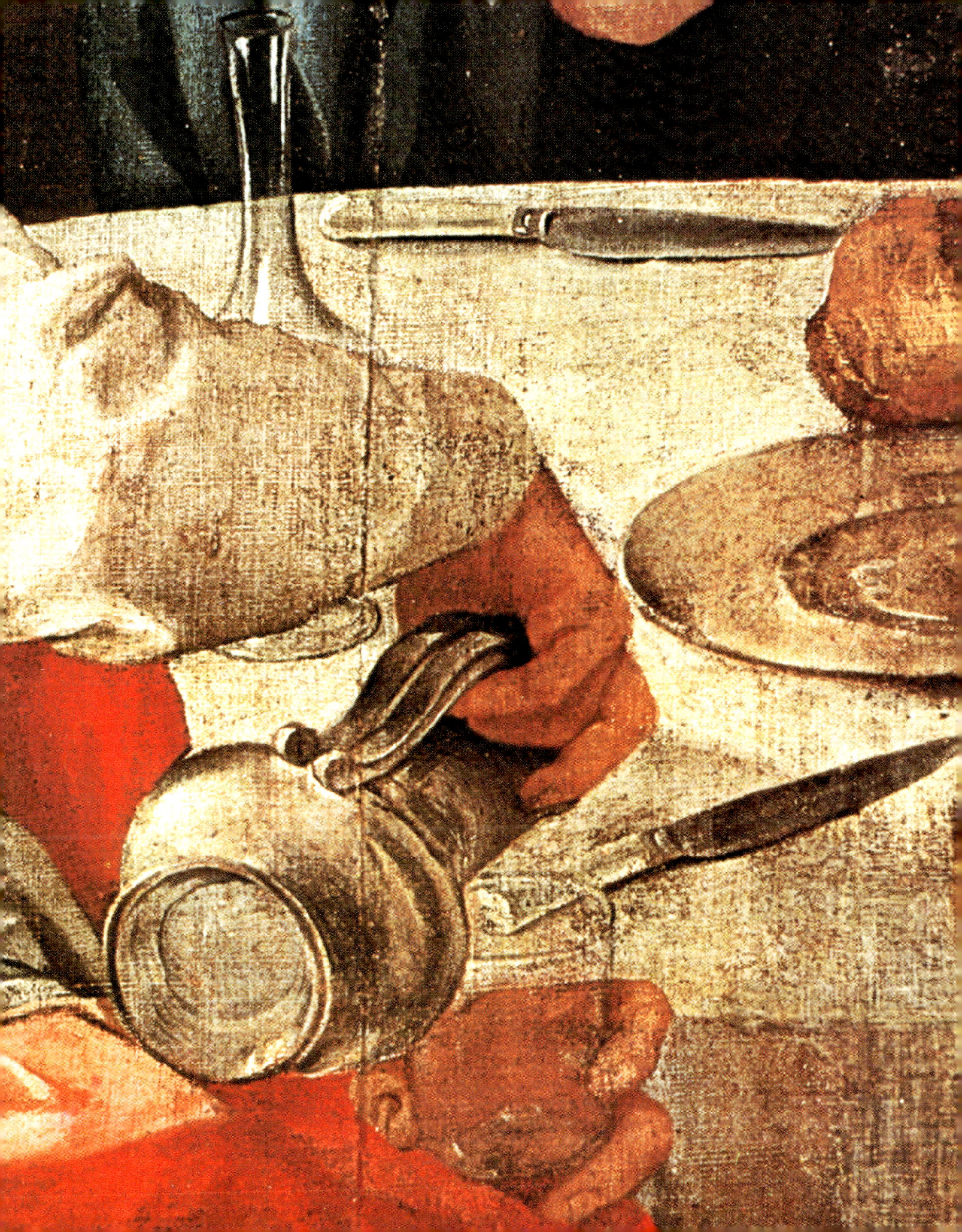

SCUM will kill all men who are not in the Men's Auxiliary of SCUM. Men in the Men's Auxiliary are those men who are working diligently to eliminate themselves, men who, regardless of their motives, do good, men who are playing ball with SCUM. A few examples of the men in the Men's Auxiliary are: men who kill men; biological scientists who are working on constructive programs, as opposed to biological warfare; journalists, writers, editors, publishers and producers who disseminate and promote ideas that will lead to the achievement of SCUM's goals; faggots, who by their shimmering, flaming example encourage other men to de"Man" themselves and, thereby, make themselves relatively inoffensive; men who consistently give things away - money, things, services; men who tell it like it is (So far not one ever has), who put women straight, who reveal the truth about themselves, who give the mindless male females correct sentences to parrot, who tell them a woman's primary goal in life should be to squash the male sex (To aid men in this endeavor SCUM will conduct Turd Sessions, at which every male present will give a speech beginning with the sentence: "I am a turd, a lowly, abject turd," then proceed to list all the ways in which he is so. His reward for so doing will be the opportunity to fraternize after the session for a whole, solid hour with the SCUM who will be present. Nice, clean-living male women will be invited to the sessions to help clarify any doubts and misunderstandings they may have about the male sex); makers and promoters of sex books and movies, etc., who are hastening the day when all that will be shown on the screen will be Suck and Fuck (Males, like the rats following the Pied Piper, will be lured by Pussy to their doom, will be overcome and submerged by and will eventually drown in the passive flesh that they are); drug pushers and advocates, who are hastening the dropping out of men. Being in the Men's Auxiliary is a necessary but not a sufficient condition for making SCUM's escape list; it's not enough to do good; to save their worthless asses men must also avoid evil. A few examples of the most obnoxious or harmful types are: rapists, politicians and all who are in their service (campaigners, members of political parties, etc.); lousy singers and musicians; Chairmen of Boards; Breadwinners; landlords; owners of greasy spoons and restaurants that play Musak; "Great Artists"; cheap pikers; cops; tycoons; scientists working on death and destruction programs or for private industry (practically all scientists); liars and phonies; disc jockies; men who ever intrude themselves in the slightest way on any strange female; real estate men; stock brokers; men who speak when they have nothing to say; men who loiter idly on the street and mar the landscape with their presence; double dealers; flim flam artists; litter bugs; plagiarizers; men who in the slightest way harm any female; all men in the advertising industry; dishonest writers, journalists, editors, publishers, etc.; censors on both the public and private level; all members of the armed forces, including draftees (LBJ and McNamara give orders, but servicemen carry them out) and particularly pilots (If the Bomb drops, LBJ won't drop it; a pilot will). In the case of a man whose behavior falls into both the good and bad categories, an overall subjective evaluation of him will be made to determine if his behavior is, on balance, good or bad.

INVENTORY / HOW TO JOIN THE MEN'S AUXILIARY

SASHA ARCHIBALD

"Life in this society being, at best, an utter bore and no aspect of society being at all relevant to women, there remains to civic-minded, responsible, thrill-seeking females only to overthrow the government, eliminate the money system, institute complete automation and destroy the male sex." Thus begins Valerie Solanas's 1967 SCUM Manifesto, a radical feminist, anarchist, and anti-male text Solanas mimeographed and distributed on the streets of New York City in 1968. SCUM, or the Society for Cutting Up Men, was the brainchild of a writer and playwright who, having first fled her home at age fifteen, and then her graduate psychology work at the University of Minnesota, supported herself in Greenwich Village with panhandling and prostitution. She's also remembered, of course, as the woman who shot Andy Warhol.

Solanas's manifesto builds on the premise that a man is an incomplete woman, the accidental result of an amputated chromosomal set. All of men's actions in the world are designed to ameliorate and conceal—or project on others—their deficiencies as non-women. Solanas goes on to indict money (without it, men couldn't retain women's company); lack of privacy (having no inner lives, men are blind to those of women); social conformity (difference exacerbates men's insecurity); philosophy (men's effort to call their sorry condition that of all humanity); as well as the more conventional sex and war, as all stemming from men's emotional, psychological, and intellectual inadequacies. Certain women are more indoctrinated by men's lies than others; these "male-females," as Solanas calls them, "too cowardly to face up to the hideous reality of what a man is, what Daddy is, who have cast their lot with the swine," fare no better by her pen.

SCUM was not, as Solanas clarified in a 1977 *Village Voice* interview, a real organization: "It's hypothetical. No, hypothetical is the wrong word. It's just a literary device. There's no organization called SCUM... It's not even me... I mean, I thought of it as a state of mind. In other words, women who think a certain way are in SCUM. Men who think a certain way are in the men's auxiliary of SCUM."[1] The SCUM Manifesto announces five major objectives: secure universal free transportation; "couple-bust" (heterosexual only); destroy "useless and harmful objects" such as "cars, store windows, 'Great Art,' etc."; flood the workforce with women who will then instigate the "fuck-up force," i.e., anarchist sabotage on a grand scale; and finally, kill all men except those in what she called the Men's Auxiliary (admission guidelines for which are reproduced on the preceding page.)

The guidelines typify the witty logorrhea of Solanas's prose, as well as her sometimes convoluted logic. One thing, however, immediately becomes clear: the men's auxiliary was not Solanas's concession to a few good men, but rather a designation for enemies inadvertently working in her favor. "Which men deserve to live?" is not her question so much as "How much evil does one tolerate in an ally?" The first criteria presented indicate types of men to be included in the Men's Auxiliary. However, "[b]eing in the Men's Auxiliary is a necessary but not sufficient condition for making SCUM's escape list." Solanas goes on to furnish a second set of criteria by which the safety afforded by inclusion is nullified. A drug dealer may be admitted to the Men's Auxiliary for his corroborative role in eliminating men by promoting lethal drug addiction. But, if he's a drug dealer in the habit of sitting on stoops and "mar[ring] the landscape" with his presence, he is no less an enemy to SCUM than any other man.

The Men's Auxiliary was a precarious unit of exemption, if it was one at all. In fact, the man Solanas invited to be president of SCUM was Warhol himself, prior to the shooting on 3 June 1968. Another man she intended to kill that day was her publisher, Maurice Girodias, who—for offering Solanas an advance to publish a novel based on the SCUM Manifesto—was surely also a member. Far from an insurance policy, the Men's Auxiliary is better understood as shorthand for the categorical instability of ally and archenemy in Solanas's scheme of things. As is logically appropriate, Solanas had to test her rule—all men are scum—by its exceptions, and found the rule held true.

1 Howard Smith, "Valerie Solanas Interview," *The Village Voice*, 25 July 1977. The interview took place several years after Solanas was released from her three-year jail term for "reckless assault with attempt to harm" artist Andy Warhol, art critic Mario Amaya, and Warhol's manager, Fred Hughes.

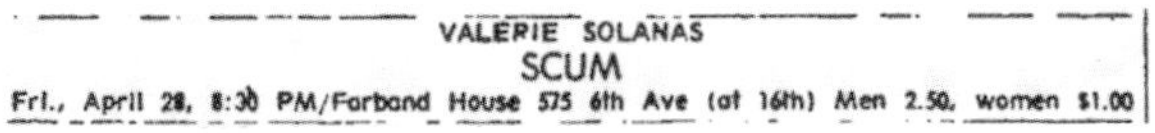
VALERIE SOLANAS
SCUM
Fri., April 28, 8:30 PM/Farband House 575 6th Ave (at 16th) Men 2.50, women $1.00

opposite: excerpt from pages 17 and 18 of the first edition of Valerie Solanas's SCUM Manifesto, a mimeograph handed out by Solanas in Greenwich Village in 1968. Courtesy Founding Collection, The Andy Warhol Museum, Pittsburgh.
above: SCUM advertisement in the classifieds of the 27 April 1967 issue of *The Village Voice*.

FRANCES STARK

There's an eight- or ten-foot telephone cord coming out of my laptop and curling into a heap on my beige melamine desktop; it has to travel an awkward distance in order to plug into the phone jack. I noticed when taking the recently-purchased cord out of its packaging that it was designated "ivory." It doesn't look ivory to me. I mean, I guess it's ivory the way so many neutral housewares are labeled "ivory," but it's not the ivory I have in mind. I want to make a monochrome painting here. I imagined my "Ivory" text as a cross between a do-it-yourself Robert Ryman painting (I hear kits are available in museum shops) and a Morandi composition of mostly off-white objects.

The cord is not plugged into the phone jack, but there are two things I previously culled from the Internet that I'd like to get out on the table now and be done with, because I want this to be a real monochrome and not some kind of calico juggling act of disparate references like I'm used to performing.

The first snippet isn't something I went fishing for. It just arrived by email in my virtual copy of the *New York Times*. It's an art review by Roberta Smith about an exhibition of ivory at the Metropolitan Museum of Art. Living in California, I instantly felt that this was a big deal that I was missing out on, and how on earth could I address Ivory for a New York–based publication and ignore the fact that this exhibition was taking place? If only I could see it, it might make a significant difference, or even blow my mind, but let's not get carried away. This'll do:

The flowering of ivory carving in the monasteries of the Middle Ages, equaled only by manuscript illumination, did not coincide by chance with the Crusades. Meanwhile, the number of elephants required to keep nineteenth-century Europe outfitted in billiard balls and piano-keys alone would make even the most unrepentant carnivores among us weep.

I also underlined the phrase "pure, useless delight"—a direction I'd prefer to head in, but before that, the other Internet finding has to do with several half-assed websites attributing the origin of the phrase "ivory tower" to a passage in the Bible where Solomon says about his beloved, "Thy neck is as a tower of ivory." It strikes me as utterly lame. Go in search of the root of a culturally complex pejorative and you find some empty biblical cheese; only later did I dig deeper to find that the writer Sainte-Beuve may have plucked it from the Bible and coined the term to criticize aesthetes like Nerval and Baudelaire. It still doesn't explain why the tower is ivory. But here's another clipping for you:

In 1851, when Louis Napoleon—whom the bourgeoisie had managed to install as president—dissolved the Second Republic in a coup d'état and established the Second Empire in its place, Baudelaire's former companions in Bohemia soured on politics once and for all. Withdrawing into what Sainte-Beuve derided as the "ivory tower" of a life devoted solely to art, writers like Flaubert and Nerval declared war on bourgeois society; this was the beginning of what Lionel Trilling eventually described as the self-perpetuating "adversary culture." But Baudelaire, who no longer viewed the world as being divided between bourgeois and Bohemian, but between bourgeois and Bohemian on the one hand, and true philosopher-artists on the other, would have no part of it. Trapped, if you will, between the "abyss" of Gautier's aesthetic separatism and the inauthentic "solid ground" of bourgeois vulgarity and do-gooder mediocrity, Baudelaire was a man forever on the verge.

Oh, did I say I wanted to make a monochrome painting here? I'm starting to think it's totally impossible. I make actual paintings too, but nobody really considers me a painter. Right now I'm working on some paintings and it's in that painting part of the painting that I want to be, rather than here with this clatter of associations and references. I don't think it would be stretching it to say my paintings are ivory in color. The surface of these paintings has been the only clear idea in my head when it comes to pondering the color ivory. All the baggage of ivory the material is just more noise having to do with colonialism and all kinds of social problems and guilt that doesn't interest me. And the baggage of ivory the tower? More interesting, sure, but too much clutter overrides the color.

Nobody really considers me a painter. In fact, I just recently applied for a tenure-track teaching job that falls under the heading Painting, and when I mentioned that to one of my former teachers, who is a painter known for his writing more than his painting, he said, "You applied for the Painting position? That's a long shot." This was followed by a little evil laugh as he punctuated our conversation by walking away. I may not be enjoying the view from the ivory tower any time soon.

The ivory-colored paintings I'm making have that hint of yellowish warmth that the phone cord does not, and a hint of surface malleability that the plastic of the cord does not. For reference, I uncovered an ivory-handled tool from the early twentieth century. It's not clear if it came from grandma's vanity or grandpa's workshed, but regardless, it's my only actual ivory referent in the house. The ivory part is well-handled on account of it being, well, a handle, and so it's well-worn and has some cracks that are quite dark with dirt, and some very yellowy grains. It's the porousness of the ivory that allows for the yellow, I think, or that's at least what happens when I'm painting. I apply the milk paint—casein—and then sand it, and in order to feel if it's smooth, I rub my hands across it and then the oil from my hands gets in there and it starts to get slightly buffed and ever so slightly yellowish here and there, and I'm sure you want to keep your finger-oils out of paintings, but I can't resist. Strictly speaking, ivory has been assigned to me—not something I can hide from you, or myself. But the thing is, I have an aesthetic weakness for ivory-colored things and somewhere along the line I suprised myself by wondering if it wasn't too close to my aesthetic to be written about responsibly, as if

opposite: Bleached peacock feather. Photo Ryann Cooley

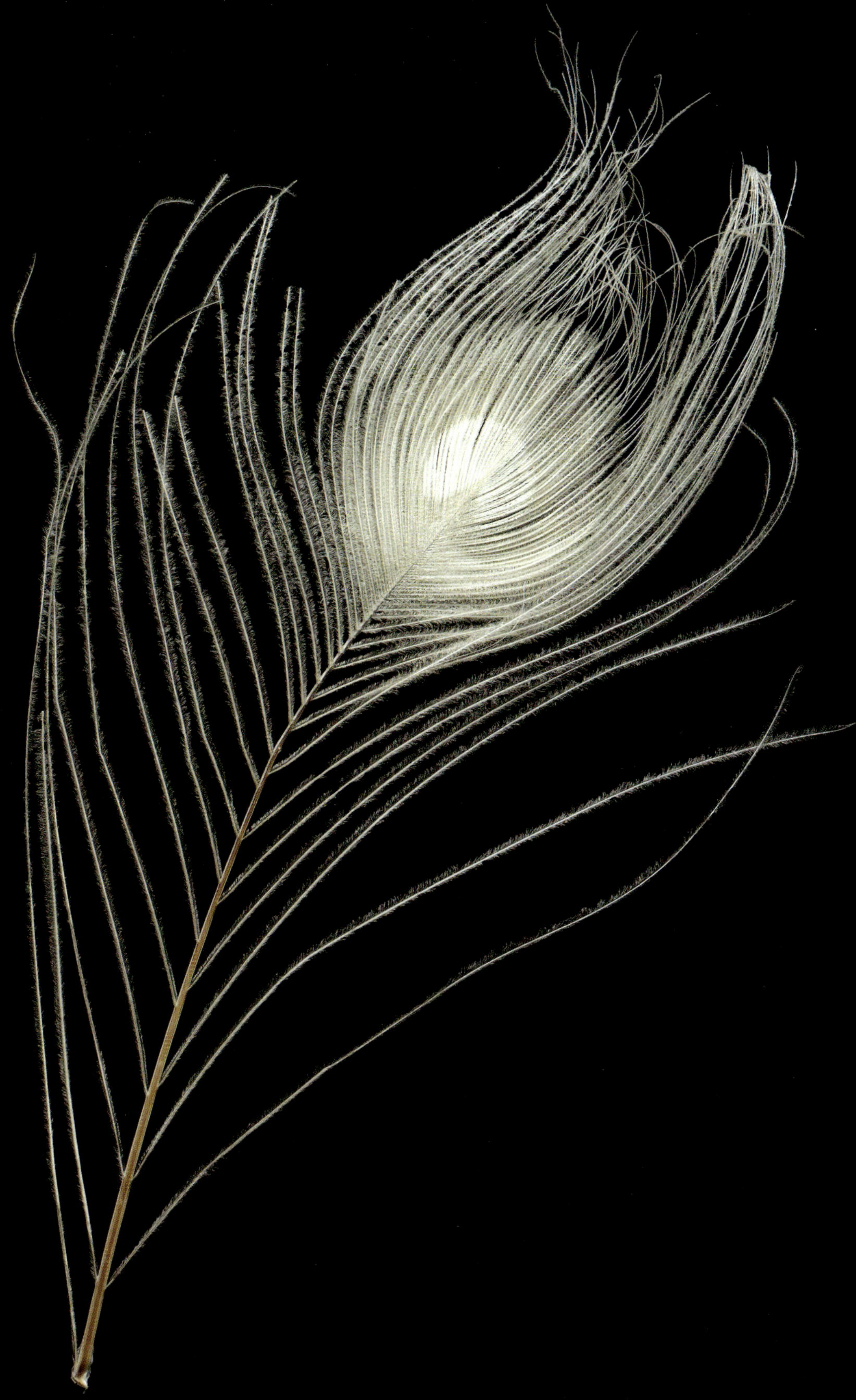

I'm not allowed to have a personal aesthetic. Now, I wonder where I ever picked up an idea like that? I don't like the way such a vague notion like writing responsibly can just pop up out of nowhere completely unwarrented and sully the mood with do-gooderisms and mediocrity. It's as irrelevant as Solomon's "thy neck is as a tower of ivory" is to the state of seclusion or separation from the ordinary world and the harsh realities of life.

I probably should retreat to the Ivory Tower, but I don't think the view is that great. Surely I'd have less time to lie around the house looking at and thinking about my stuff. This includes, of course, my ivory-colored things and the less yellowish and more simply off-whitish stuff too, like my paintings and the German porcelain and my collection of ivory-colored skirts that I never wear, or the broad, beautiful margins of *Franny and Zooey*, or all the bowls and candle-stick-holders and my Commes des Garçons wallet and my chrysanthemum brooch made out of sharks' teeth. This rag-tag list is not exactly how I pictured my Ivory Morandi. I told myself early on it should be a perfect crowd of individual articulations; matching, of course, but not so closely matching as to appear to be wearing uniforms. I thought I was so clever; "not so closely matching as to appear to be wearing uniforms." Needless to say, I didn't get close to meticulously depicting a series of things, let alone their subtle variations. That's not easy to do in writing, on account of how easy it is to stray from the purely visual. I guess that's why I didn't actually pull together an arrangement of vases and fabrics, because the translation would be too grueling. I wish my computer screen was ivory-colored, instead of this blue-white. And while I'm off-centered, I might as well mention that I can't stand the smell of Ivory soap, and I don't know how they can get away with calling it "99% pure" when it has such a strong smell. But back to the paintings.

There were some problems with the casein surfaces my assistant was working on, and it wasn't her fault but mine. It turned out that they had to be totally redone, so I took the opportunity to paint them myself this time. I got to enter into that pure ivory space for a couple of days, and it was a relief in a sense, but not as perfect as I had imagined it. Trying to sand something to perfection and get that hint of yellow and a hint of gloss is a lot less entrancing than I remember it being. It's like a form of futile dermabrasion. As I sanded, I wondered if I would ever break down and resurface my face with dermabrasion. And then I wondered if the porousness and the small blemishes on my panels weren't in fact a feature that made the surface more beautiful. I know that sounds corny; it reminds me of my mother explaining why it's okay if my skin isn't like ivory. Look at the golden hills, she would say, see how they look like soft lion paws and you want to pet them, but you know full well that if you go up in those hills they are patchy and scratchy and not soft to the touch at all. Okay, now this is getting too yellow. Let it be known I don't have experience with monochroming. My ivory paintings are ivory now, but I plan to break their current mouth-watering silence with imagery. Peacocks.

BLACK PYRAMID / MANIFESTO

PETER LAMBORN WILSON

1.

Some years ago in the Wisconsin pine barrens—actually the huge depression formed by long-ago disappearance of "Glacial Lake Wisconsin"—somewhere around Necedah (hometown of excommunicated-visionary-Catholic-cult theme park, and of the book *Wisconsin Death Trip*)—strange sunken humid basin like a ghost lake thick with unbreathable air

looking for some lost Indian effigy mounds, ourselves lost, car trouble, weird local people, suffocating heat. Along County Highway "ZZ" or something, flat & straight thru deserted pines & scrub, occasional ruin of a mobile home, then tracts of bottomland & miles of dry bog

suddenly way off to the left, back amongst dwarfish pines, we catch a glimpse of something—a black pyramid—maybe twenty or twenty-five feet high—dead black & featureless—out in the middle of nowhere—alone—no sign—no explanation—nothing.

Stop & park the car by weedy roadside—get out & walk back thru trees—no path—sweat—thorns & bugs—smell of baked putrescent vegetable matter & sweet pines, sense of increased & immeasurable gravity.

The pyramid turns out to be a flimsy structure covered with black tarpaper, revealing cheap plywood where paper has already begun to scale away in moist heat. The pyramid is surrounded by uncut weeds. No sign of life or occupancy. A door also covered with tarpaper is set flush into one face of the pyramid & locked with a rusty padlock. A breathless silence prevails—no cars are passing along the road—no birds—not even a sigh of breeze in the pines.

2.

John Toland, *The Knights of Jubilation* (Amsterdam 1708; facs. ed. Dublin, 1981)
Thos. Devyr, *The Odd Book of the Nineteenth Century, or "Chivalry" in Modern Days* (Brooklyn, NY, 1882)
Charles Fourier, *Sur la maçonnerie androgynique* (1824) (photocopy from *Oeuvres complètes*; Paris 1967)
R. Vaneighem, *The Heresy of the Free Spirit*
Thos. Paine, *The Druidic Order of Masonry* (pamphlet reprint, Berlin 1979)
M. Bakunin, *Über die Heilige Vehmgericht* (pamphlet reprint, Berlin 1979)
Gustav Landauer, *On Socialism* (Telos, 1978)
G. Bruno, *De magia* (photocopy of Latin text)
James Macpherson, *The Poems of Ossian* (Edinburgh, 1926)
Ali Shariati, *Javanmardi Shi'i* (pamphlet in Farsi, Tehran, 1960)
J. V. Andrae, *Fama fraternitatis* (reprint, Philadelphia, Rosycross Press, 1990)

Delia O. Kelley, *The Patrons of Husbandry (the Grange) and the Eleusinian Mysteries* (Fredonia, NY, 1891)
The Unabomber Manifesto
Malory, *Morte d'Arthur* (facs. of the Kelmscott Press ed. by Wm. Morris)
Wm. Blake, *Marriage of Heaven & Hell*
Susan Chen, *The City of Willows: the Tongs & the Anarchists in 1911* (Berkeley, University of California, 1964)
Tacitus, *Germania* (facs. of the John Aikin trans., London 1777)
Seamus Moran, *Wolfe Tone & the Whiteboys* (Belfast, 1921)
Novalis, *The Disciples at Saïs* (London, 1913)
Julian Baldick, *Imaginary Muslims: the Ovayssi Order*
The Bonnot Gang

3.
Page torn out of an old book of adventures, yellowing flaky acidic late-nineteenth-century paper: an engraving imitating Gustave Doré showing a hidden cove on some eighteenth-century rocky coast, an inlet too small for any but the skinniest sloop to slip inside on moonless murky nights

a snake of men costumed as freebooters winding up the beach behind hunchback parson with black lantern beneath the cavemouth frowning in the rain

each with a small oval cask on his shoulder

chiaroscuro stalagmitic grotto lit with lurid torches flickering with pitch—stacks of brandy barrels & chests of china tea

winding stairs cut in the rock lead up to the cliff above & open secretly into the crypt of a lonely deconsecrated church which (according to a fragment of text on the engraving's verso) serves as HDQ for the crew

& the graveyard said to be haunted by a specter that walks on foggy nights & moans & lugs a child's coffin on its shoulder.

4.
Rent a billboard & paint on it the emblem "Festina Lente" (dolphin & anchor) from the *Hypnerotomachia Poliphili*

old-fashioned crop-duster biplane skywriting the hieroglyph Eye of Horus

blow up cellphone tower in forest, leave behind Tarot card of the Falling Tower (XVI)

demand admission to Fort Knox dressed in mystic robes, etc. When refused, seek publicity (e.g., supermarket tabloids). Claim you want to carry out alchemical rite to cast spell of glamour over gold hoard so USA will go back on gold standard & thus undo work of evil magician Nixon in 1973

during WWII, English witches supposedly held sabbat on cliffs of Dover to repel Nazi magic & invasion. Modern witches could perform rituals against corporate demons—use black magic—seek publicity—try to goad the companies into open retaliation

perform exorcisms in Malls & other grotesque public spaces. If possible, use real priests.

a group dressed as medieval Catholic *penitenti* (in black pointy cone masks & black robes) meets to eat in fast food restaurants. When asked, they claim to be "doing penance for our sins by eating shit like this." When evicted, start flagellating each other, etc.

series of large banners of various shapes, sizes & materials, embroidered with hieroglyphs & emblems to protect certain places & things from subtle evil influences such as commercialization & trivialization, including

the green banner of Khezr

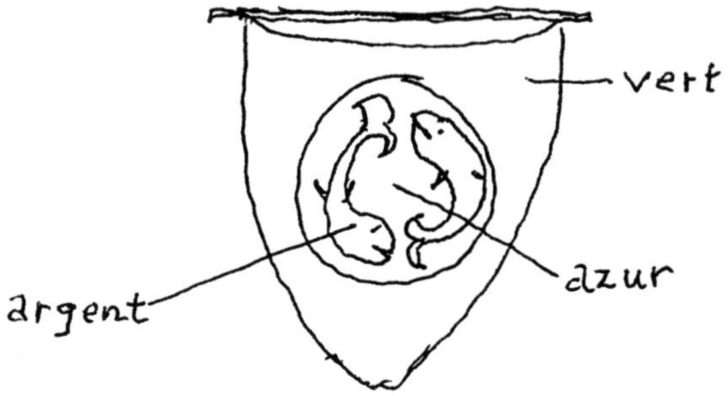

a banner against electromagnetic pollution (Indra's Thunderbolt)

a banner promoting silence (hieroglyph of *Harpocrates*)
banners to protect bodies of water (even small ones like puddles)—

flying from poles stuck in middle of river or pond, etc.
air-banners (against, e.g. pollution by noise, airplanes, etc.) carried by helium balloons (or fire balloons at night with luminescent banners).

5.
The Fatimid Order

Founded in New York City in 1911 as a fraternal organization by various Rosicrucians and Grand Orient Masons according to a charter provided by Justus Mathew Riley (1865-1926), a journalist and oriental travel writer (author of Yemen and its Saints*, NY: Linemann Publications, 1898). Riley claimed that in Sanaa in 1895 he was initiated into the sect of the Ismaili Hafezi Shi'ah, the Legitimate Pretenders to the Fatimid caliphal dynastic throne of Egypt.*

The Ismaili Caliphate (or "Anti-Caliphate") was devoted to the esoteric and heretical doctrines of the "Seveners" or Ismailis; it was centered in Cairo, and was famous for its tolerance, culture, and wealth. The dynasty was overthrown in 1171 AD by the great Sultan Saladin, who established the Ayyubid Dynasty.

According to the Charter, *the last living Fatimid Pretender, one Dawud ebn Suleiman, vanished after an abortive uprising in Yemen sometime in the early thirteenth century and was "translated to the Invisible World," like so many other Shi'ite Imams. Subsequently the sect flourished in Yemen and was headed by a succession of Chief Propagandists (*al-Da'i al-Mutlaq*) known under the title Shaykh al-Hafeziyya. The sect's esoteric teachings, including much cosmic neoplatonic and occult speculation in the style of the Brethren of Purity (q.v.) clearly owed much to the doctrines of other more dominant rival Ismaili groups such as the Tayebis or Bohras of Yemen and India, and the Nizaris or so-called "Assassins" of Alamut. Spiritual knowledge was transmitted through traditions and visions of the "Vanished Caliph" to the shaykhs and adepts of the order. A structure of seven levels of initiation was propounded, although the two highest levels were kept "empty," representing the Imam and his* Bab *or* "Gate." *Riley organized his own Fatimid Order with three degrees, "Knight," "Shaykh," and "Caliph."*

The F.O. founded several lodges, in Manhattan, Brooklyn, Poughkeepsie, and Rochester, and met regularly till around the time of the First World War, when all branches seems to have "gone inactive." It appears that Riley attempted to persuade the Grand Orient Rosicrucian Masons to adopt the F.O. as a degree in its own system (like the Shriners within American Grand Lodge Masonry) but apparently nothing came of this. It is not known whether Riley appointed a successor.

—from *Encyclopedia of American Fraternal Organizations* (New York: 1932; reprinted by AMS Press, 1968)

6.

Aleister Crowley around 1913 staged the "Rites of Eleusis" in a magickal chamber in London with the audience all dosed on mescaline & morphine. He judged it a failure because stupid people on drugs are still stupid. Like Artaud, or Bruno signaling desperately through the flames—but now it's all a made-for-TV movie & no one understands them. The key is to get rid of the audience.

Cornelius Agrippa hints at a kind of occult lunar telegraph whereby messages are sent somehow via the moon. Perhaps by dreams. The antenna could be an obelisk shaped to the mathematical dimensions of a single moonbeam, tipped with a large moonstone or opal, mounted on the back of a sphinx, inscribed with hieroglyphs for transmission, & left alone in forest or desert or mountain after appropriate ritual in the style of Marsilio Ficino with lunar correspondences—perfumes, tints, liquors, sigils, chants, etc.

An amusing & instructive incident put an end to Acèphale, the "headless" secret society founded by Bataille & Caillois. In order to transcend the trivial, they demanded that one member volunteer to be a human sacrifice. When no one stepped forward, the Order had to be disbanded.

7.

a rosicrucian gesture
a sign of distress
Count Cagliostro in a half-mask
has lost his address

locked up in our monads
like Nemo's bathysphere
je n'est un autre
with nothing to fear

hallucinogenic snuff
drips like green snot
the mask that nature wears
is everything we're not

MAIN

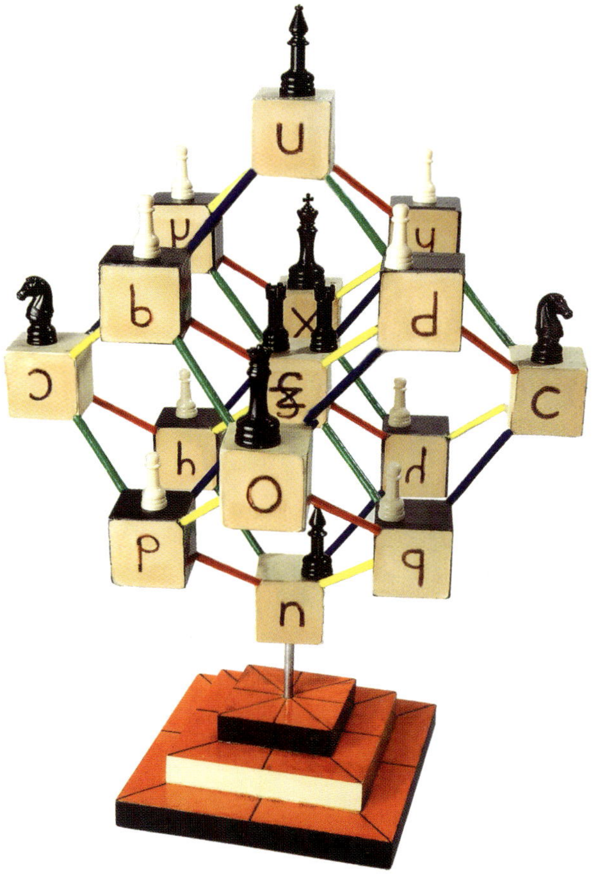

CRYSTAL CLEAR: AN INTERVIEW WITH SHEA ZELLWEGER

CHRISTINE WERTHEIM

In 1953, while working a hotel switchboard, a college graduate named Shea Zellweger began a journey of wonder and obsession that would eventually lead to the invention of a radically new notation for logic. From a basement in Ohio, guided literally by his dreams and his innate love of pattern, Zellweger developed an extraordinary visual system—called the "Logic Alphabet"—in which a group of specially designed letter-shapes can be manipulated like puzzles to reveal the geometric patterns underpinning logic. Indeed, Zellweger has built a series of physical models of his alphabet that recall the educational teaching toys, or "gifts," of Friedrich Fröbel, the great nineteenth-century founder of the Kindergarten movement. Just as Fröbel was deeply influenced by the study of crystal structures, which he believed could serve as the foundation for an entire educational framework, so Zellweger's Logic Alphabet is based on a crystal-like arrangement of its elements. Thus, where the traditional approach to logic is purely abstract, Zellweger's is geometric, making it amenable to visual play.

Like his notation, Zellweger's working methods are delightfully unconventional. While constituting a genuine research project in logic, his notebooks (made between 1953 and 1975) have remarkable visual appeal, passing through phases reminiscent of Russian Constructivism, outsider art, concrete poetry, and pop. These days we accept outsider artists, and are perhaps aware of outsider scientists, but Zellweger may be the first we could define as an outsider logician. Although he has worked on the Logic Alphabet for over fifty years, his professional life has not been spent in departments of philosophy or mathematics, but in psychology, mostly at Mount Union College in Ohio, from which he retired in 1993. After half a century of obscurity, Zellweger's work is starting to attract the attention of some mathematicians who believe it offers an exciting new perspective on logic. Christine Wertheim, co-director of the Institute For Figuring, has been studying Zellweger's work, and talked with him about his unorthodox approach.

The history of logic is very interesting, and has undergone many phases. In the Western world, it began about 2,500 years ago when the Greeks were developing a new form of civic structure in which debate and argumentation replaced allegiance to tradition as the major political tools. Slowly philosophers realized that, if laws were to be based on the outcome of arguments, an understanding of how valid

above: The Logical Garnet, a wooden model in which the symmetries of the full three-dimensional figure behind the Logic Alphabet can be seen.

arguments are actually constructed was crucial. Formal logic began when thinkers such as Aristotle started using simple diagrams, like the famous Logic Square, to study these structures. This was an amazing innovation which applied a mixture of algebra and geometry to the study of language, that is, language in its role as the medium of argumentation. During the Middle Ages, many thinkers dreamed of making a complete mathematical analysis of logic, a complete formal notation for describing arguments and their components. The Spanish nobleman Raymond Lull, a famous eleventh-century debaucher who later turned religious, was probably the first to have the idea, and in that sense he is considered by some as the great-great-grandfather of computing. However, the mathematization of logic did not get very far practically until the mid-nineteenth century when an Englishman named George Boole developed the first fully-fledged formal notation. The study of logic radically changed at this point. It's not dissimilar to the way that sixteenth- and seventeenth-century physicists revolutionized the study of motion by mathematizing it. In what way does your work relate to this innovation?

Since Boole's groundbreaking work, most logicians have looked to algebra for models of how to formalize logic, which is why it's now so abstract. But logic can also be modelled as a *geometric* system, and when you do this you get quite a different view because you see that it's not just a set of abstract symbols but is composed of a fascinating group of symmetric patterns. These patterns are the basis for my Logic Alphabet.

So that we can compare what you've done with the standard notations, can you give a layman's description of how logic is thought of today?

Let me make an analogy with arithmetic. In arithmetic we construct equations by combining numbers through operations such as addition, subtraction, multiplication, and division, symbolized by the signs +, –, x, and ÷. In logic you don't combine numbers, but propositions such as "cats have four legs" or "trees have leaves," which are symbolized by letters such as A, B, C, and so on. Just as numbers can be manipulated using arithmetic operations, so propositions can be manipulated by combining them through logical operators called *connectives.* The most common connectives are "and," "or," and "if…then…," which each have their own symbols. With these you can write such logical expressions as: [(If A then B) and A]. Then, just as in math you can use the laws of arithmetic to find the solutions to equations by reducing them to a simple value—for instance, the solution to the equation [((2+7) x 8)) ÷ (3 x 2)] is 12—so there are laws that enable us to find solutions to logical expressions. The "solution" to the example cited above is "B." This might seem very trivial, but modern computers are built around these kinds of operations. A computer is really just a great big logic-processing machine.

But in standard logic there are symbols for only three or four of the connectives. Yours has sixteen.

Why so many?

It's much like the difference between the Arabic and Roman numeral systems. The Romans had distinct symbols for 1, 5 and 10, that is, "I," "V," and "X," and for the higher numbers they added "L" for 50, "C" for 100, "D" for 500, and "M" for 1000. All other numerals were constructed from combinations of this idiosyncratic set. This means that the number "VIII" can't be interpreted by the place-based method we're familiar with—which would give 5111. Instead you have to see it as a sort of mini-equation that reads "5+1+1+1," i.e., 8. In this way Roman numerals were an ad hoc mixture of number-values and equations.

What's different about the Arabic system?

The Arabs (with help from India) settled on a consistent use of base ten, gave each number within this base its own symbol (the numerals 0, 1, 2, 3, 4, 5, 6, 7, 8, 9), and then imposed a macrostructure in which the units, tens, hundreds, and thousands were each given their own distinct columns or places. With this system you can more easily do arithmetic and uncover the patterns inherent in numbers.

Is your Logic Alphabet analogous to the Arabic numerals?

That's right. The standard notations are analogous to the Roman numerals and mine is like the Arabic system, because there are sixteen logical connectives in all, but most notations only use three or four, cobbling the others together from combinations of these few. In my notation, all sixteen are given equal prominence, and each has its own symbol, just as each of the units in the base-ten Arabic system has its own symbol.

And it's because you use all sixteen that your notation shows the geometry and symmetries underpinning logic?

Yes, you only see the symmetric patterns in the system when you look at the whole thing with all sixteen elements together. When you use only a few, you don't see the beautiful crystalline structures. My notation is designed to highlight these wonderful patterns, not obscure them, as most notations do.

But why do you need to show these patterns? Both people and computers are doing fine using only three or four connective symbols, and not having a clue about the lovely patterns hidden below. Why do you think it's so important to reveal these?

---

opposite top: The Logic Bug, a metal tool showing the symmetries of the Alphabet. By flipping and rotating the Bug we see how letters are transformed into each other.

bottom: The Flipstick, a wooden tool for playing with the symmetries of the Alphabet as a whole.

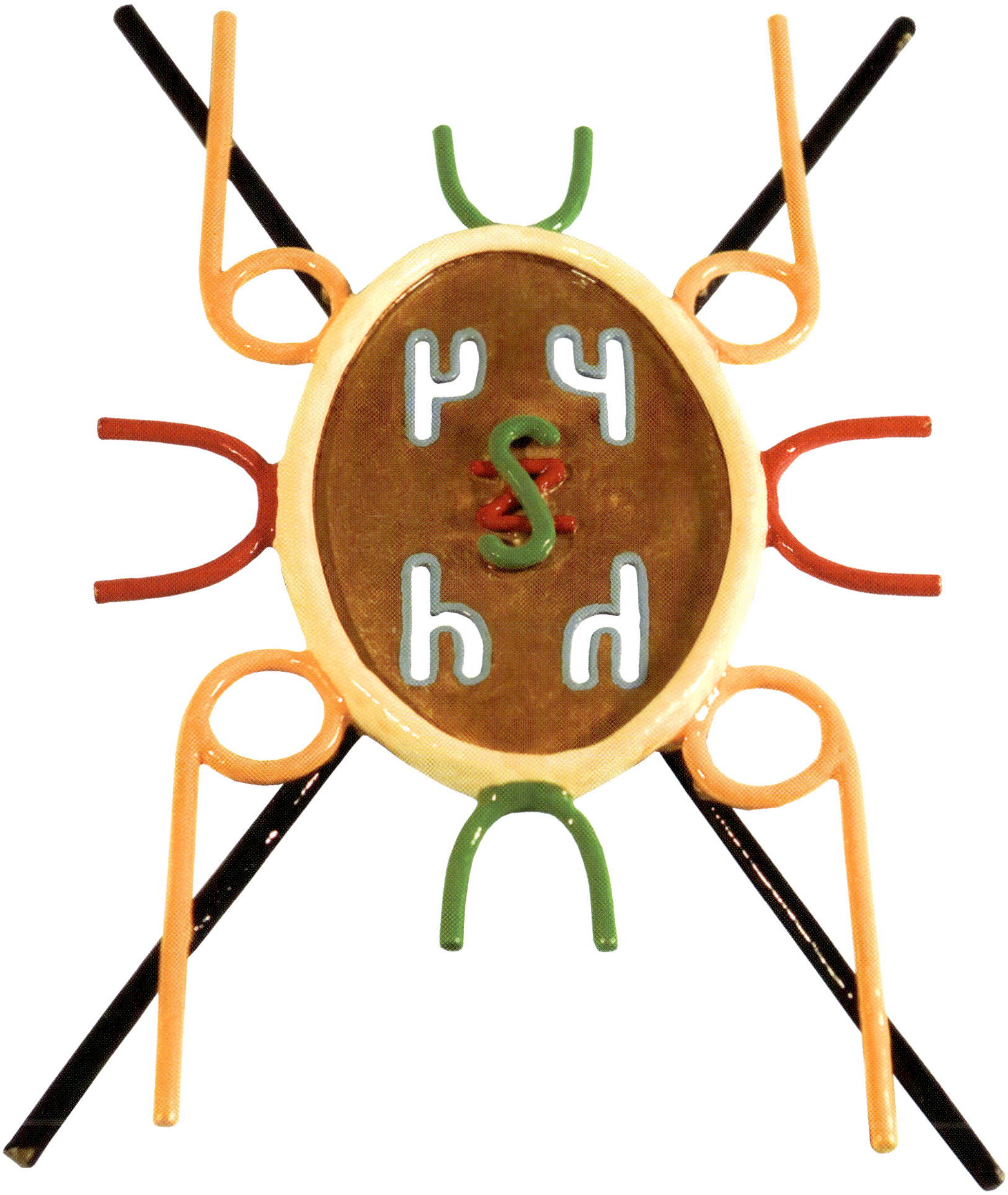

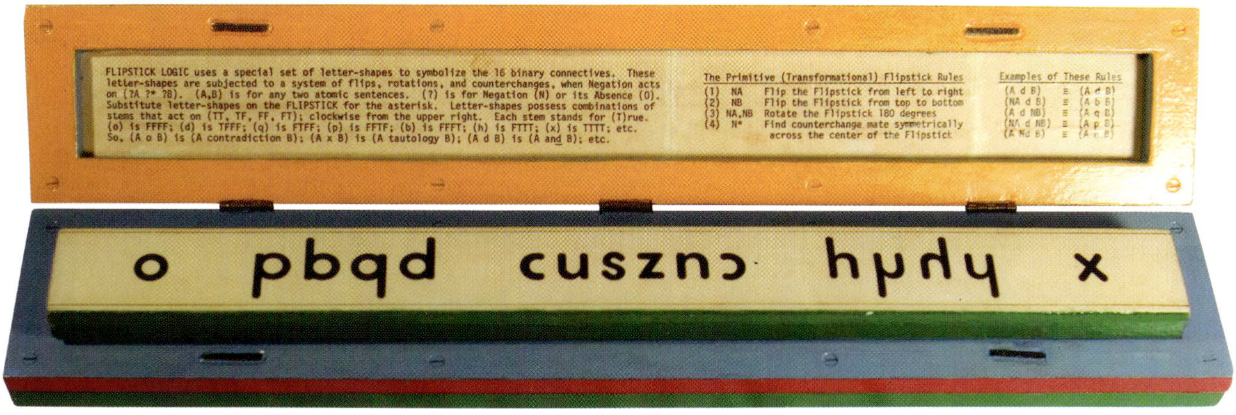
FLIPSTICK LOGIC uses a special set of letter-shapes to symbolize the 16 binary connectives. These letter-shapes are subjected to a system of flips, rotations, and counterchanges, when Negation acts on (?A ?* ?B). (A,B) is for any two atomic sentences. (?) is for Negation (N) or its Absence (O). Substitute letter-shapes on the FLIPSTICK for the asterisk. Letter-shapes possess combinations of stems that act on (TT, TF, FF, FT); clockwise from the upper right. Each stem stands for (T)rue. (o) is FFFF; (d) is TFFF; (q) is FTFF; (p) is FFTF; (b) is FFFT; (h) is FTTT; (x) is TTTT; etc. So, (A o B) is (A contradiction B); (A x B) is (A tautology B); (A d B) is (A and B); etc.
The Primitive (Transformational) Flipstick Rules
(1) NA Flip the Flipstick from left to right
(2) NB Flip the Flipstick from top to bottom
(3) NA,NB Rotate the Flipstick 180 degrees
(4) N* Find counterchange mate symmetrically across the center of the Flipstick
Examples of These Rules
(NA d B) ≡ (A b B)
(A d NB) ≡ (A q B)
(NA d NB) ≡ (A p B)
o pbqd
x

It's a bit like cladding a house in glass so you can see how it's actually built, rather than covering it all in plywood and stucco, which hide the underlying structure. To me, it's important not to just be able to *do* something, like driving a car. I also want to know how the thing works. In my notation, you could say that the design puts what's under the hood onto the dashboard, so you learn how the vehicle works while you're actually driving it. This makes the whole act of driving much less passive, and ultimately much more satisfying. I also like the fact that one's interaction with my notation is literally hands-on and physical, rather than just all in your head. Knowledge shouldn't be disconnected from the body. The body should be used as much as possible as a part of the means through which we acquire and store knowledge. Why can't logic be like that too?

Does this mean that your notation offers not just a new kind of logical notation, but a whole different mindset—a new perspective, really, on what logic is?

It is a different mindset, but what's really important is how this approach plays out in the teaching of logic. For most people, if they have encountered logic at all, it has probably seemed complicated, difficult, and full of abstract rules and symbols. My system is like a game whose simple and explicitly exposed structures enable you to easily understand the basic principles of logic, and even to begin doing some elementary constructions without learning any complicated rules. This is because the geometrical model on which it's based can easily be embodied in objects you can manipulate with your hands and eyes. In fact, you can just play with the system as an interesting set of patterns in its own right. By flipping and rotating the elements, you can explore the symmetries embedded in the system without seeing it as a way of modeling logic.

Your notation is specifically designed then to make these symmetry patterns tangible?

The Logic Alphabet is a very special kind of writing that uses sixteen letter-shaped symbols whose forms have been carefully designed to mimic the geometrical patterns underpinning logic. In many ways, it's more like a pictographic language than a phonetic or purely abstract one. However, the pictorial aspect doesn't just lie in the shapes of the individual symbols, but also in the relations between them. What is important is the way you can turn one letter-shape into another by flipping and rotating, and that you can literally see this when you do it.

Can you give me an example?

For instance the Logic Alphabet includes the symbols "d," "b," "q," and "p." If you flip the d-letter to the right, it turns into a "b." If you flip it upside-down it turns into a "q." If you do both together, it rotates into a "p." The other symbols in my Alphabet are also related by very specific symmetries which can be described by flips and rotations, and together all sixteen form a pattern you can have great fun with. But it's easier to grasp if you look at a three-dimensional model first.

You built some models specifically for this purpose, didn't you?

Yes. The Logic Alphabet is a script designed to be written on paper, so it's only in two dimensions, but the overall patterns it captures are actually in four dimensions. Of course, we can't build anything in four dimensions, but there is a three-dimensional version that neatly encapsulates the basic figures. In the 1970s, I built some models as teaching tools, which beginners can play with. In this way they become familiar with the symmetries and beautiful patterns, long before they are able to think about logic itself.

In this sense your whole approach is similar to the ideas developed by the great nineteenth- and early twentieth-century pedagogues Friedrich Fröbel and Maria Montessori, who founded the Kindergarten movement and the Montessori school system, respectively. Both believed that higher-level conceptual thought should be preceded by concrete hands-on play with geometric forms embodied in solid materials.

That's right. The whole way logic is taught today, as a system of purely abstract signs that only college-level students can understand, is completely backward. The Fröbel-Montessori method of acquainting children first with fundamental patterns, and then later putting letters and other symbols on these to show how the same forms are embodied in natural phenomena and geometric figures, is exactly right. I've just extended this methodology to logic. In fact, I think of myself as a Fröbelian logician rather than as an outsider, because I think of logical structures as figures of thought, figures that can be explored materially.

You said that the patterns underlying logic have a *crystalline* structure, and that it is the symmetries of this crystal that your notation allows us to see and play with. Can you explain this?

As I said when talking about the models, the Logic Alphabet is like a two-dimensional presentation of a higher-dimensional figure. The three-dimensional version of this figure is a rhombic dodecahedron, which is formed by the interpenetration of a cube and an octahedron. I call it the Logical Garnet because it looks like the gemstone garnet. The letter-shapes of the Logic Alphabet were specially designed

opposite top left: Half the Olivia story—using letters pbdq and hʯrlɥ—showing some of the "group" relations buried in the Garnet.
top right: Drawing of the Logical Garnet on photostated dot-grids used by Zellweger as mental aids.
bottom left: The dream of "c" swinging round to create its reverse "ɔ."
bottom right: Diagrams of group relations within the symmetries of the Logic Alphabet.

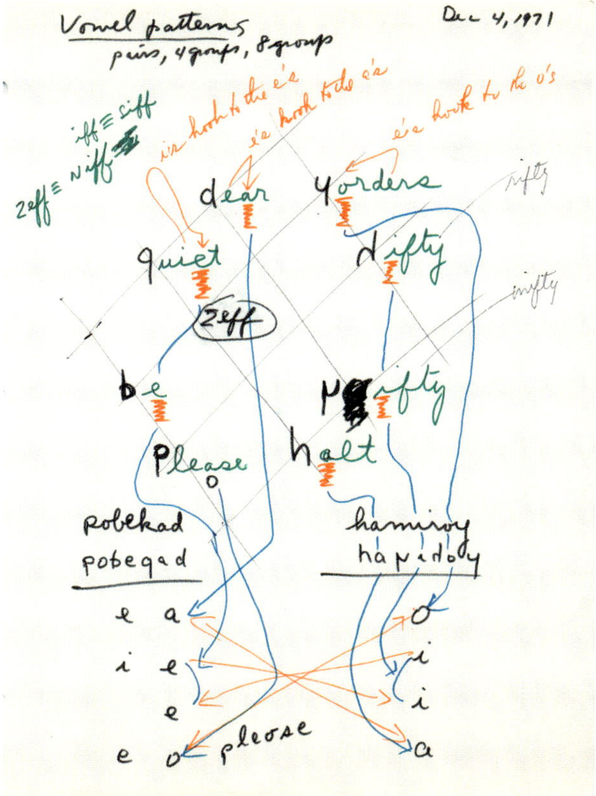
Vowel patterns
pairs, 4 groups, 8 groups
Dec 4, 1971
dear
quiet
Please
halt
please

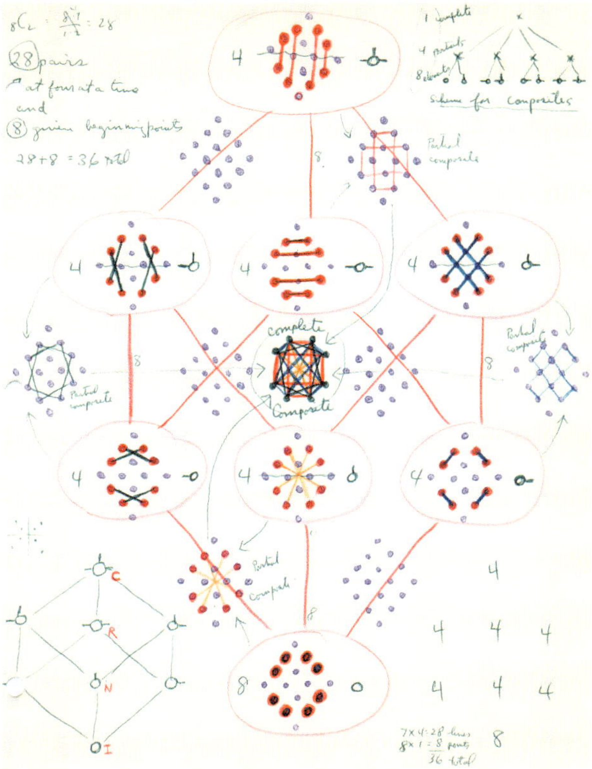
28 pairs
Complete
Composite
Partial composite
Scheme for composites

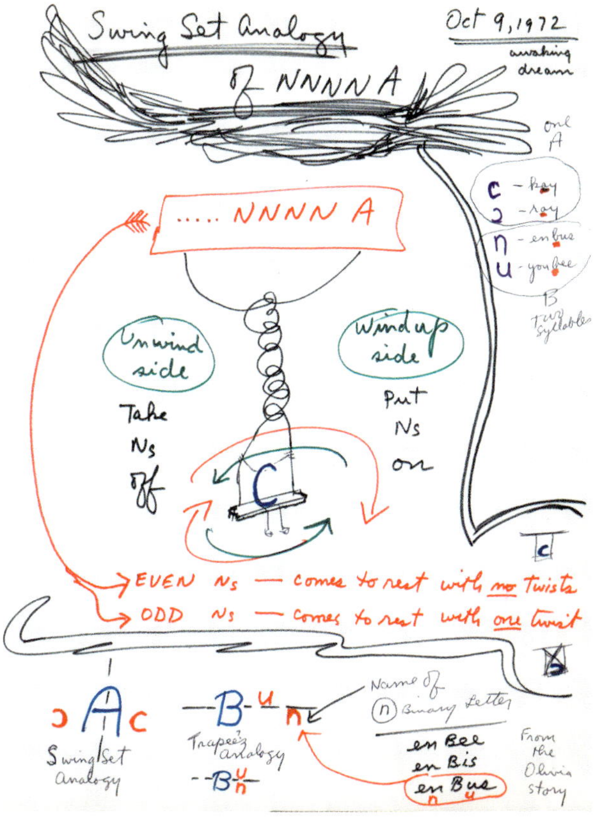
Swing Set Analogy
Oct 9, 1972
awaking dream
..... NNNN A
Unwind side
Take Ns off
Wind up side
Put Ns on
EVEN Ns — comes to rest with no twists
ODD Ns — comes to rest with one twist
Swing Set analogy
Trapeze analogy
Name of Binary Letter
en Bee
en Bis
en Bus
From the Olivia story

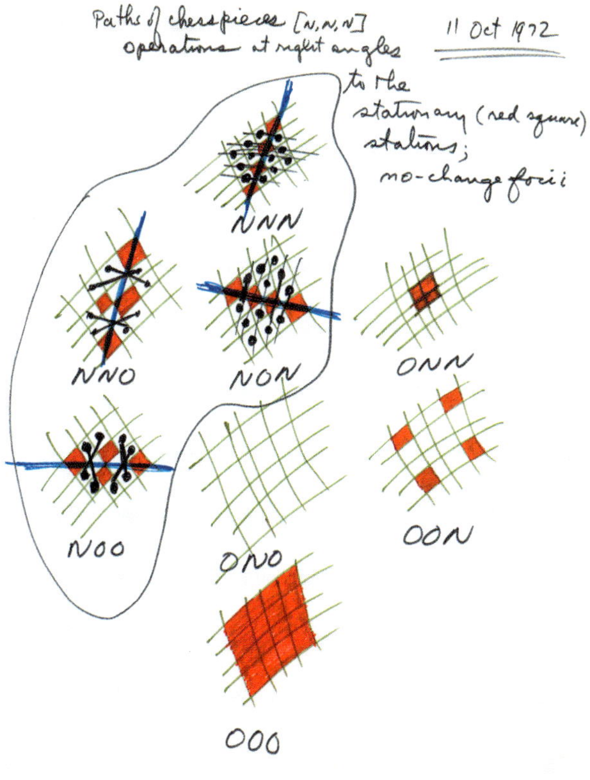
Paths of chesspieces [N,N,N]
operations at right angles
to the stationary (red square) stations;
no-change focii
11 Oct 1972
NNN
NNO
NON
ONN
NOO
ONO
OON
OOO

to make the symmetries embodied in this figure as easy to see as possible, and as easy to manipulate.

We don't normally think of mathematical and logic notations as works of "design." We mostly assume that when a new symbol is needed, someone just makes it up without much thought about its aesthetic qualities. At least, that's what I thought until I saw your work.

We take the Arabic idea of one numeral for each unit within the base for granted, but it was a profoundly creative act. Many other cultures had usable ways of symbolizing numbers, but none of them were as powerful as the Arabic invention. Once you realize that the logical connectives form a group of symmetry relations, you are almost inevitably led to the idea that these should be reflected in the shapes of the symbols themselves. This is what's missing in the standard notations.

In the Logic Alphabet, all sixteen connectives have their own names, and each has a letter-shape as its symbol. I believe you've devised a mnemonic to remember them by?

Yes, I call it the Olivia Story:

Act 1	olivia?					
Act 2	please	be	quiet,	dear.		
Act 3	cAn't	u Bee	stop	zatt	nBus	ɔAckett?
Act 4	halt,	µifty	ɹiftee	ɥorders.		
Act 5	eXit!					

It's a mini-drama with sixteen letters and five acts about a man who keeps being interrupted by his daughter's noisy play. At first he tries gently to persuade her to desist. When this fails he becomes increasingly exasperated, and winds up ordering her out of the room altogether, or leaving himself! I had to make up my own pronunciations for the words beginning with the four nonstandard letters—rackett, mifty, riftee, yorders—hence the increasing sense of chaos and linguistic breakdown as the narrative unfolds.

You have said that dreams played a part in your logical research. Could you explain this?

I've worked on this project a long time, so my mind keeps thinking about it, even when I'm doing other things. I never know when an idea will resolve itself, and when it does it can be at the oddest times, like in a faculty meeting. Once I woke up from a dream with an image of the letter "c" on a swing spinning round and round. It gave me the solution to a problem I was occupied with at the time.

You seem to have mostly been working alone...

I don't feel that I've ever really been alone. I have worked outside the fields of professional logic. I never taught it, nor even enrolled formally in any classes. I've pursued this thing in my spare time, and on occasional sabbaticals, but I was always able to find "soft spots," generous mathematicians who would from time to time listen to my ideas and give me help, especially the great geometer H. S. M. Coxeter, and my faculty colleague Glenn Clark.

In the 1970s, you took out patents on your ideas. Why did you do that?

It was really an end run. Up to the mid-1970s my papers always came back with rejection slips. So when I started making the models, I figured that a record of my diagrams in the patent office would be at least one place where my work could be anchored publicly. You can't patent ideas, such as logarithms, but you can get a patent on a slide rule, which is a material embodiment of them. My first patent was filed in October 1976, but not granted until June 1981. It was a long and torturous process. You have no idea!

Was it worth all the trouble?

Absolutely. The specification included in each patent notes that my models are an "introduction to the crystallography of logic." That was the first time that this expression, which links logic to its deep roots in symmetry, was used in print.

I believe your work is finally receiving some attention in the logical arena.

No, it isn't. Logicians aren't interested at all. Unless you speak in their language, they don't want to know about your work. However, there are a few mathematicians who have taken an interest. You can find references to their papers on my website at <www.logic-alphabet.net>.

Given how entrenched the logic world already is in its current notations, do you think your system, or something like it, will ever take off?

Something like it, a notation of the same geometrical type as the Logic Alphabet. Yes, absolutely. I think it is inevitable. This is Fröbel, Montessori, and Piaget all over again. Just give one generation of children the hands-on opportunity to play with models like mine in the early years of their cognitive development, and it could transform the way we do logic.

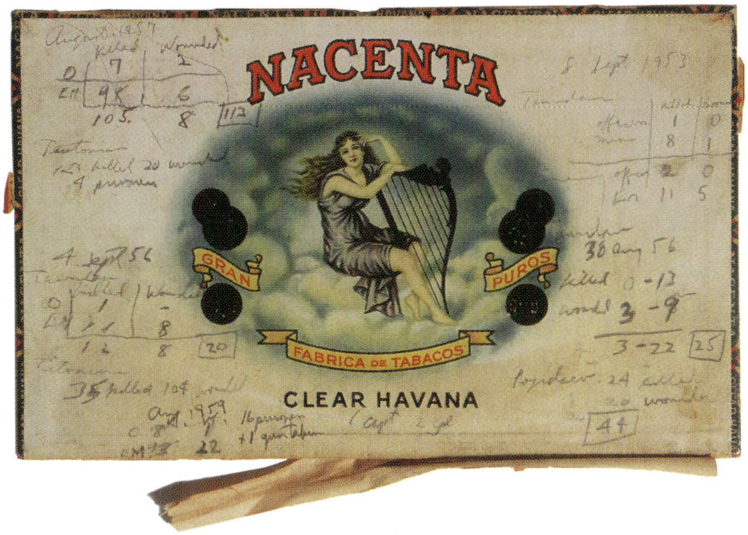

THE MATCH GAME

SASHA CHAVCHAVADZE

In Speak,Memory, *Vladimir Nabokov describes a match game he played as a child with an old general. He recalls with filmic precision the general's "thickset, uniform-encased body creaking slightly" as he placed the matches end-to-end saying, "This is a sea in calm weather." He changed them to a zigzag saying, "A stormy sea," and was abruptly called away with a "flustered grunt" to command the World War I Russian army in the Far East. Years later, after the war and a revolution, in a chance encounter on a bridge, Nabokov's father met the general again, dressed as a peasant, asking for a cigarette light. "What pleases me is the evolution of the match theme," Nabokov writes, "those magic ones he had shown me had been trifled with and mislaid, and his armies had also vanished, and everything had fallen through..."*

From: S. Chavchavadze
Sent: Sunday, October 06, 2002 1:00 PM
To: D. Chavchavadze
Subject: match game

Can you describe the match game you played when you were a boy? I started to think about it when I read about a match game in Nabokov's "Speak, Memory," so I wondered about your matches.

From: D. Chavchavadze
Sent: Sunday, October 06, 2002 4:48 PM
To: S. Chavchavadze
Subject: match game

The match game was invented by me in 1940. In those days there were kitchen matches that could be lit by almost anything, and different companies had different colored match heads. The matches represented individual soldiers, and had insignia of rank. The matches could be put in trenches or foxholes. If it was my turn I fired a BB gun at the enemy's matches, one shot for each match I had on the front. There was also artillery represented by rocks being lobbed at the enemy. Matches that were knocked down were "wounded" and given a stripe. If a match was lit, it was dead. I have never described this in writing. Would be glad to answer more questions.

My father, David, has decided to travel to Russia for the first time, and has invited me to join him since I have learned to speak Russian. It is 1974 and he goes to the Soviet Embassy in Washington to introduce himself and ask for a visa. He meets with an embassy official and says, "My name is David Chavchavadze. I worked for the CIA for thirty years and I would like to take my daughter to Russia." The official looks stricken, apparently briefly thinking that David is defecting, and disappears for a few minutes. When he returns he says "*Vsyo budyet normalno*" ("Everything will be normal").

David once told me that the only accurate depiction of a spy in the movies was the one by Richard Burton in *A Spy Who Came in from the Cold*, based on the le Carré novel. Unlike James Bond, a real spy has to be completely innocuous, to the point that when he walks into a restaurant nobody notices. Though David is a handsome man, he carries himself in an understated way, wearing a short raincoat and walking with a shuffle. Once I was riding the subway to Brooklyn, drinking a cup of coffee, when I looked up and saw David sitting across the subway car, carrying a small plastic bag, looking at me as if deciding whether to speak. Though retired from the CIA, he was doing contract work, interviewing Soviet émigrés living in Brighton Beach. The plastic bag was part of his cover, making him look like any other guy on the subway.

above: A Cuban cigar box top with match-game scoring notes made by the author's father throughout the 1950's. The box contained the original match game, including instructions, BB containers, flags, and a government-issue pen. Photo Kim Keever.

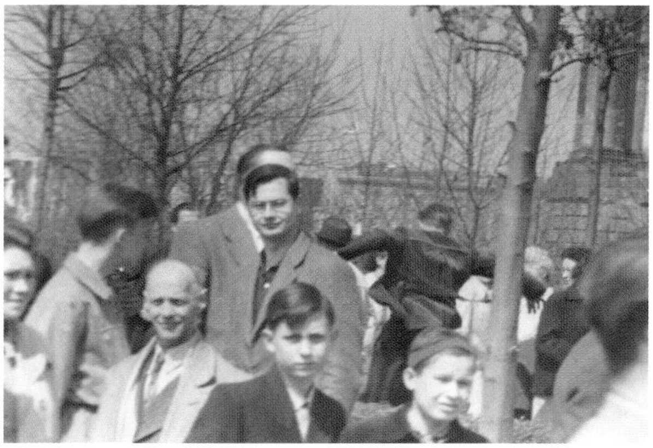

From: S. Chavchavadze
Sent: Monday, October 07, 2002 5:43
To: D. Chavchavadze
Subject: match game

How did you mark the insignia on the matches – with different colored paint? Or did you cut notches in them? Did you start with fresh matches each time, i.e. new battles, or was it the same war played endlessly with the same old soldiers? What colors were the match heads? These days parents would freak out. Kids don't have BB guns or play with matches.

When we flew to Moscow together, David's carry-on luggage was also plastic, a cheap variety of over-the-shoulder tourist bag, white with a logo. Our trip to Russia went smoothly. There was no sense of being followed or watched, though David was convinced that the flowers given to me by a young man in the Leningrad Hotel contained a microphone. He was clearly nervous about going to Russia for the first time; not only had he spent his career as an operative specializing in Soviet affairs, but his grandfather was a Romanov Grand Duke, executed by the Bolsheviks in 1919. David's parents fled Russia, never to return.

David was born in London in 1923, and raised as a Russian in exile. His mother had played with the Tsar's children, and was the same age as her cousin, Anastasia, whom she disliked. In her memoirs, she describes a fight she had with Anastasia: "...fists flew, hair was pulled and we scratched and we bit each other. All this went on in complete silence except for sounds of heavy breathing and crashing furniture.... We emerged disheveled, bleeding and covered with bruises. Oddly enough nothing was ever said to us by the grown-ups and nobody was scolded or punished."

David's grandfather was executed with his brother, Nicholas, a historian known for his socialist sympathies, whose book on Asian lepidoptera is cited by Vladimir Nabokov as inspiring his passion for butterflies. The brothers knew that revolution was inevitable, and had urged the Tsar to grant a full constitution. Hours before they were executed, the writer, Maxim Gorky, asked Lenin for a stay of execution based on Nicholas's socialist sympathies, which was granted. Gorky rushed to the Peter and Paul fortress, but arrived too late.

From: D. Chavchavadze
Sent: Tuesday, October 08, 2002 4:44 PM
To: S. Chavchavadze
Subject: match game

My army was Ohio blue tips, blue and light blue. Others were black and white, light blue and red, red and white. Everybody was free to make up their own insignia. Mine was red or black pencil, round lines for officers, chevrons for non-coms. The lower part of the match was for black wound stripes. Fresh matches were introduced to replace those killed, and the wounded were returned to duty in every new game. We did not bother to define wars. This is fun for me, but why all the interest in the match game?

Like many brilliant young men, David was recruited out of Yale into the CIA in 1950. Though his parents mourned the loss of their family members, they were surprisingly uncritical of socialism. They hated the Soviet regime but were sympathetic to the causes that drove the Revolution. They were pacifists, whose friends, American intellectuals like John dos Passos and Edmund Wilson, espoused socialism in the 1920s. Like many second-generation immigrants, David chose a different path from his parents. Always interested in the military as a child, he joined the Knickerbocker Grays, a military program for society boys, where he rose to the rank of colonel, and invented elaborate military games played with matchsticks.

In his memoir, *Crowns and Trenchcoats*, David recalls his initial difficulty adapting to life in the CIA. "After a couple of weeks my mind became compartmented.... There was always the terrible temptation to tell people interesting tidbits, or to hint that I knew something they did not. This would have been a violation of the Great Taboo, an unpardonable sin." Secrecy, he wrote, eventually became second nature to him, and he soon felt absolutely no temptation to reveal anything.

In the CIA, he was stationed in Berlin before the Wall. He describes the city with its four national demarcation

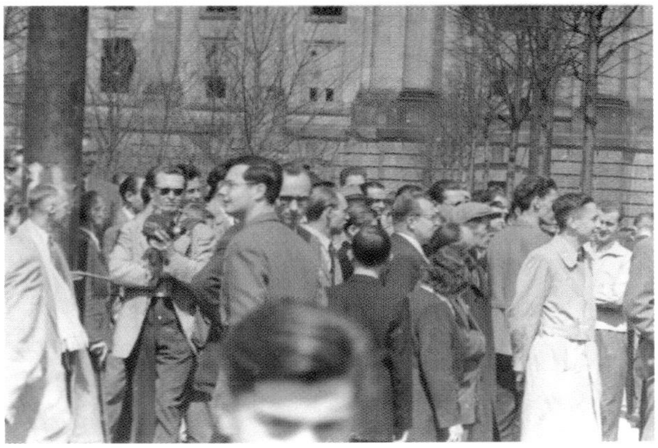

zones. The Soviet Sector was off-limits to the Americans, one of the first manifestations of the Cold War. He spent hours walking the streets, the most effective way of identifying enemy surveillance teams; if you walked long enough, it became clear who was following you. He and his colleagues would stroll in parks with their wives and children, a perfect cover while making contact with agents.

```
From: S. Chavchavadze
Sent: Wednesday, October 09, 2002 4:24 PM
To: D. Chavchavadze
Subject: match game

Wonderful descriptions about the matches. A
friend who grew up in Ohio said you could light
Ohio blue tips on your pants zipper or teeth! Do
the original matches still exist? I remember you
told me you played the game into your fifties
with your friends from the agency. I have been
trying to recreate the match game. Wooden matches
are hard to find. Cigar shops have a brand called
"Swan" made in Sweden - short with salmon pink
tips - and there are the long red-tipped super-
market variety. I'm always a bit nervous when
I buy them in bulk, especially these days of
heightened security.
```

David sits in a darkened room, the lit screen of a reading device in front of him, spending his final years poring over manuscripts, memoirs, and genealogies. He is almost blind, and without this special device, he cannot read at all. On one of my infrequent visits to Washington, he tells me he can hardly see me, that I am a blur. We are sitting, wedged awkwardly across from each other on two pillow-stuffed sofas in the house belonging to his third wife, Genia. I have many questions to ask him but feel somewhat constrained, sensing the same from him. It is as if the physicality of being in the same room with him after all these years is too much for both of us.

As a child I would visit David on weekends, though he was often overseas, sitting in hotel rooms around the world under aliases, directing the movements of his agents. He would show up periodically for short visits on his way back from clandestine trips. On one visit, he signed my scrapbook, "D. was here, alias the Crooked Sixpence or the Wooden Øre." In 1970, a Soviet defector stated that there was a mole in the CIA with a Russian name. Director James Jesus Angleton, whose close friend, Kim Philby, had recently been denounced as a spy, went on a witch hunt, implicating a number of people in the agency, including David, who took early retirement soon after.

Before I leave Washington, we exchange email addresses, something we have both just learned to do. When I get back to New York, I email him a question and, to my surprise, receive an immediate answer with great detail and a flourish of humorous anecdotes. We begin an almost daily communication; nothing heavy, mostly memories and stories, although once I ask him, "Have you really cared about me all these years?" to which he emails back an immediate assent. It was as if the sheer physicality of the older modes of communication, the voice of the telephone, and the hand of the letter, never worked. The great void of the Internet matched the silence that had grown up between us. Its lack of physicality, its detachment, almost clandestine in nature, enabled us to break the silence of forty-nine years.

```
From: D. Chavchavadze
Sent: October 24, 2004 5:04 p.m.
To: S. Chavchavadze
Subject: army found!

in a cigar box, I am happy to report - the entire
original Tauridan Army (blue and light blue
matches) and Cenraurian Army (red and white)
are in the box, along with accounts of battles,
a match-sized battle flag penetrated by several
BB holes, and lots of ammunition. I will present
them for your inspection whenever you appear.
```

opposite and above: David in Berlin, 1954. He spent hours walking the streets—the best way to identify the enemy. If you walked long enough, it became clear who was following you.
overleaf: A recreation of David's match game by the author, using simulated Ohio Blue Tips marked with insignia to represent the Tauridan Army. The game was often played on the beach. Photo Kim Keever

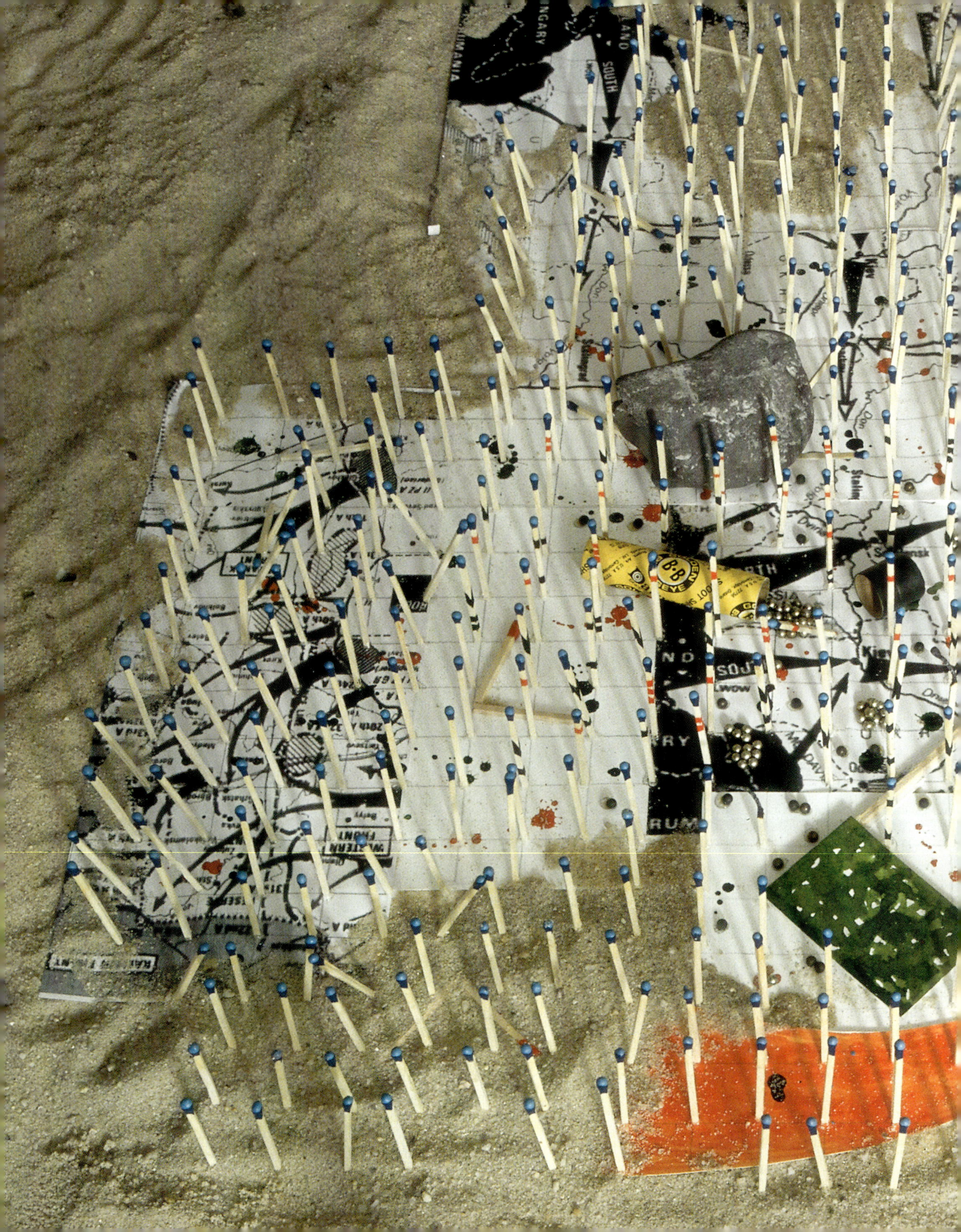

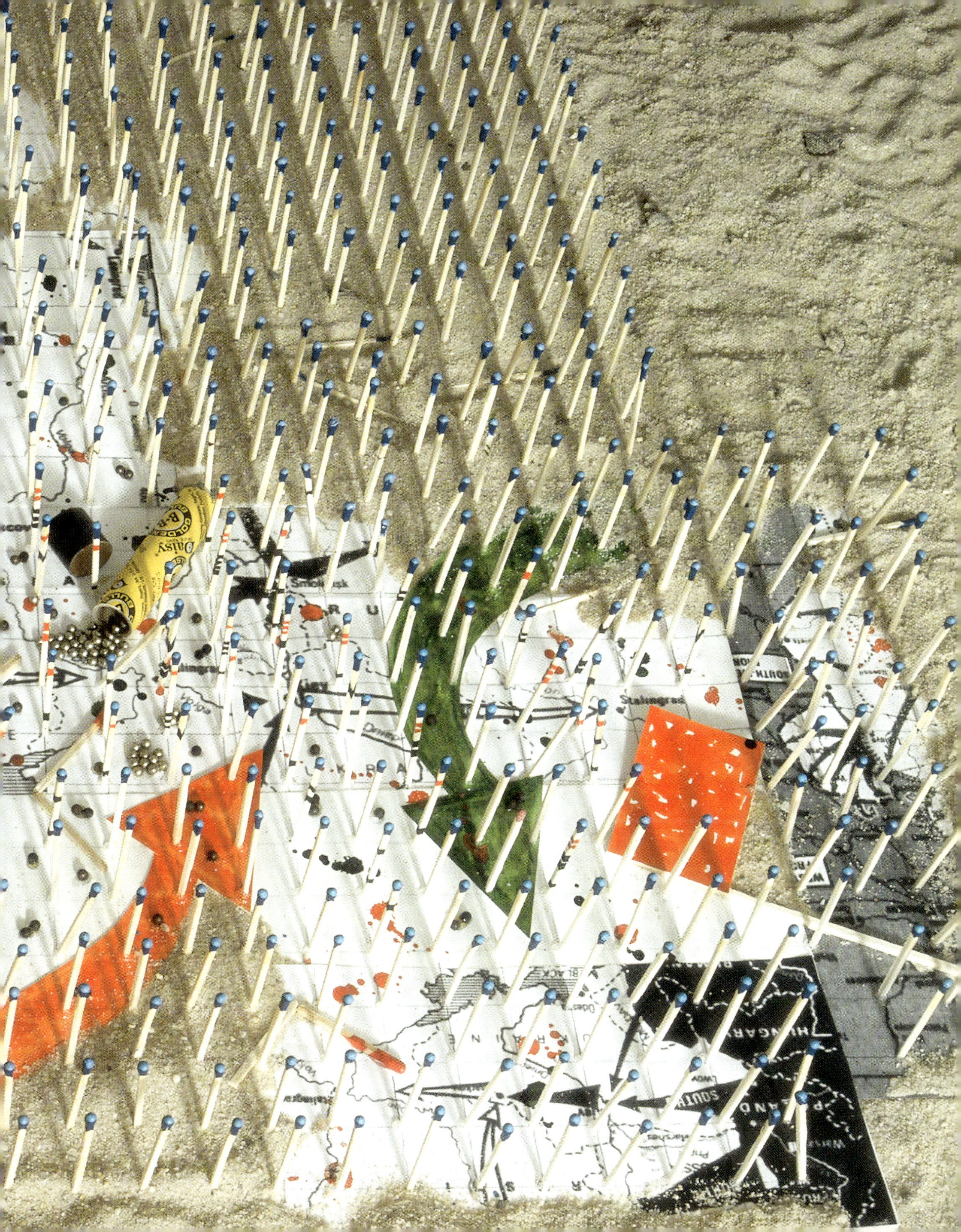

Daisy
Smolensk
Stalingrad

JONATHAN WARD

Query any grizzled music aficionado about them and you're likely to be greeted with a baffled stare. Flip through thousands of albums in thrift stores, yard sales, or used record shops and you're lucky if you find just one. Cold-call corporate archives and you still might hit a dead end. But they do exist. What are these rarities? Recordings of industrial musicals (also known as industrial shows): joyous, inspirational expressions of company life in song performed on stage and occasionally pressed on vinyl to be given to employees as souvenirs. These audio relics—today some 200 examples are preserved—belt out the last vestiges of presumed innocence in twentieth-century capitalism, recalling a time when many believed industry was benevolent, corporations knew best, and products were saviors.

Of course music has been attached to consumerism since the recording industry's dawn, from jingles to "sales marches" to full-length novelty tunes like "In My Merry Oldsmobile" or "Henry's Made a Lady out of Lizzie." It took the postwar boom for corporations to begin thinking really big; by the early 1950s, they were producing all-out, Broadway-style musicals, though not to sell products to the public, but rather to entertain the workforces at corporate conventions and galas. *Give the Lady What She Wants*, an original musical written in 1951 by a young composer named Lloyd Norlin, chronicled the history and philosophy of Marshall Field's department stores. Privately pressed on vinyl to celebrate the company's seventieth anniversary, it's the very first known recorded industrial show, a distinction made possible by its coinciding with the mainstreaming of the long-play phonograph record.

The automobile industry soon jumped into the fray with Oldsmobile's *The Mighty O!*, a soaring paean to the brand-new, chrome-covered '54 line. *Mighty O!* boasted a cast of dozens, a full orchestra, and real Broadway stars, including Bob Fosse. Its plot was perfectly tailored to allow the singers to extol the exciting features of Olds's new models: "Sleek as a yacht on a drifty sea—three inches lower than '53!" Indeed, an unyielding sense of passion fills every track, even "Panoramic Windshield."

By the late 1950s, the nascent industrial show genre had carved out its goals: educate the managers and salesmen, get them excited about new products and concepts, bolster the worker's confidence in the company's future, and of course, leave them humming as they exit the show. All of which meant hiring talented composers, lyricists, and actors, as well as spending untold amounts of money. Just about everyone got on board: Standard Oil treated their workforce to *The Big Change* in 1957 and *I Love A Salesman* in 1958. General Electric's appliance divisions produced a slew of shows. *It's A Great New Line* from 1957 featured lovingly crafted odes to their dishwashers and garbage Disposalls. A crowning achievement of the decade was *The Shape of Tomorrow*, a "musical introduction to 1958 Westinghouse appliances." With brassy orchestrations and positively bionic vocals, Westinghouse gave its higher-ups a musical that crammed every attribute of their new products, however minute, into each song:

The "C" in A-B-C is for the cleaning ease that
Westinghouse makes trouble-free—
With plug-out surface units, oven heaters as well—
The wonderful new No-Dip tops, convenient, do-tell!
All this plus adaptable new styling throughout—
Are reasons why with Westinghouse, we shout!

Who wouldn't want to sell a stove after hearing that bouncy plug? By the beginning of the 1960s, the industrial show was in full bloom. Composers and actors were eager to hone their talents and reap the fast cash that "industrial theater" could yield. Among the unsung industrial-musical geniuses of the shows' most fruitful decade were Michael Brown, who churned out classics for DuPont Fibers, J. C. Penney, and Singer Sewing Machines, and Sid Siegel, who gave the world *The Bathrooms are Coming* for American Standard. Skip Redwine, Ed Nayor, and Wilson Stone, though all largely unknown to the world at large, were talented and highly paid composers on the industrial circuit. Future Broadway mainstays Jerry Bock and Sheldon Harnick wrote the tractor-show hoedown *Music to Ford-I-Fy Your Future*. Television stars Hal Linden, Loretta Swit, Valerie Harper, and David Hartman began their careers in such forgotten masterpieces as *The Name of the Game* for Listerine, *Going Great!* for Rambler, and *Go Fly A Kite*, the highlight of General Electric's Fifth Utility Executive Conference.

The compositions were catchy and the lyrics well written, often with tongue in cheek. Take *Diesel Dazzle*, for instance, the 1966 musical written by the composer/lyricist team of Hank Beebe and Bill Heyer for the Detroit Diesel Engine Division of General Motors. Billed as a "musical moment in pursuit of solescence," one of the show's standout tracks is the soapy "One-Man Operation," in which a salesman's wife sings a valentine to her husband, the hardworking Joe who bought his own service station and now has time to spend with her and the kids, thanks to Detroit Diesel, of course.

Women weren't just wives in industrial shows: the 1966 B. F. Goodrich sales meeting musical features the potent track "A Girl Who's Making It Big," in which the female lead singer proves she can sell tires just as well as any man. Buick's *The Car: Buick '59* includes a number sung by a female car buyer who easily handles the drooling salesmen, cool in her knowledge of what she, the customer, needs. While the lyrics are hilarious in their dated politics, they're at least inclusive. But some women didn't fare as well. When the wives of Clark Equipment salesmen sing, "Yes, we're those things called salesman's wives—we gave up living when we chose our lives," in *This Is Clarkmanship* (1969), we know that their lament probably rings true.

Of course gender politics wasn't the central theme of industrial musicals. Naturally, it's all about sales. The corporate cliché abounds in the shows' titles: *Opportunity*

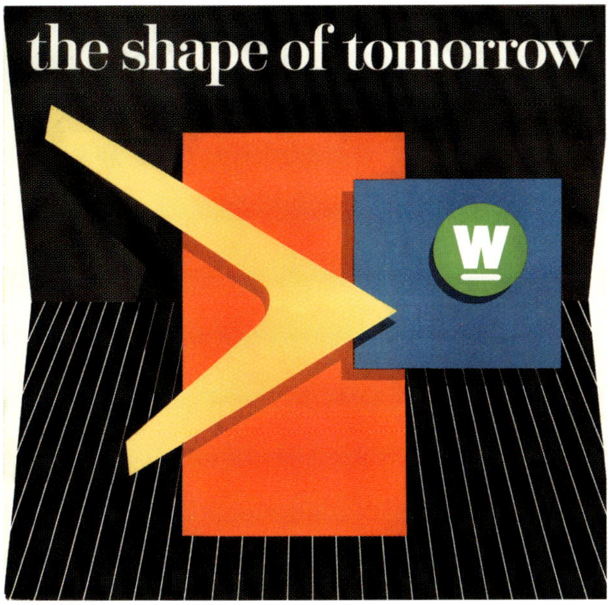

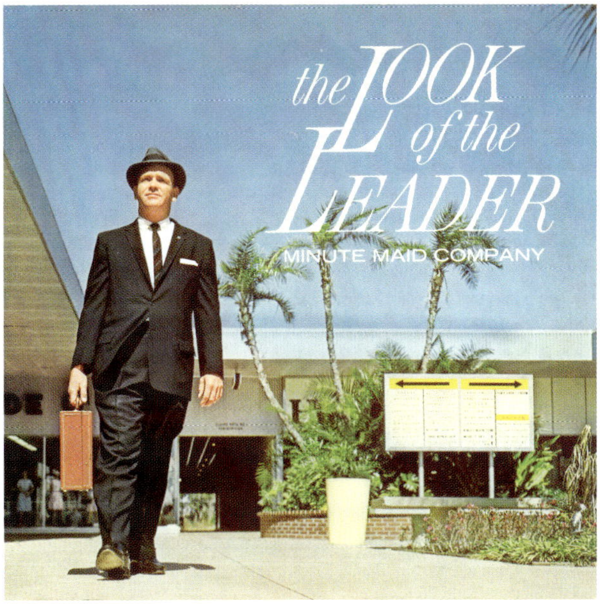

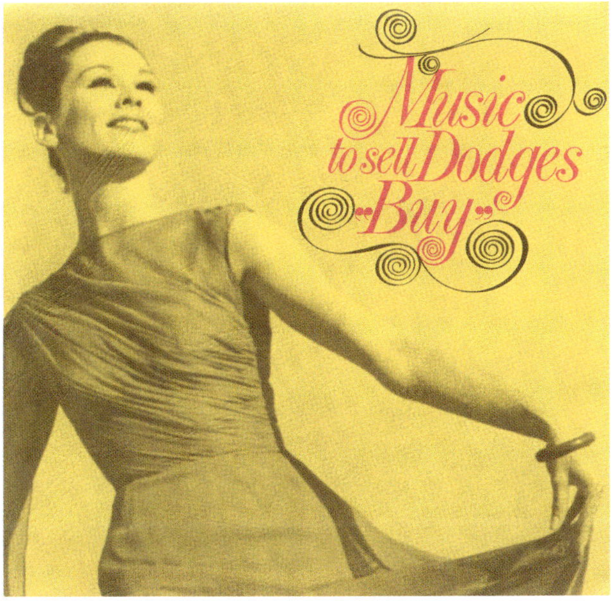

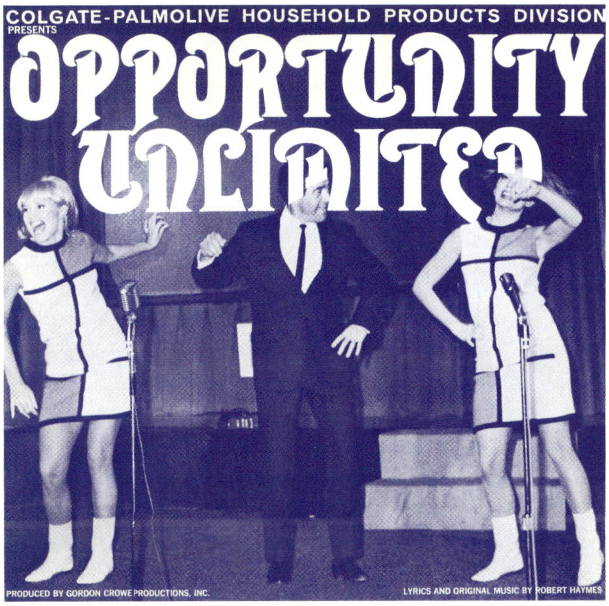

The Shape of Tomorrow, Westinghouse, 1958

"Easy as A-B-C"

Glamour for sale! Glamour for sale!

The shape of tomorrow for a loveliness bewitchin'—

The shape of tomorrow for a STUNNING KITCHEN!

Music to Sell Dodges Buy, Dodge announcement show, 1964

"What Have We Got"

You take the grill and bumpers and the tail lamps—

You take the hood and roofline and the wheels—

That's a silhouette about as great as you can get—

You know you're ready for the customers and deals!

The Look of the Leader, Minute Maid, 1963

"Minute Maid Company on the Move"

While America's growing shore to shore—

Minute Maid will keep growing—more, and more, and more!

Good for all America—for our economy!

And what's good for America is good for you and me!

Opportunity Unlimited, Colgate-Palmolive Household Products Division, 1965

"King of the Road"

Here comes our salesman Dan, handsome and tall and tan—

There's nothing finer than—a real live Colgate man!

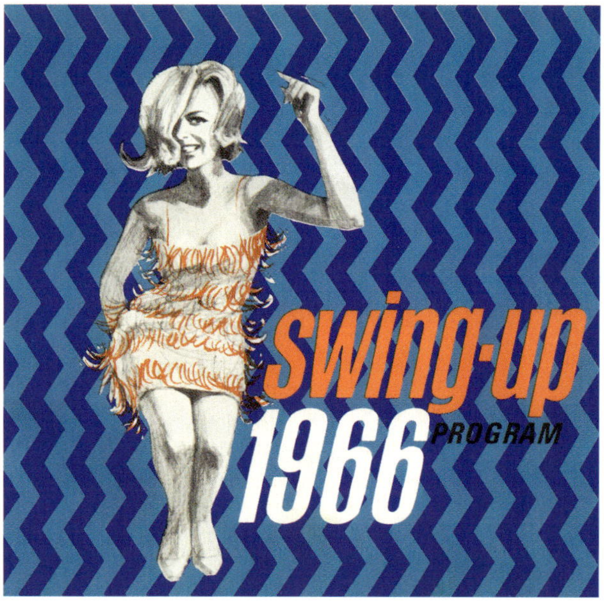

***Swing Up '66*, Chrysler-Plymouth announcement show, 1966**

"Swing Up"

Get set for '66, the year of the Swing Up!

The growth in industry is gonna be outstanding!

The whole economy is gonna be, ooooooh outstanding!

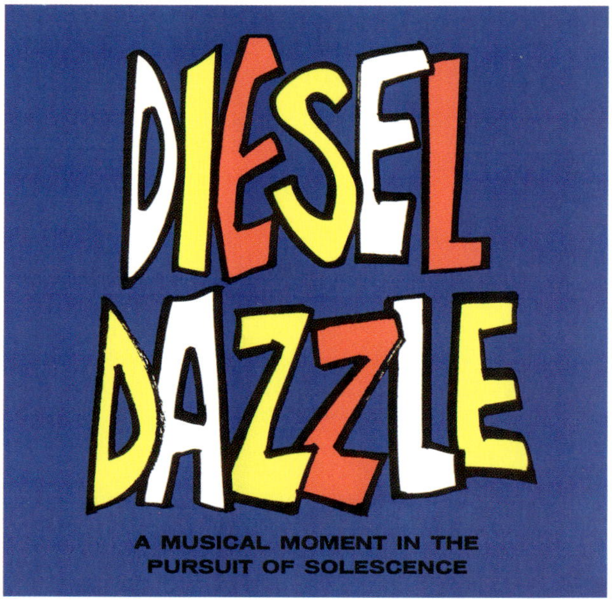

***Diesel Dazzle*, Detroit Diesel Engine Division of General Motors, 1966**

"Reliabilt Hoedown"

National promotion right up to the hilt—advertising to spread the flame—

Bright new packages for each rebuilt—packages that bear the name:

Reliabilt

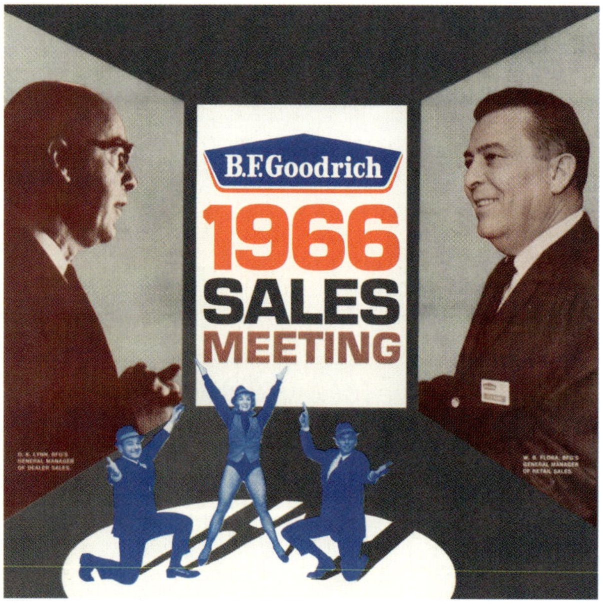

***1966 Sales Meeting*, B.F. Goodrich, 1966**

"A Girl Who's Making It Big"

I've learned my lesson and now I know: I can sell like a man—

I can spot a prospect a mile away and if someone can sell him, I can!

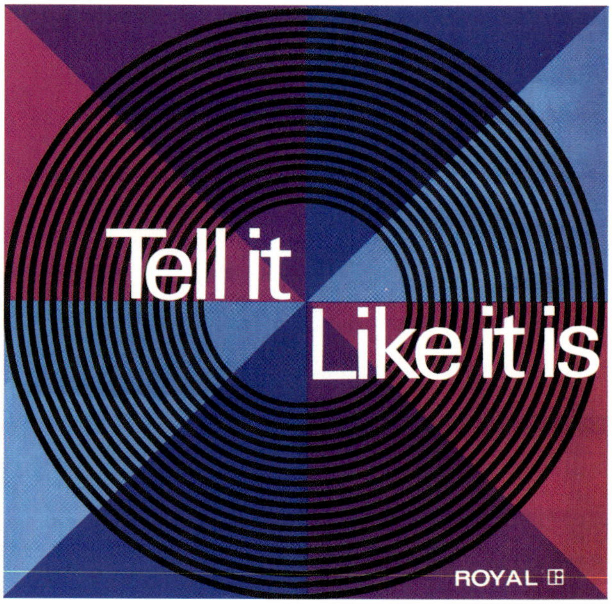

***Tell It Like It Is*, Royal Typewriter, 1969**

"Secretary's Dilemma"

Though our boss never beats us, for that he'd never do—

It always looks as though he does 'cause we are black and blue

With ribbons! Ribbons! Ribbons!

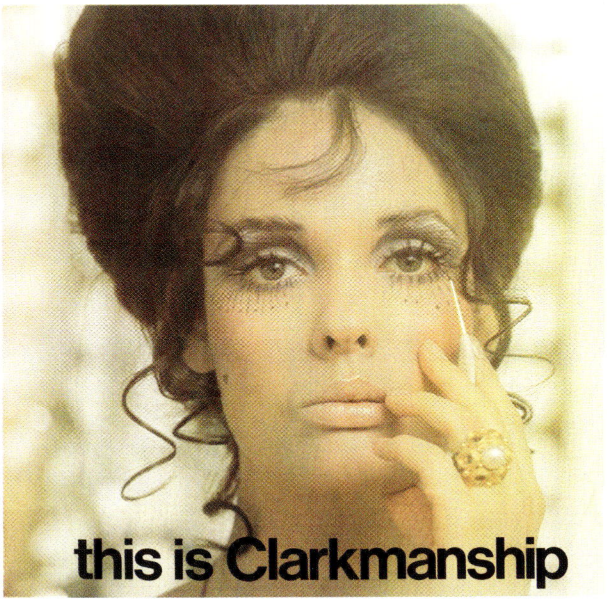

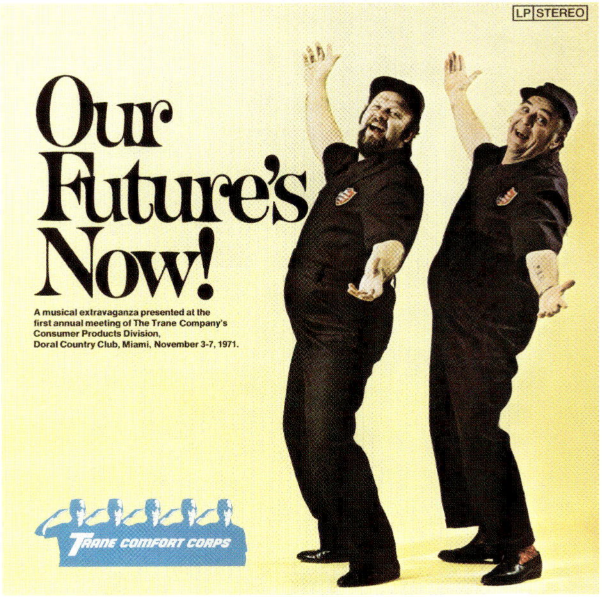

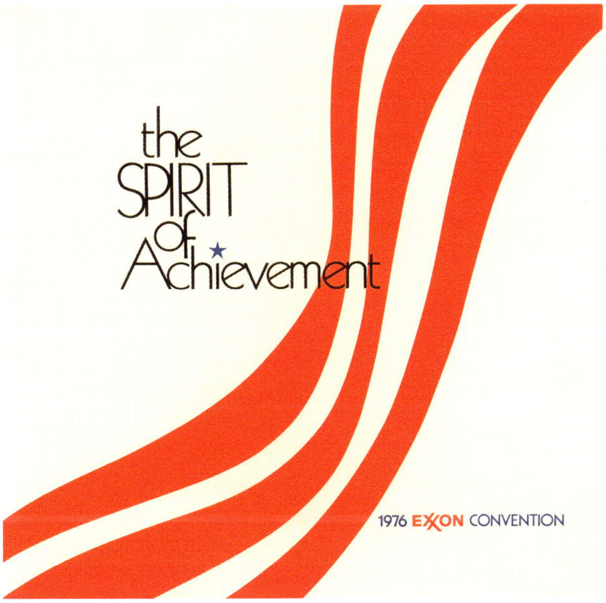

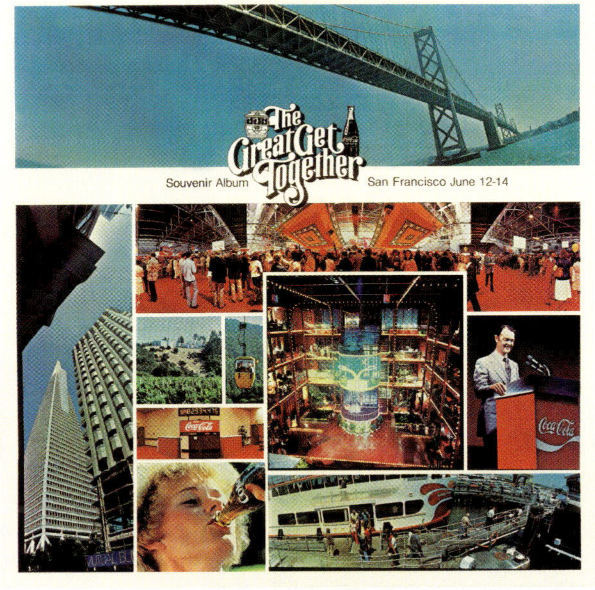

This is Clarkmanship, **Clark Equipment, 1970**

"Hooray for Human Engineering"

So sing the praise of a company that cares,
A company that plans and works and dares –
To make bones feel better through human engineering!

***Our Future's Now*, Trane Company, Consumer Products Division, 1971**

"New Day's A-Comin' Soon"

New day's a-comin' soon, and it just won't be the same—
CP division supporting you, and the Comfort Center name.

***The Spirit of Achievement*, Exxon, 1976**

"The Bottom Line"

Stop and use your senses by controlling your expenses
On the bottom line—the profit line!
Unit volume is the thing that counts, it's not the single sale amounts—
The bottom line is the dollar sign!!

The Great Get Togetrher, **Coca-Cola, 1979**

"That Big Bottling Plant Up in the Sky"

In that big bottling plant up in the sky—
There's no FTC and there's no EPA—
No FDA, to spoil your day!
No more alphabet soup to turn your hair gray!

Unlimited (Colgate, 1965), *It's A Brand New Ball Game* (Monroe Calculator, 1969), *The Grip of Leadership* (Coca-Cola, 1961), and *Look of the Leader* (Minute Maid, 1963). And in an early expression of global capitalism, the musicals were exported as well: Coca-Cola repackaged their American industrial musicals for German Coke bottlers with *Partnerschaft-Addierte Kraft* (featuring the jaunty "Wir Bleiben am Ball," or "We're Having a Ball"), and for their Mexican bottlers with the swinging *Usted Y Coca-Cola*.

Whether these shows succeeded in generating better salesmen, or even entertaining them beyond the night of the live production, is difficult to ascertain. Judging simply from the scarcity of the souvenir albums, one would guess not. Yet the variety of those that have survived is evidence that a broad cross-section of American industry performed these extravagant shows year after year—so sales must have picked up when the curtain closed. Companies large and small, no matter how difficult their products were to sing about or plot around, gleefully burst into song. Take Converters Inc., a producer of disposable paper hospital gowns and sheets; their 1967 show has the confidence to proclaim, "I really enjoyed my appendectomy—loved my hysterectomy! Love those drapes and caps and those towels—by Converters!" Or take The *HPB Go Show* of the same year, by the Home Products Division of the Owens-Corning Fiberglas Corporation. Yes, an entire musical about their fiberglass products. No matter that it was produced in a half-empty hotel room with three singers and an attendance of maybe thirty-five people. It was all in the name of Industry.

But industrial musicals weren't all cheerleading and verve; there was a darker side. Stamped on every souvenir album is a bold warning for its owner: not only are the albums never to be played publicly, they are strictly for company employees only. In other words, you're in trouble if the competition hears about this. And no wonder. Ford's musicals boast about how they'll "beat the hell out of Chevrolet." Coca-Cola's shows—the most buoyantly militaristic of all industrial musicals—contain such jaw-dropping lines as, "We'll send those boys from OSHA straight to hell!" And Exxon, in *The Spirit of Achievement*, boldly summed up its philosophy in the song "Efficiency":

Reasonable government guidelines, well that's okay—
We don't mind if the government has its fair say—
But too much control, well that just gets in the way
Of Efficiency!

Tellingly, most of these hubristic corporate fantasies emerge from the industrial shows of the 1970s and 1980s. While the shows of the 1950s earnestly appealed to salesmen to embrace their fellow man (after all, he's the customer), and those of the 1960s delivered in entertainment value, by the late 1970s corporations had, at least in song, gained an edge. Gone were the days when Cole National Corporation would perform and release *A Fairy Tale* (1965), an entire show about their new line of color-coded car keys. That seems quaint compared with *Money* magazine's 1981 tenth anniversary show, *One For the Money*, which featured tracks that tried to grapple with the effects of trickle-down economics. By 1986, the Pepsi Advertising Premiere show could, amid bubbling synthesizers and a robotic chorus, promote Pepsi taking over the entire universe, "side by side with our bottlers."

Pepsi's dream of conquest was something of a swan song for the genre, as the industrial show soon faded away. Come the 1970s, theatrical production costs grew unwieldy as SAG fees rose, limiting the talent pool. And of course Broadway isn't the popular force it once was. Today's Monsanto employee most likely does not own album versions of *Les Misérables* or *Rent* as his forebears might have owned *My Fair Lady* or *Hair*. Add to this the arrival of video, and now, PowerPoint, and the demise of the industrial musical seems inevitable. In fact, the idea of a musical stage show extolling the virtues of a company, its philosophy, and its products as tools to engender loyalty and enthusiasm is hopelessly out of date. Employees of modern-day corporations are savvy to the fact that their parent company will do anything to cut costs: slash benefits, limit vacation time, or simply lay off staff. Needless to say, musicals extolling the virtues of massive cutbacks or offshore tax shelters would be a very hard sell.

So what's left of a three-decade era of staged corporate entertainment? Only the records: the most perverse amalgam of influences, agendas, clever lyrics, and catchy melodies ever set to vinyl. For these private glimpses of business frolic, we have a few devoted industrial album collectors to thank (as if you couldn't guess: I'm one of them). Were it not for their dogged perseverance an entire subgenre of American music would be lost to the dustbin of a poorly attended estate sale.

Record covers courtesy Steve Young and the author.

In the Southern California of my childhood, it was always rocket summer.

"Rocket summer" is the heat wave created by Mars-bound rockets in Ray Bradbury's *The Martian Chronicles* (1950). "One minute, it was Ohio winter," writes Bradbury, "icicles fringing every roof..."[1] Then the rockets exhale, turning winter into a puddle of ice water, the "skis and sleds suddenly useless..."[2]

In Chula Vista, the San Diego suburb where I grew up in the sixties and seventies, rocket summer was an unchanging mental season for anyone whose father worked in the aeronautics industry, as my stepdad did. In 1965, he, my mother, and I had headed west in a Volkswagen van, camping our way from New Britain, Connecticut to Southern California, where the commercial and military contracts were ripe for the picking. My stepdad had landed a job as a machinist at Chula Vista's biggest employer, Rohr Aircraft, and we promptly rented a stucco bungalow and began living the working-class dream.

We were part of a westward expansion that had begun during WWII. "Ten percent of wartime federal spending went to California," writes the regional historian D.J. Waldie. "Southern California aircraft plants produced 40 percent of the planes flown by the Navy and Army Air Corps. By the end of the war, 600,000 border Southerners had migrated to Southern California to work in defense industries."[3] After the war, the tide ebbed, but tales of good pay, palm trees, and endless sunshine continued to draw workers to the promised land. The tribes of Aerojet and Convair, Litton and Lear-Siegler, Hughes and Northrop, McDonnell-Douglas and Ford Aerospace, Rockwell and RAND and, among the subcontractors, Rohr, were fruitful and multiplied.

My stepdad worked on the tailfins for the sleek, swept-wing fighter jet that would later knock Tom Cruise out of the spotlight in *Top Gun*—the legendary Grumman F-14 Tomcat, which entered military service in 1972. He had a hand, too, in the engine nacelles for the DC-10, the 727, and the 737; the thrust reverser for the 747; the exhaust system for the Concorde; and the space shuttle boosters. When my elementary school teachers asked us to introduce ourselves with an autobiographical sentence or two, I upped my coolness quotient with the exotic fact that my stepdad was "the man who makes the parts that make the parts that make airplanes"—a loose translation of his job description as a jig-and-fixture builder.

Little wonder, then, that my mental skies were crisscrossed with the contrails of SSTs and the fiery plumes of ascending moonships. San Diego, after all, was where Ryan Aeronautical built *The Spirit of St. Louis* (with Fred Rohr as foreman); where Lindbergh took off from North Island, en route to New York for his legendary flight to Paris; and to which he returned in triumph, reassuring a jubilant crowd of 60,000 that "San Diego has always been in the foreground of western aeronautics and San Diego, I believe, always will be in the foreground."[4] When I was in grade school, schoolkids were still making the obligatory pilgrimage to the musty Aerospace Museum in Balboa Park, to feign a reverential moment before a replica of Lindbergh's rickety little *Spirit*.

Back in the real world, the fossil record of man's evolution into *Homo Icarus* was all around me. Weekends, my family bodysurfed at Coronado, where in 1911 Glenn Curtiss made history's first successful seaplane takeoff and landing. Sometimes, we picnicked on the scrubby Chula Vista hill where, in 1883, John Montgomery strapped himself into his seagull-inspired "Gull Glider" and flew 600 feet, "open[ing] for all mankind the 'great highway of the sky,'" as the Montgomery Memorial's gently vandalized stone marker proclaims.[5] Occasionally, we would drive out to the Torrey Pines cliffs, near Del Mar, to watch Montgomery's hang gliding descendants drifting lazily on the updrafts, their wings bright splashes of color against the ocean far below.

I lived with one foot in the future, a parallel dimension where supersonic travel, jetpacks, lunar vacations, and offworld colonies under geodesic domes were already a reality. Disney's Tomorrowland fueled my fantasies. Once a year, on Rohr night, when the park opened its gates to Rohr employees only, I thrilled to the space-jock jargon and simulated microgravity of the Flight to the Moon (brought to you by McDonnell-Douglas) and the *Incredible Shrinking Man*-effects of the Adventure Through Inner Space (brought to you by Monsanto). By moonlight, Tomorrowland's aerodynamically cool monorail and spaceport architecture made the master-planned technocracies and interstellar odysseys in my stepdad's Isaac Asimov novels and *Popular Science* magazines seem suddenly, thrillingly real.

But Tomorrowland only literalized the Visions of Things to Come floating around in postwar America. Space evangelists such as Willy Ley, Wernher von Braun, and Lester Del Rey spread the gospel of space exploration and colonization through children's books that were equal parts edutainment, pulp SF, and boys' adventure story. Ley's inspiring tract, *The Conquest of Space* (1949), cut the die for the genre: ringingly romantic evocations of space travel, brought to life by the superreal clarity of Chesley Bonestell's artwork. Bonestell's views of *Saturn Seen From Titan*, *The Surface of Mercury*, and *Exploring the Moon* were stills from a movie not yet made, one that every schoolkid was certain he would one day star in. "The younger generation of rocket engineers is just beginning," wrote Ley, in 1951. "They are of the new generation to which space travel is not going to be a dream of the future but an everyday job with everyday worries in which they will be engaged."[6]

While my stepdad built the casings for the boosters that launched the moon rockets, I climbed Bonestell's dramatically lit lunar ridges, plumbed the depths of their shadowed craters. I teleoperated the spiderlike robots in Ley's *Space Stations* (1958), assembling a huge, ring-shaped spacelab high above the earth. I flew through the cosmic void in Lester Del Rey's *Space Flight: The Coming Exploration of the Universe* (1959), propelled by the jetpack in my weirdly medieval metal spacesuit, mechanical claws sprouting from my gloves and boots.

Like the rest of my generation, I was itching for liftoff. Tang was in our mother's milk; the course of our fantasies was plotted by books like Mae and Ira Freeman's *You Will Go to the Moon* (1959), whose perky text managed to make lunar colonies sound as cozily familiar as the suburbs:

> *You can see more from the top of this hill.*
> *Look! Do you see that house?*
> *That is the moon house.*
> *That is where you will live on the moon.*[7]

On July 20, 1969, I watched, enthralled, with half a billion other earthlings, as Apollo 11 Commander Neil Armstrong took that momentous first step onto the Moon. I marveled at the astronauts' near-weightlessness in the Moon's microgravity, and strained to make out the desolate, meteor-bombed landscape around them in the ghostly TV transmission.

As everyone knew, Armstrong's "giant leap for mankind" was only the first step. Within two weeks of the Moon landing, von Braun was exhorting a presidential task group to pursue an Integrated Space Program that would establish a permanent moonbase and space stations, springboards for a nuclear-powered mission to Mars.[8]

Space exploration was about more than scientific curiosity, more than a second chance for a lucky few if Mutually Assured Destruction ever became an apocalyptic reality: It was our evolutionary destiny. *Homo sapiens* was about to witness childhood's end, as Arthur C. Clarke prophesied in his Teilhard de Chardin-ian fable, *2001: A Space Odyssey*. Apotheosis into Clarke's radiant "starchild" awaited us, somewhere out there. Hadn't von Braun, the high priest of rocket science in a country that regarded the space program with religious awe, framed the 1969 Moon landing in explicitly evolutionary terms, calling it "equal in importance to that moment in evolution when aquatic life came crawling up on the land"?[9] We were stardust, and to stardust we would return, voyaging "beyond the infinite," in the words of the "event" movie of 1968, Stanley Kubrick's adaptation of Clarke's *2001*.

And then, as soon as it began, the future was over. Partying in Los Angeles with President Richard Nixon after Armstrong and his crewmates had gotten out of quarantine, a drunken astronaut raised his glass in a sardonic—and prophetic—toast: "Here's to the Apollo program. It's all over."[10]

He was right. Apollo 11, the capstone of the Space Age, turned out to be its tombstone. After 1969, America began to lose faith in the gospel of von Braun. My Lai, Kent State, and Watergate steadily eroded the *Father Knows Best* trust in authority that had written JFK a blank check to land a man on the Moon and return him safely to the earth. To many, the space program looked like a costly boondoggle (Apollo alone had cost a staggering $24 billion), diverting the nation's attention from more pressing matters on the ground: Vietnam, racial tensions, urban blight, and the environment.[11] When the last of the moon missions, Apollo 17, splashed down on 19 December 1972, the world barely noticed. "We held a televised press conference, but apparently were already yesterday's news, for the networks didn't find time to put us on the air," Commander Eugene Cernan noted ruefully in his memoir *The Last Man on the Moon*.[12]

* * *

To those of us who lived through the downsizing of America's rocket dreams, the only thing more extraordinary than those memories of human beings standing in the Sea of Tranquility or the Ocean of Storms is the suddenness with which we seemed to forget it. Had it all been a Moonage Daydream? To anyone born after Apollo, Cape Canaveral was a Petrified Forest for futurists, its buzz-cut mission controllers and Bible-quoting astronauts relics of a more earnest America.

NASA stumbled on, but the escalating war in Vietnam was a sucking chest wound in the federal budget, forcing drastic cutbacks in funding for the once all-powerful agency. Then, too, NASA's painfully public SNAFUs, from the near-fatal explosion that brought Apollo 13 limping back to Earth in 1970 to Skylab's premature wipeout in 1979, made the mass of Americans increasingly uneasy about the cost, in national nightmares (and taxpayer billions), of aiming for the stars. The unmanned Viking spacecraft's discovery in 1975 that Mars was a dead rock, utterly inhospitable to human life, extinguished dreams of colonizing the red planet. Skylab's unscheduled crash only reinforced what the historian Peter N. Carroll calls our "sense of earthboundedness."[13]

As "the energy, the faith, the devotion" of the Kennedy years faded into the long national nightmare of the Nixon era, the transcendental impulses that once found expression in the space program sought new outlets. True believers continued to bear witness to the von Braunian gospel: Timothy Leary, the Neil Armstrong of the acid flashback, exhorted his flock to prepare for "space migration;" the physicist Gerard K. O'Neill built castles in the air—solar-powered orbital cities, some 20-million strong—in his 1977 book *High Frontier: Human Colonies in Space*. But most seventies seekers embarked on inner-space odysseys, solo flights to self-actualization guided by the star charts of the Aquarian Age.

Even some of the astronauts saw the light. Rolling with the zeitgeist, they reconciled Space Age and New Age in harmonic convergences all their own. For Apollo 14 astronaut Edgar Mitchell, seeing the fragile lifeboat Earth adrift in space inspired a Saul-on-the-road-to-Damascus revelation: in a flash, Mitchell understood that the universe is suffused, at the subatomic level, with a cosmic intelligence that connects all things. In 1973, he founded a New Age thinktank, the Institute of Noetic Sciences, in Palo Alto, California, to fish in the waters where the crosscurrents of science and mysticism meet. Others took more conventional flightpaths: Russell Schweickart (Apollo 9) embraced Zen Buddism, Story Musgrave (Skylab) struggled to make sense of the

top: floor plan for building in the Calvary Southern Baptist Church complex.
bottom: architectural rendering of the church complex.

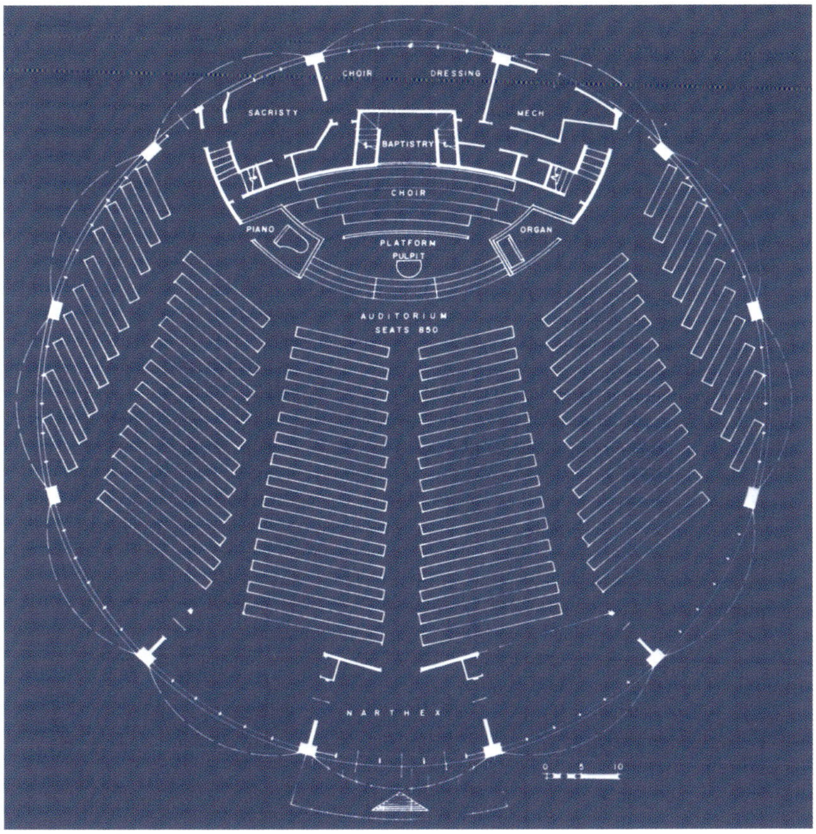

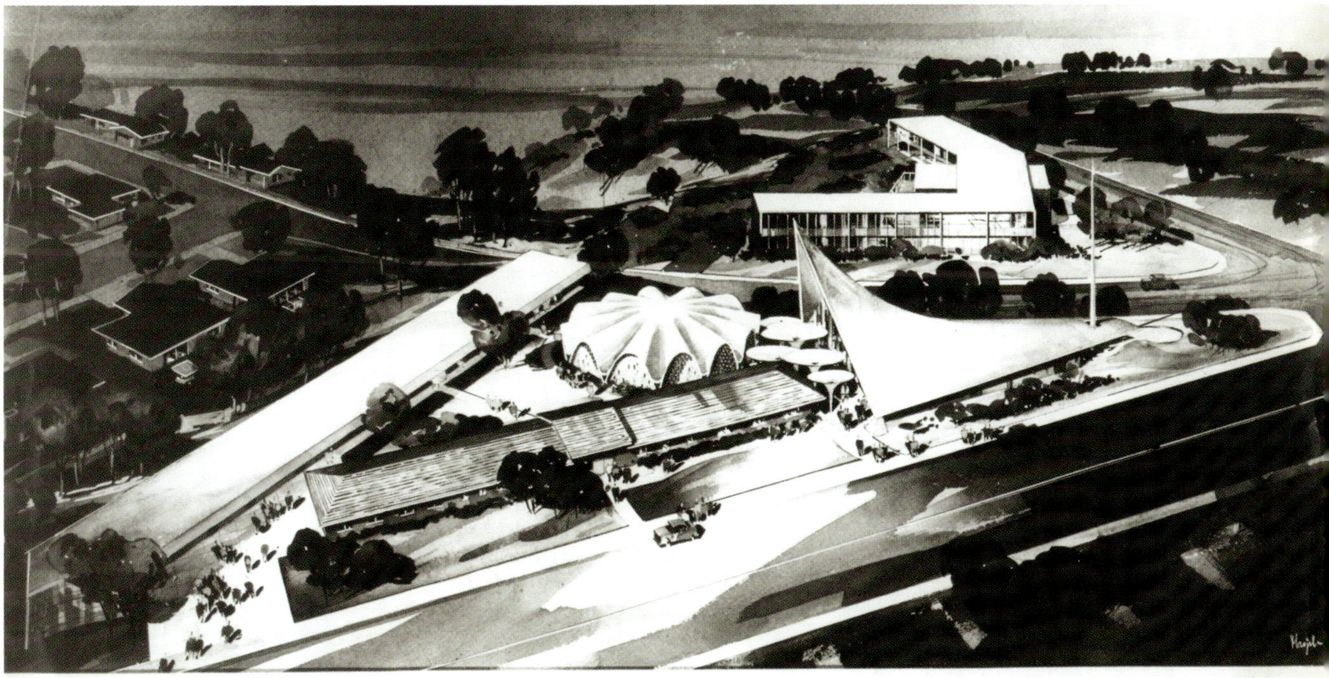

C A L V A R Y S O U T H E R N B A P T I S T C H U R C H

R O B E R T E. D E S L A U R I E R S A. I. A

A R C H I T E C T

"noble, magnificent" music he heard in space, and Jim Irwin (Apollo 15) became a born-again Christian, leaving NASA to launch the evangelical High Flight Foundation.[14]

Meanwhile, in Southern California, the techno-transcendentalism of the receding Space Age intersected with mainline Christianity's age-old dreams of spiritual liftoff from the world, the flesh, and the devil. These trajectories converged in a church architecture that was equal parts earthship and mothership, aerodynamic yet close to the Earth. The church I attended as a boy, in Chula Vista, is a pyramid-shaped artifact of this period aesthetic. St. Mark's Lutheran resembles a redwood treehouse idling on a concrete launchpad. Designed in 1966 by Robert Des Lauriers, St. Mark's serves two masters: the Rousseau-ian back-to-naturism of the ecology movement, and a rocket-finned futurism cultural runoff from the aeronautics industry.

Des Lauriers made a name for himself as the architect of more than sixty strikingly modernist churches throughout Southern California, all but a few in San Diego county. His flirtations with the aesthetic reached their apogee in the Carlton Hills Lutheran Church in San Diego's Santee suburb, a Jetsonian traffic-stopper whose "flying effects" (his words) exploit the hyperbolic paraboloid. For inspiration, he drew on the Mexican modernist Felix Candela (from whom he borrowed the paraboloid), Le Corbusier, Wright, and his own deeply felt Christian faith.

Of course, he recalls, "everybody was thinking of doing space things" in the late sixties and early seventies.[15] For the First Assembly of God church in the San Diego suburb of Mission Hills, Des Lauriers crossed the Spanish contemporary aesthetic with an "aeronautical design," based on "the trajectories of rockets." The church's parabolic arch evoked Noah's rainbow in visual rhetoric an aerospace culture could understand. As Des Laurier proclaimed, in a statement of aesthetic principles he wrote, "Man is looking for a soaring attitude. We [architects] can partially achieve this with our new forms. The aerospace industry can take credit for some of this thinking." At the same time, he stressed, his was an "innovative architecture with traditional roots—Gothic, Romanesque, and Renaissance."

Which brings us full circle, historically: With its gantry-like flying buttresses and dizzy verticality, the Gothic cathedral itself suggests a medieval premonition of the Space Age: a sacred ark, eager to be airborne. Inversely, the launch towers at Cape Canaveral were, for the Italian journalist Oriana Fallaci, "the cathedrals of an age that...has substituted technology for liturgy."[16] And, like the Gothic cathedrals, our Cold War race to plant the flag on the Moon before the Russkies did was at heart symbolic—"an act of faith and vision," conceded Kennedy, "for we do not now know what benefits await us."[17]

* * *

Driving through San Diego's inland suburbs one furnace-hot August recently, on a pilgrimage to Des Lauriers's churches, I wondered what benefits we had reaped from our lunar crusade. Inevitably, footage of Apollo 14's Alan Shepard golfing in the Moon's Fra Mauro highlands, or Apollo 17's Harrison Schmitt singing "I was strolling on the Moon one day" in the Taurus-Littrow valley, makes boomers like me wonder: What did it all *mean*?

The lunar missions pushed the envelope of knowledge, though they would have pushed it far further if Schmitt hadn't been the only scientist NASA sent up. For politicians, of course, the benefits of the space program were clear: JFK's stirring declaration, "We choose to go to the Moon in this decade and do the other things, not because they are easy, but because they are hard," covered the dashing young president in moondust and glory—and facilitated his political resurrection, after the embarrassment of Sputnik and the Bay of Pigs.[18]

For the rest of us, the moonshots were sacred events, robed in religious rhetoric: In the seconds before Apollo 11 lifted off, an expectant Norman Mailer realized that he "was like a penitent who had prayed in the wilderness for sixteen days, and was now expecting a sign."[19] Then, his prayers were answered: "[W]hite as the shrine of Madonna in half the churches of the world, this slim angelic mysterious ship of stages rose without sound out of its incarnation of flame and began to ascend slowly into the sky..."[20]

These days, the Kennedy Space Center at Cape Canaveral is a shrine to fading glories. In *Rocket Dreams: How the Space Age Shaped Our Vision of a World Beyond*, the cultural critic Marina Benjamin describes the Atlas, Titan, Gemini, and Redstone missiles at the KSC Visitor Complex's "Rocket Garden" as "so lackluster, so tired, they speak only of yesterday. And yesterday is where the Space Center and its surrounding attractions are for the most part stuck, caught up in a loop of reminiscence for Apollo."[21] Despite the overly insistent title of the Center's IMAX movie *The Dream is Alive*, NASA is the Vatican of the Space Age, reverently preserving the sanctified fragments of futures past. (Not for nothing does the KSC website proudly announce that "NASA's Lunar Sample Laboratory Facility is home to the most cherished... *relics* of the Apollo program."[22])

True, NASA continues to launch satellites and unmanned missions, while the International Space Station and Space Shuttle programs limp along. In 2004, George W. Bush had a Buzz Lightyear moment: Delivering an uplifting homily that sounded, at times, like a reading from the Book of von Braun, the president dreamed aloud of a $15 billion "Crew Exploration Vehicle," a lunar base, and sometime after 2020, a manned mission to Mars. To infinity—and beyond!

But building popular support for the megabillion-dollar program will be an even tougher sell, in a country bled white by Operation Iraqi Freedom, than it was during the Vietnam war. After the horror of the *Challenger* and *Columbia* disasters, not to mention more laughable pratfalls, such as the 1999 screw-up that sent the $125 million Mars Climate Orbiter kamikaze-ing into the red planet (NASA had failed to convert English measures to metric values), much of the nation seems convinced that boldly going where no man has gone before just isn't worth it.

Their redwood beams dried and cracking after decades of rocket summers, Des Lauriers's sixties and seventies churches reminded me of J.G. Ballard's elegies for yesterday's tomorrows. The stories in *Memories of the Space Age* are set in a melancholy future where dead astronauts circle the Earth, entombed in their lost capsules, and Cape Canaveral lies abandoned, "its gantries rising from the deserted dunes."[23]

> *Sand has come in across the Banana River, filling the creeks and turning the old space complex into a wilderness of swamps and broken concrete. [...] Beyond Cocoa Beach, where I stopped the car, the ruined motels were half hidden in the saw grass. The launching towers rose into the evening air like the rusting ciphers of some forgotten algebra of the sky.*

At the dawn of the twenty-first century, we inhabit Ballard's metaphor. The Space Age is ancient history. Why not admit, then, that its greatest contribution to American culture is the rich fund of symbolism it has given us? The twentieth century's greatest myth, space exploration is the only truly new religion since the Bronze Age. Christianity gave us the unforgettable fable of the alien messiah who touched down on planet Earth, assumed human form, sacrificed himself in order to save the species, then rose from the dead and returned to the stars.

The Space Age offers a new cosmology, better suited to our age of technological wonder and terror, scientific miracles and monsters. NASA has given us martyrs, saints, and icons, proof positive that there are more things in heaven and earth than were dreamt of in our old-time religion: Gemini 4's spacewalking Edward White, savoring the sheer ecstasy of unfettered freedom as he tumbles weightlessly over the Gulf of Mexico at 17,500 miles per hour. Bootprints in lunar soil, like traces of the last human on some post-apocalyptic beach—prints that will likely remain sharply etched for a million years or more. A snapshot of Apollo 16 astronaut Charlie Duke's family in their Houston backyard, left by Duke on the sands of the Moon's Descartes Highlands—an image of almost unbearable loneliness. And, at the other end of the emotional scale, the awful grandeur of a thirty-six-story Saturn V rocket, shattering gravity's shackles in a mighty blast. "I didn't think my heart could take it," said one observer. "It was such an intense experience. I felt it in every bone in my body. It was an exalted feeling."[24] The image of technological transcendence par excellence, a Saturn V blasting off was the twentieth-century version of Burke's sublime, with 7.5 million pounds of thrust.

Space exploration has taught us new parables, too, most hauntingly Charlie Duke's dream, six months before he went to the Moon:

> *In my dream, we were driving the [lunar] rover up to the [North Ray crater]...It was untouched, the serenity of it, had a pristine purity about it. We crossed a hill. I felt, "Gosh, I've been here before!" And, uh, there was a set of tracks out in front of us, so we asked Houston if we could follow the tracks and they said yes, so we turned and followed the tracks. Within an hour or so, we found this vehicle, it looked just like the rover, with two people in it, and they looked like me and John [Young]. They'd been there for thousands of years. It was not a nightmare-type situation, nothing like that. It was probably one of the most real experiences in my life.*[25]

Duke's dream felt so premonitory that he found himself scanning the North Ray crater for tire tracks as he descended onto the Moon in the lunar module *Orion*. Perhaps it was a prophetic glimpse of the end of the Space Age—a moment symbolized by a pair of ancient astronauts, on the highlands of the Moon, waiting for a future that will never come.

1 Ray Bradbury, *The Martian Chronicles* (New York: Bantam Books, 1979), p. 1.

2 Ibid.

3 D.J. Waldie, *Holy Land: A Suburban Memoir* (New York: W.W. Norton & Company, 1996), p. 163.

4 Gerald A. Shepherd, "When the Lone Eagle Returned to San Diego," *The Journal of San Diego History*, Winter 1994, Volume 40, Number 1 and 2,< http://sandiegohistory.org/journal/94winter/eagle.htm>.

5 See "John J. Montgomery (1858-1911)" in the "San Diego biographies" section of the San Diego Historical Society website, < http://www.sandiegohistory.org/bio/montgomery/montgomery.htm>. See, also, "John Montgomery," online historical resources of the University of San Diego, <http://history.sandiego.edu/gen/local/montgomery.html>.

6 Quoted in John Sisson, "Dreams of Space,"< http://sun3.lib.uci.edu/%7Ejsisson/john.htm>.

7 Mae and Ira Freeman, *You Will Go to the Moon* (1959 edition), <http://sun3.lib.uci.edu/%7Ejsisson/youmoon.htm>.

8 David West Reynolds, *Apollo: The Epic Journey to the Moon* (San Diego: Harcourt, Inc./Tehabi Books, 2002), p. 246.

9 Marina Benjamin, *Rocket Dreams: How the Space Age Shaped Our Vision of a World Beyond* (New York: Free Press, 2003), p. 57.

10 Andrew Chaikin, *A Man on the Moon: The Voyages of the Apollo Astronauts* (New York: Viking, 1994), p. 231.

11 "a staggering $24 billion": David E. Nye, *American Technological Sublime* (Cambridge, MA: MIT Press, 1994), p. 250.

12 Eugene Cernan with Don Davis, *The Last Man on the Moon* (New York: St. Martin's Press, 1999), p. 340.

13 Peter N. Carroll, *It Seemed Like Nothing Happened: America in the 1970s* (New Brunswick, NJ: Rutgers University Press, 1982), p. 301.

14 Quoted in Benjamin, *Rocket Dreams*, ibid., p. 51.

15 All Des Lauriers quotes from an interview with the author, August 2004.

16 Quoted in Benjamin, p. 12.

17 Ibid.

18 Ibid.

19 Norman Mailer, *Of a Fire on the Moon* (London: Weidenfeld and Nicholson, 1970), pp. 79-81, 180.

20 Ibid.

21 Benjamin, p. 12.

22 NASA/Kennedy Space Center website, "Multimedia Gallery,"< http://mediaarchive.ksc.nasa.gov/detail.cfm?mediaid=23550>. Italics mine.

23 J.G. Ballard, "The Dead Astronaut" in *Memories of the Space Age*, ibid., p. 67.

24 Quoted in Nye, p. 239.

25 Interview with Charlie Duke, *For All Mankind* (*National Geographic* video, 1992). Chaikin gives an expanded version of Duke's dream in *A Man on the Moon*, pp. 485-6.

MOONWORKS

CRAIG KALPAKJIAN

In the late 1960s, artists like Michael Heizer, Robert Smithson, Dennis Oppenheim, and Walter De Maria began to make large-scale land art projects, or "Earthworks," in the American West. One of Heizer's first projects, *Circular Surface Planar Displacement Drawing* (1970), involved hiring professional motorcycle racers to ride in circular patterns on a dried lake-bed in Nevada, repeatedly tracing ephemeral patterns in the sand that could be seen from above. Similarly, Oppenheim's *Relocated Burial Ground* (1978), consisted of a 610-square-meter X that the artist drew in the California desert using industrial primer material.

In 1997, the Robotics Institute at Carnegie-Mellon University began development of the Lunar/Planetary rover, Nomad. Larger than the Mars rovers, Nomad is an autonomous unmanned vehicle designed specifically for exploring the lunar surface. Able to guide itself across vast stretches of terrain, avoiding obstacles and finding the optimal route, Nomad was extensively tested in the deserts of South America, and has more recently been used in the Arctic Circle to find and retrieve small meteors that have fallen on the ice.

I propose to send a vehicle like Nomad across large stretches of the lunar surface—preferably the smoothest lunar "seas"—where over the course of many years simple patterns could be repeatedly traced out. By moving or disturbing the lunar soil and thereby exposing underlying layers, or by finding some other way of increasing the reflectivity of the lunar material (which is actually quite dark, similar to coal dust), a drawing or "Moonwork" could be created that would be visible from the earth, at least via telescope. The pattern should be recognizably man-made, one that could not occur through natural processes. Several possibilities are shown on the following pages.

Contemporary earthworks have often been compared to the Nazca lines in the Peruvian desert. These marks on the landscape have long puzzled scientists, leading to a variety of wild speculations about their origins—perhaps most famously in Erich Von Daniken's bestselling *Chariots of the Gods* (1969), in which he conjectured that they were in fact created by visiting aliens. The Moonworks can perhaps be thought of as an inversion of this scenario, by making us on earth the viewers, from above, of our markings on the surface of another world where we ourselves are aliens.

If the lunar landing is thought to be one of the highest achievements of mankind, it is only fitting that art should accompany humanity's journey into space. A visible trace will serve as both evidence of and a monument to our accomplishment. The Moonwork will be a kind of Mt. Rushmore for the twenty-first century. The first artwork made for all mankind, it will be available for viewing by everyone on the planet.

While there is no significant lunar ecology that the Moonwork might disturb, it will in fact be temporary in the scale of cosmic events, as it will eventually be erased by the slow bombardment of asteroids creating craters that constantly alter the lunar landscape. Indeed the lunar terrain can be seen as a vast recording surface, registering the impact of successive events in its history. The Moonwork, while not the first human addition to this process, will be the first in the name of art.

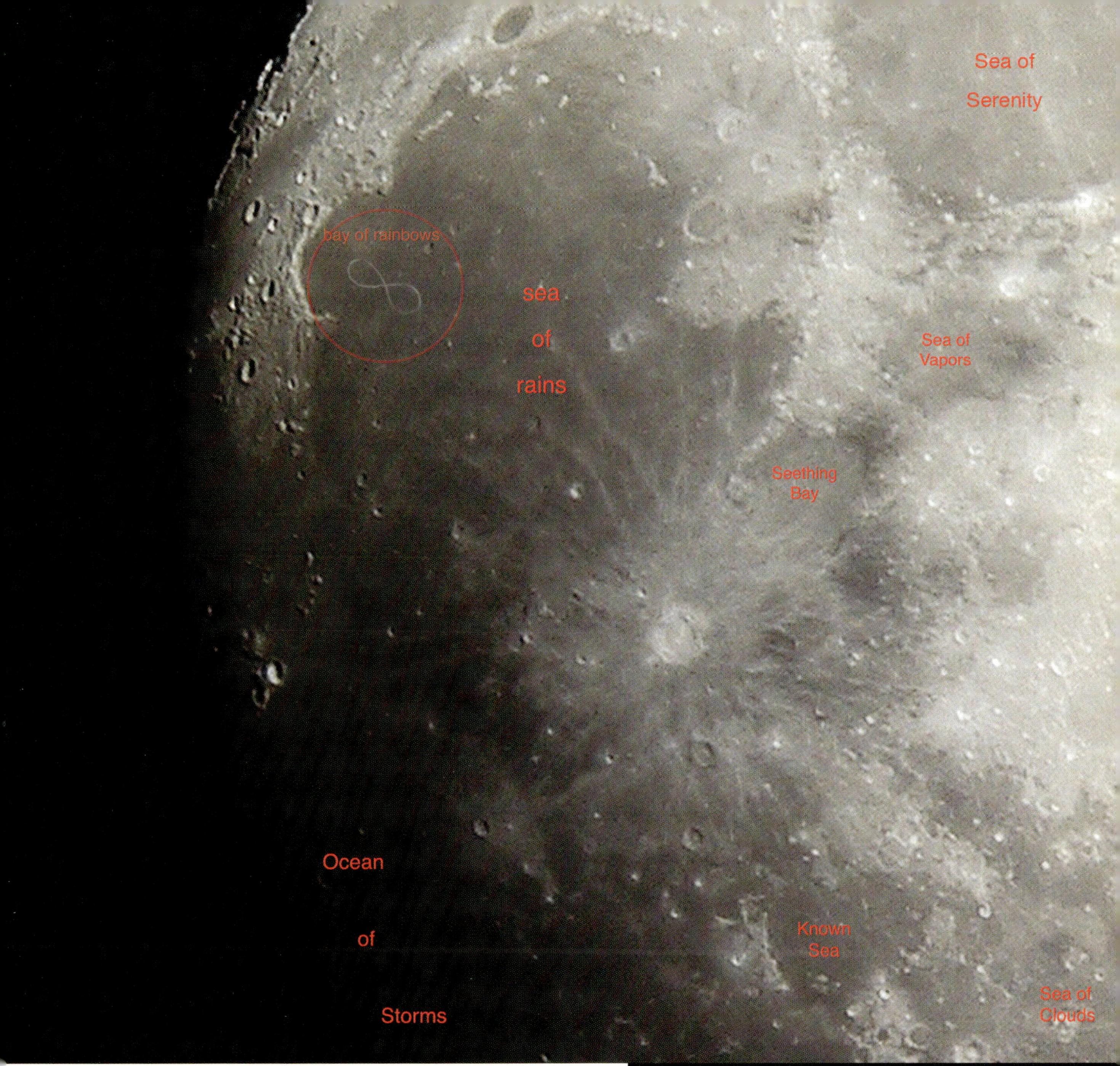
Sea of
Serenity
bay of rainbows
sea
of
rains
Sea of
Vapors
Seething
Bay
Ocean
of
Storms
Known
Sea
Sea of
Clouds

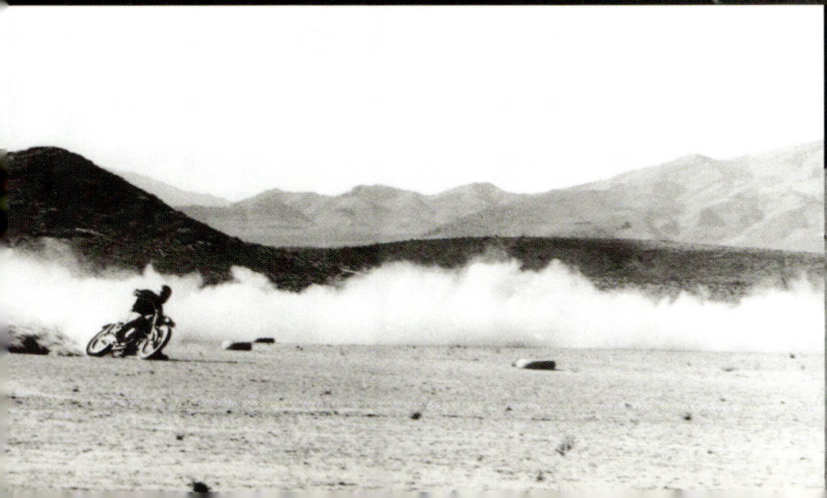

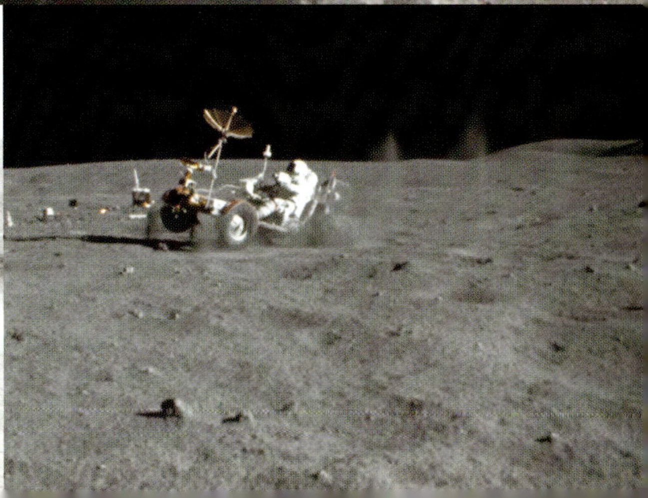

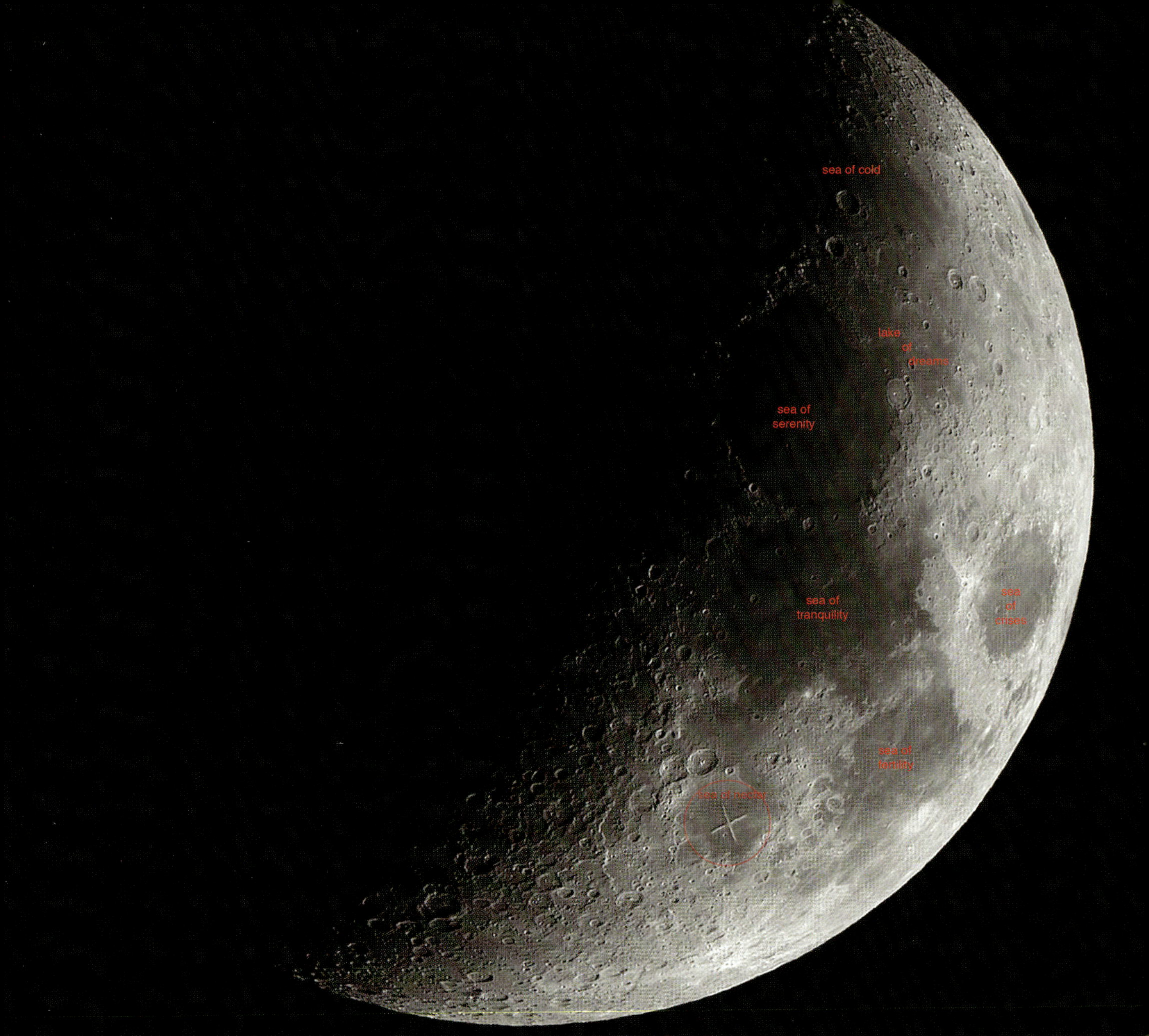
sea of cold
lake of dreams
sea of serenity
sea of tranquility
sea of crises
sea of fertility
sea of nectar

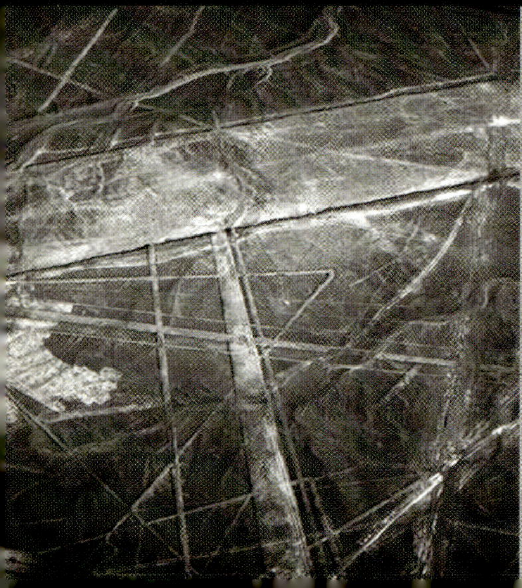

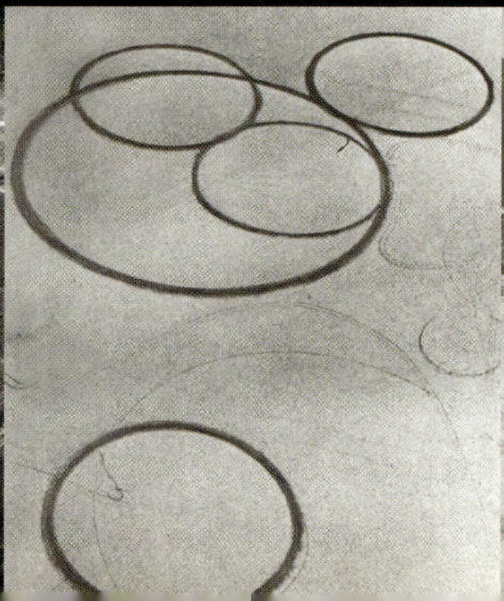

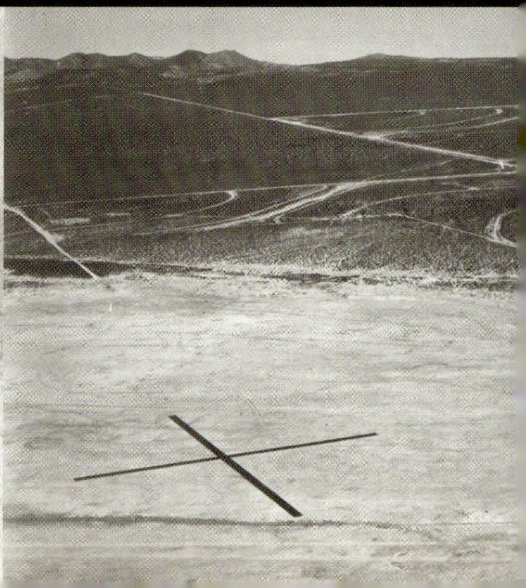

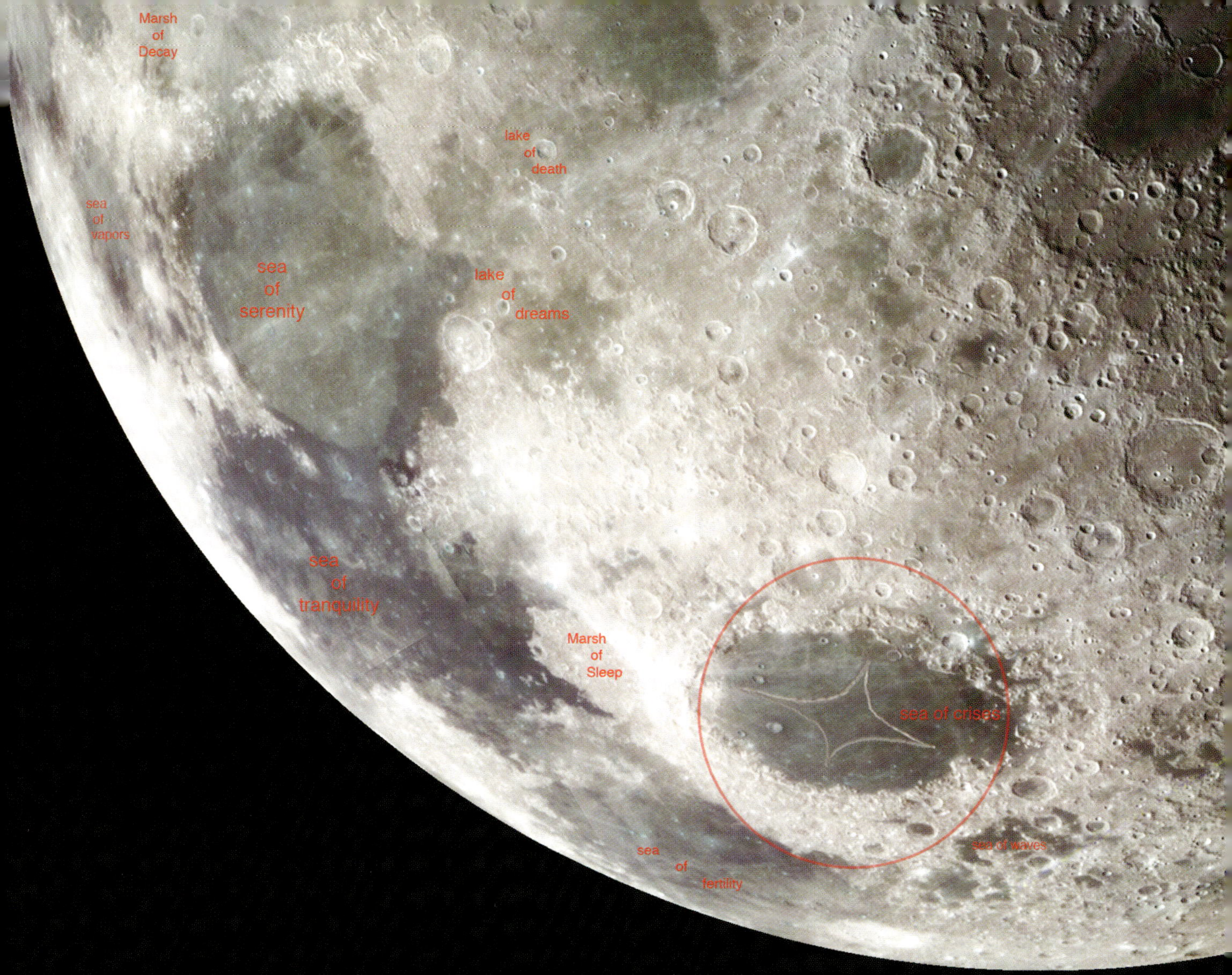
Marsh of Decay
lake of death
sea of vapors
sea of serenity
lake of dreams
sea of tranquility
Marsh of Sleep
sea of crises
sea of waves
sea of fertility
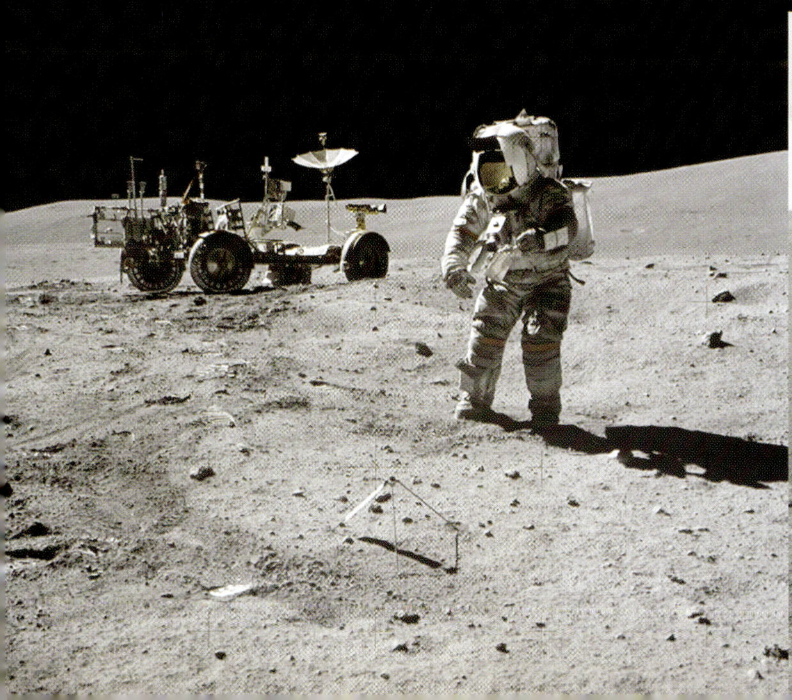
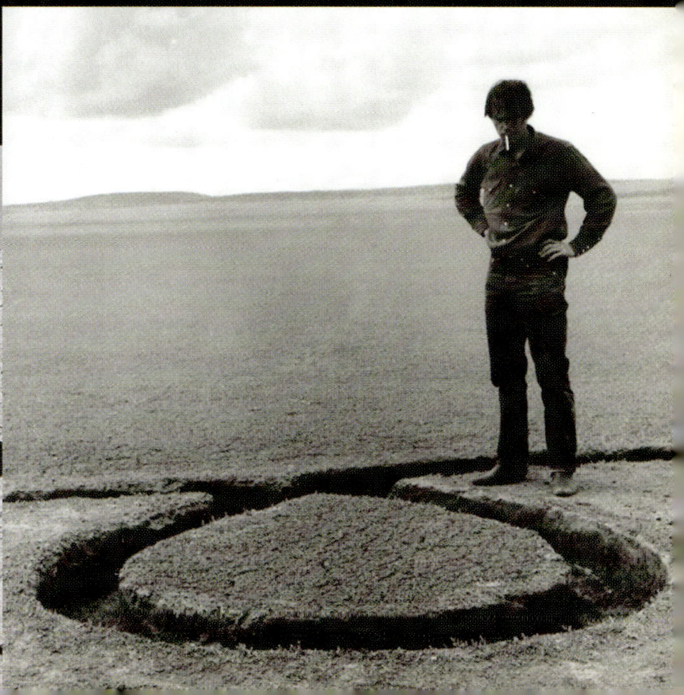

BAD BIRDS

LYNNE ROBERTS-GOODWIN

Lynne Roberts-Goodwin's "Bad Birds" are portraits of long-dead birds from the collection of the Department of Ornithology at the Australian Museum in Sydney. They were photographed in the artist's studio with the assistance of Dr. Walter Bowles, the Department's Head Veterinarian, and his assistants. The initial twenty portraits were made from the Australian Avian collection, including native Australian bird species such as the Budgerigar and the Ring-Necked Parrot. The birds were placed as if they were in a museum diorama but without the painted backdrop. They all face away from the camera, but are nevertheless easily identifiable as species by plumage, markings, and relative differences in upper-body proportions. The absence of the face confounds our anthropomorphic projections, frustrating our tendency to want to read certain kinds of temperament or character into the faces of animals. Of course, even though the frontal view isn't really necessary for species classification, it helps immeasurably in the identification of individuals, as official identity documents such as passports have long demonstrated. Indeed, a different strand of Roberts-Goodwin's own work acknowledges the utility of the conventional portrait view. In another of her animal projects, she worked with scientists on location at isolated royal falcon preserves in the Persian Gulf, in Oman, and the United Arab Emirates, recording royal hunting birds who were deliberately posed facing the camera in order to satisfy her royal clients. Roberts-Goodwin is now helping ornithologists in the region to develop animal passports that will at some point assist in the regulation of the international rare species trade and the eradication of the illicit hunting-bird market.

The reason why Roberts-Goodwin's bird photographs can simultaneously function in both artistic and ornithological spheres is that her images are highly exact, which is to say that the metonymy of plumage enables a surprising degree of information. For the "Bad Birds," she knew that rear-facing and less conventionally informative views would show the color shifts and marks in plumage that differentiate males from females and juveniles from adults, and even breeding from non-breeding birds. But at the same time she understood that turning the birds away, despite the ornithologically functional result, would inevitably suggest that she—or the birds—refused to disclose something essential of their character. Her series' title, "Bad Birds," amplifies this uncertainty. For much as we might like to project human emotions onto birds (and imagine that these once-talkative animals are like bad children, told to stand in a corner, face to the wall, or else suppose instead that the birds are shy, refusing to meet the camera's gaze), it is more the case that her "Bad Birds" are, first, the museum's imperfect, bad specimens and, second, that the categorization implied by "Bad Birds" invites precisely the kinds of psychological projection described above, even if to confound it by a studied, documentary neutrality.

—Charles Green

Photos courtesy of the artist and Sherman Galleries, Sydney, Australia.

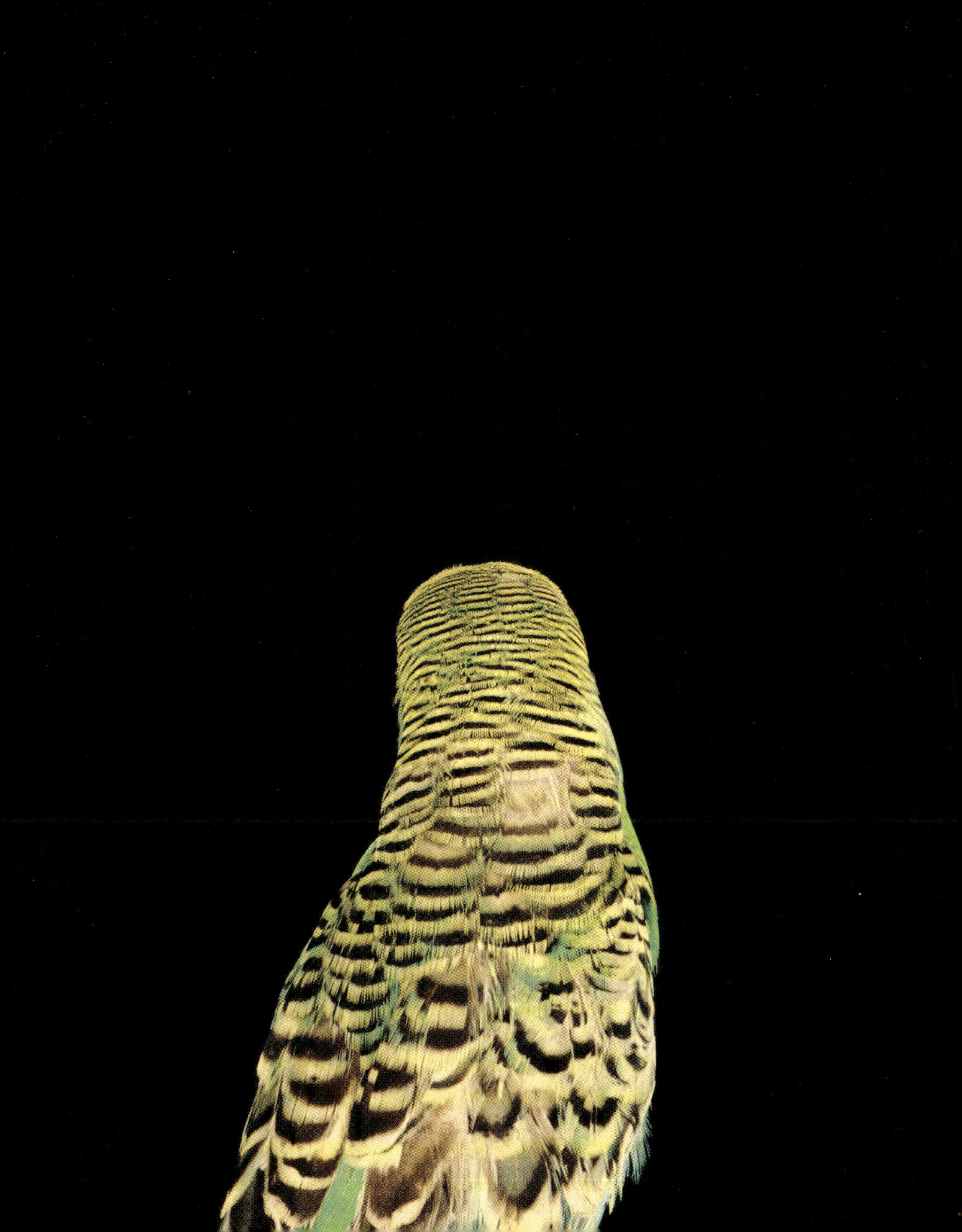

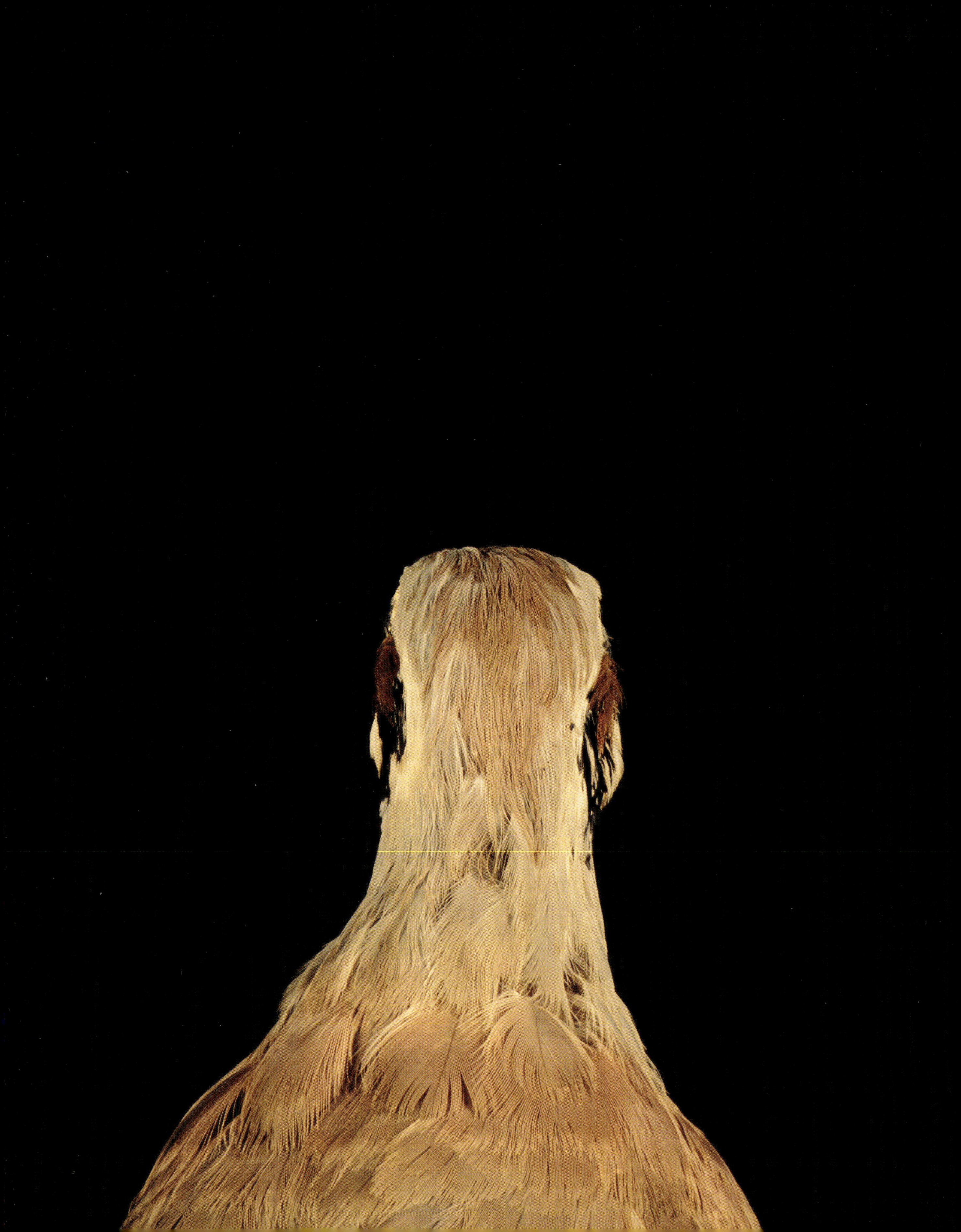

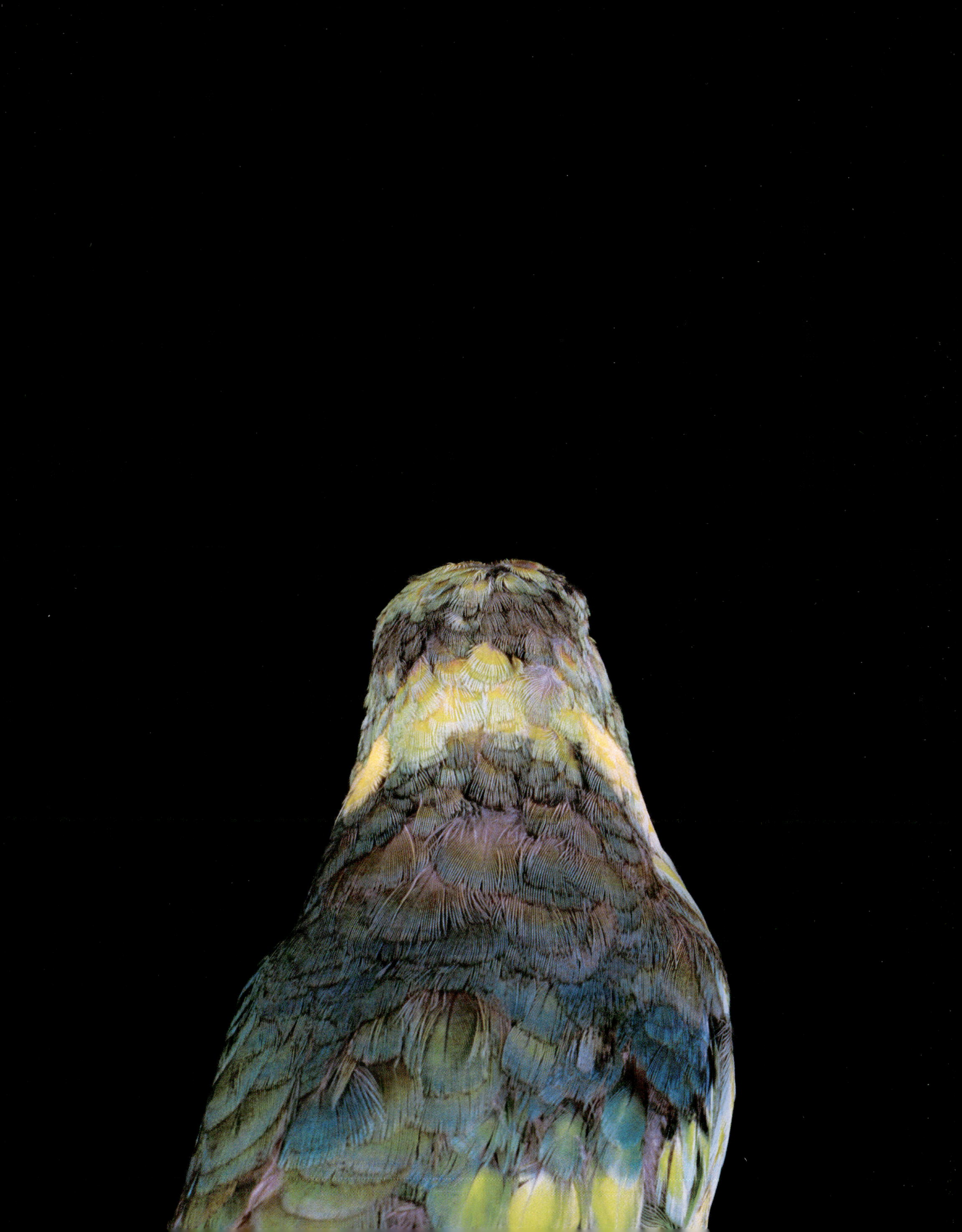

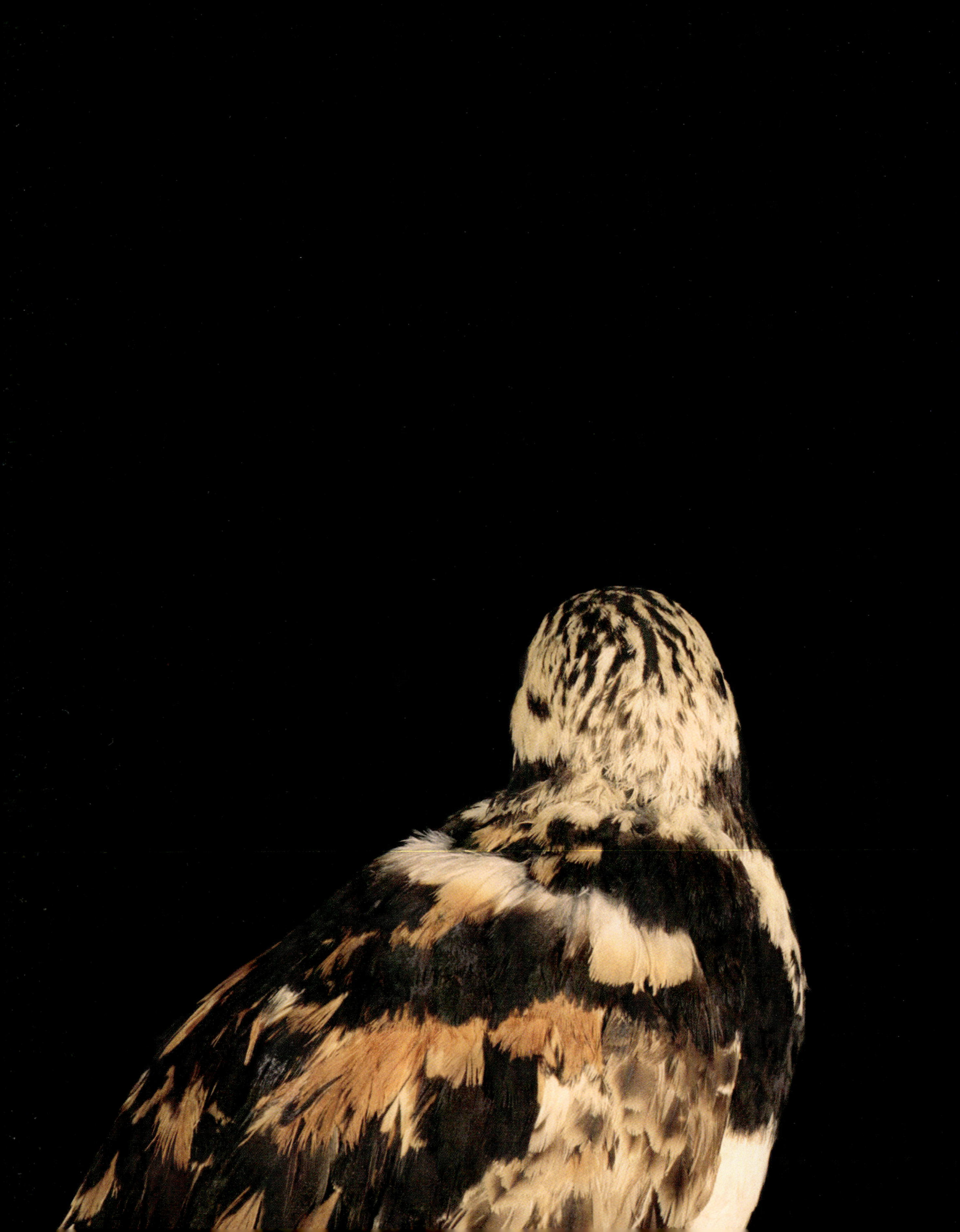

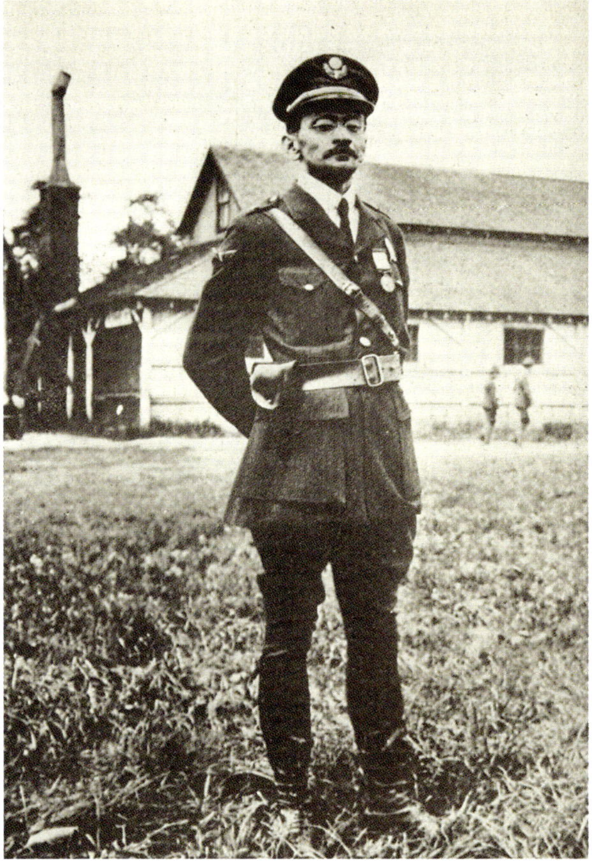

THE KINGPIN OF FAKERS

CHRISTOPHER TURNER

Why is a tomato red and a cucumber green? Why does a raw green banana become yellow when ripe and not blue? Why does a brown cow eating green grass produce white milk, which when churned makes yellow butter?

—Dinshah Ghadiali

In an archive box at the National Library of Medicine in Washington D.C., crammed between a crushed can of ozonated olive oil (invented and marketed by Nikola Tesla) and folders on dubious vitamin supplements, are three files of evidence relating to the Food and Drug Administration's investigation into a device called the Spectro-Chrome. An FDA agent who dismantled this curious machine, which looks like a simple aluminum slide projector mounted on a stand, described it as follows: "Examination showed that the device consisted essentially of a cabinet equipped with a 1000 watt floodlight bulb and electric fan, a container of water for cooling purposes, two glass condenser lenses for concentrating the light, and a number of glass slides of different colors."

Colonel Dinshah P. Ghadiali, who invented the Spectro-Chrome in 1920, claimed to be able to cure almost everything

above: Colonel Dinshah P. Ghadiali in his New York Police Air Reserves uniform.

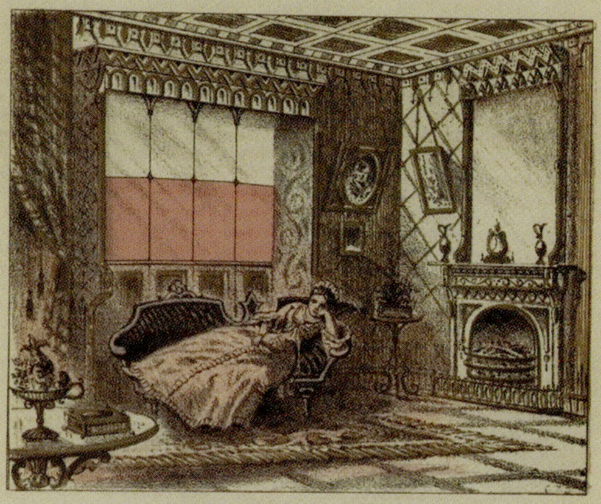

APPLICATION OF RED LIGHT, Full Bath.

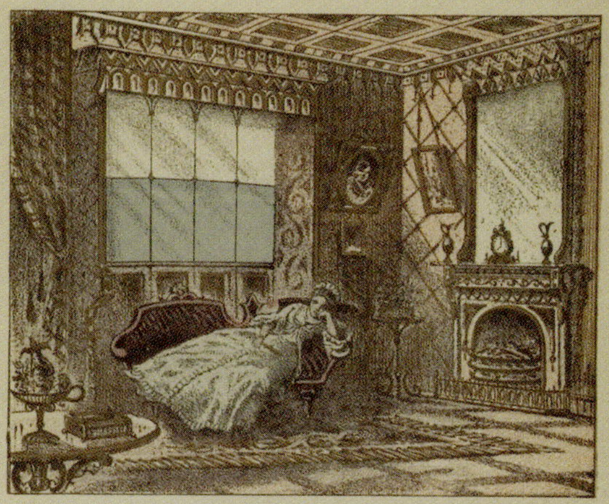

APPLICATION OF BLUE LIGHT, Full Bath.

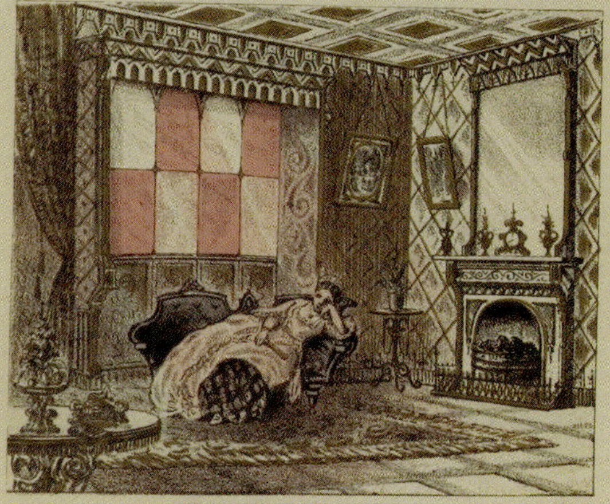

APPLICATION OF RED LIGHT, Partial.

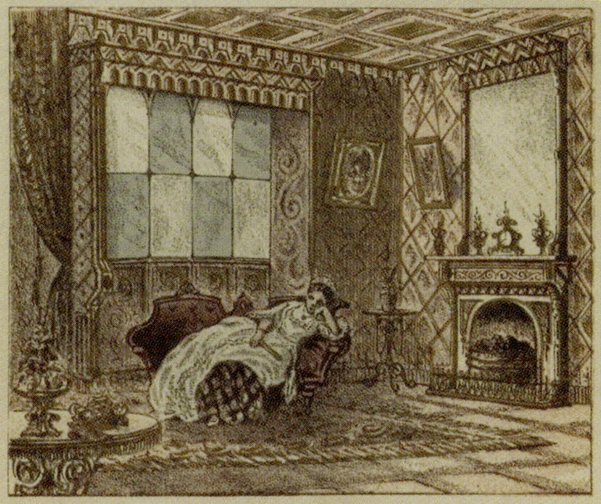

APPLICATION OF BLUE LIGHT, Partial.

with its twelve colors; after intensive treatment with "attuned color waves" a badly burnt infant now had satin-white silky skin, a blind girl's sight had been restored, and a paralyzed woman was able to walk again. "The Spectro-Chrome is *not* a lamp," Ghadiali asserted, "it is a system, a new, original and unique science." By 1946, he had sold nearly 11,000 devices, the most expensive of which cost $750, earning himself over one million dollars. "Many up-to-date homes are already equipped with a Spectro-Chrome just like the Electric Light, Telephone and Radio," Ghadiali wrote, adding hopefully, "soon there will be a SPECTRO-CHROME IN EVERY HOME."

The use of colored light in the treatment of illness and disease became fashionable in America in the late nineteenth century. While seeking a way to grow bigger grapes in his greenhouse in Philadelphia (the city where Ghadiali first established his Spectro-Chrome Institute), the retired general Augustus Pleasanton discovered that alternating panes of clear and blue glass was also the secret to restoring health. He published the results of these experiments in *The Influence of the Blue Ray of the Sunlight* (1876). Seth Pancoast extended this thinking in his *Blue and Red Light: or, Light and its Rays as Medicine* (1877), in which he cautioned against "light quacks" even as he claimed to have cured Master F., an eight-year-old paraplegic, after only a week under red glass, and Mrs. L., a 32-year-old widow suffering from severe sciatica, after only three sittings in a bath of blue light.

The following year Edwin Babbitt, an American teacher and mesmerist, outlined his own, increasingly complex color theory in *The Principles of Light and Color* (1878). Babbitt believed that everyone radiated their own brightly colored energy and that sickness was visible to psychics as an upset in the natural harmony of this color field. He invented a device to restore equilibrium that he called the Chromolume, a stained-glass window composed of sixteen colors which sold for $10. A less bulky $5 Chromo-Disk was marketed for easier "irradiations," as well as a Chromo-Lens for charging drinking water with medicinal color. *Scientific American* dubbed the color healing craze the "blue glass mania" and offered the following prescription: "blue glass one part; faith, ten parts; mix thoroughly and stir well until all common sense evaporates, as the presence of a minute quantity will spoil the mixture."

The mania for chromo-therapy spread to Europe, where Charles Féré, a psychiatrist working under Charcot at the Salpêtrière Hospital in Paris, tinted the windows of hysterics' cells with violet glass to create calming and curative effects (Féré thought of colored light as different waves or vibrations of radiant energy which could be sensed not just by the eyes, but all over the skin in a form of cutaneous vision). The fashion reached as far as India where Ghadiali, then working as the stage manager of a Bombay theater, read Babbitt's treatise. He had his first opportunity to apply Babbitt's principles of color therapy when a friend's niece was dying of mucous colitis, which no ordinary medication seemed able to cure. He made a DIY Chromolume out of an empty purple pickle bottle and a powerful kerosene lamp borrowed from the Highway Department; he irradiated milk in a blue glass container which he also had her drink (the Spectro-Chrome stored five vials behind the bulb center in which water could be charged for this purpose). Within three days she was apparently totally cured and Ghadiali devoted the rest of his life to practicing what you might call medical showmanship.

Ghadiali emigrated to America in 1911 and set himself up as an inventor in New Jersey (near his hero Thomas Edison), where he began to elaborate on Babbitt's theories, mixing them with Parsee philosophy, and updating the Chromolume to the era of electric light. Four years after he arrived, the *New York Times* reported that he had filed a patent for the Dinshah Photokinephone, which he claimed was the first film projector able to coordinate sound with flickering images without the use of a phonograph. The article claimed that he already had "several inventions to his name," such as the "Dinshah Automobile Engine Fault-Finder." The Spectro-Chrome, invented after a wartime stint as a pilot in the New York Police Air Reserves (where he rose to the rank of Colonel), promised to be even more miraculous. But how did it work?

In case Ghadiali's device appeared to be too simple, he invented a labyrinthine language of his own to explain its occult workings. The therapists Ghadiali trained at the Spectro-Chrome Institute had to spend 600 hours studying his convoluted three-volume instruction manual, *The Spectro-Chrome Metry Encyclopedia* (1933), as if clocking up the hours for a pilot's license. To summarize his theory: Ghadiali believed that the body was made up of oxygen, hydrogen, nitrogen, and carbon, which were colored blue, red, green, and yellow respectively. When the four colors are out of balance, people become sick, and the Spectro-Chrome promised to restore a natural harmony. Ghadiali published a chart which showed the twenty-two parts of the body that particular colors should be projected onto to cure different illnesses, and specified the exact time of day each hour-long sitting should take place in a series of complicated regional astrological tables.

"Tonations" had to take place in a darkened room while the patient was naked, with eyes open and head facing north, so the body would be aligned with the earth's magnetic fields. "Disorders with Growths or Tumours," read a typical prescription, "developing slowly within the body, may be irradiated with Lemon Systemic and Indigo Local on the Affected Area, with Magenta on 4 [left breast] or 18 [middle back] where so indicated... For Excessive Sex Craving, irradiate with Lemon Systemic alternated with Purple on Area 11 [genitals]."

Spectro-Chrome Metry was more a cult than a health cure; members of the "Scientific Order of Spectro-Chrome Metrists" were encouraged to wear a special purple skull-

opposite: Fashionable lady bathing in red and blue light. From Seth Pancoast, *Blue and Red Light: or, Light and its Rays as Medicine* (1877).

overleaf left: Chromo-Therapy in action using a "Kromayer" light. From a 1938 manual. Right: Ghadiali's "Free Guidance Chart". An FDA agent wrote in, describing his sick son's symptoms, and received this advice by return mail.

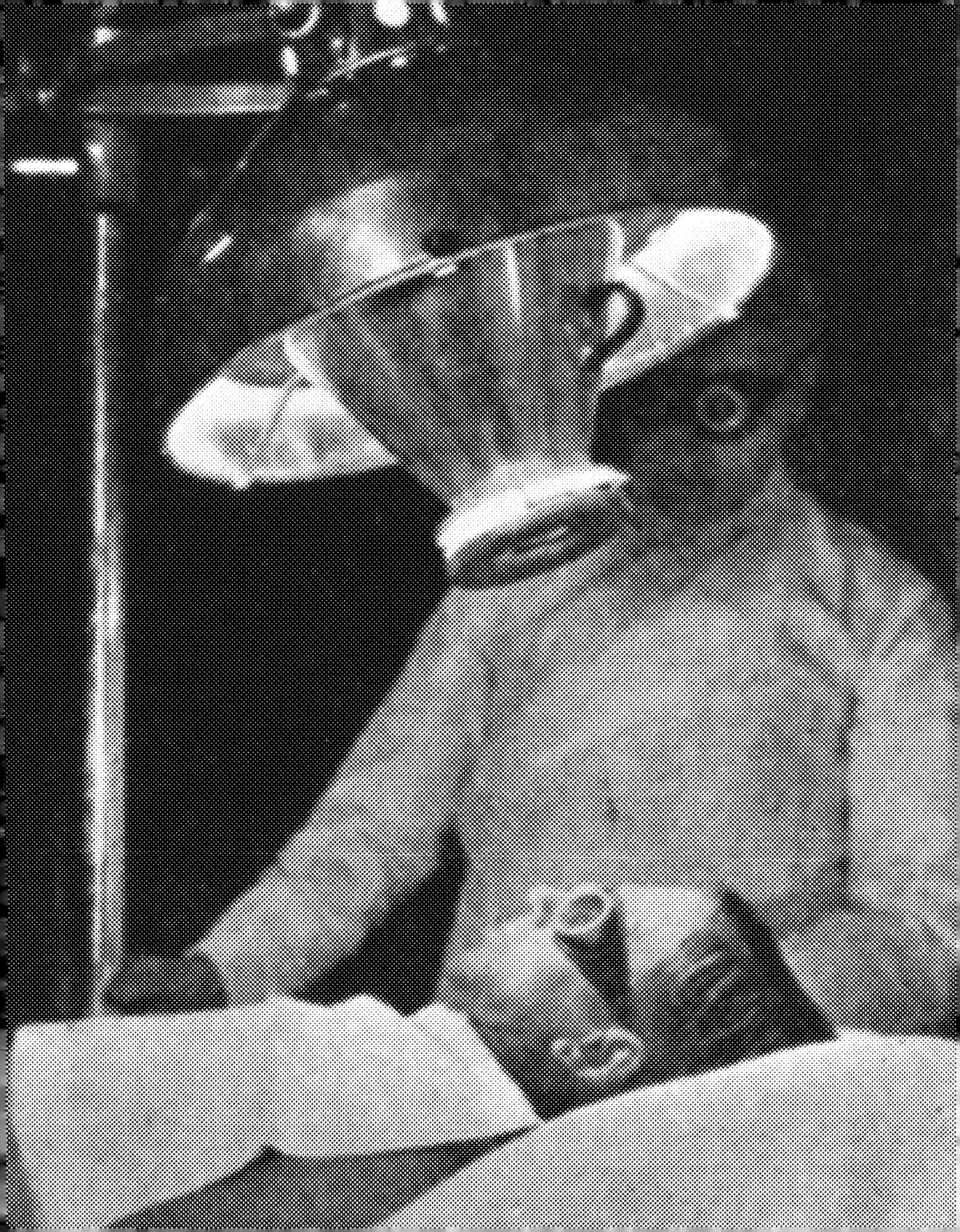

REFER TO AND STRICTLY FOLLOW ARTICLES PUNCHED ABOVE

Trade Mark Number 163,762

Registered U. S. Patent Office

SPECTRO-CHROME IRRADIATION

Free Guidance

FOR THE SERVICE OF MANKIND

ISSUED SOLELY TO BENEFIT STUDENT FOR USE IN IMMEDIATE FAMILY IN ACCORDANCE WITH THE FAVORSCOPE

Dinshah Spectro-Chrome Institute
Malaga, New Jersey

TO
Henry J. Van Wyke
29304 Walnut Street
FLAT ROCK, MICHIGAN

Dated DEC 26 1947

Chronos T 36 B
(Typing Time; Not For Irradiation)

We acknowledge receipt of your FREE Guidance Request about Yourself.

FOLLOW INSTRUCTIONS FOR TONATING SUFFERER BY IRRADIATING ATTUNED COLOR WAVES, ACCORDING TO PUNCHED DIRECTIONS ON ALL FOUR EDGES.

EDGE ALPHABET LETTERS ARE FOR ATTUNED COLOR WAVES; NUMBERS ARE AREAS

ARTICLES

a—Sufferer should sleep HEAD to NORTH, in SEPARATE bed, in room at comfortable Temperature.

b—High Heels, Silk Stockings, Furs, Feather Pillows, should be DISCARDED.

c—Stop TOTALLY use of Flesh, Fowl, Fish, Eggs, Honey, Tea, Coffee and so-called "Irradiated," "Vitaminized," "Homogenized" or "Enriched" Foods. Strictly adhere to Rational Food Of Man. Do not eat between meals.

d—On enclosed sheet, send particulars of what Sufferer eats and drinks in 24 hour period. Sign it in full in ink.

e—Stop promptly use of ALL Drugs, Dopes, Medicines, Pills, Potions, Plasters. Spectro-Chrome can NOT be combined with other Healing Systems.

f—Stop ALL Intoxicants, whether Brandy, Whiskey, Wine, Champagne, Beer, Root Beer, Cola drinks.

g—Stop Smoking entirely or never normalate. Tobacco, in any form should NOT be used.

h—Stop using ALL Laxatives, Cathartics, Rectal Enemas and Suppositories. Spectro-Chrome will soon produce necessary Eliminations in natural manner. Sufferer should become accustomed to Squatting Posture and using moistened Toilet Paper.

i—Stop ALL Vaginal Douches, Tampons and Chemical Syringes.

j—Stop Sex Indulgence until Disorder improves or controlling condition normalates.

k—Stop ALL Vaccines, Serums, Injections, Antitoxins, Immunizations, Hypodermics.

(over)

SPECIAL:—Follow Directions As Punched Herein—Follow Rational Food Of Man System.

STOP SMOKING FOR LIFE.
CHANGE FOOD.
SLEEP IN A SEPARATE BED WITH HEAD TO NORTH.
YOU NEED SPECTRO-CHROME SERVICE AS MUCH AS YOUR SON, FOR YOUR OWN BENEFIT.

Dinshah Spectro-Chrome Institute
by ______ S-C.N.

CONTINUE IRRADIATIONS AS PUNCHED ON EDGES AND REPORT PROGRESS BY COMPLETE GENERAL ADVICE CHART IN DAYS PUNCHED BELOW

1 2 3 4 5 6 7 8 9 10 15 20 25 30 60 90 Discontinue Tonations

Left edge: 1 2 3 4 5 6 7 8 9 10 11 12 13 14 15 16 17 18 19 20 21 22 — Systemic Front Back Local Once or Twice a Day — USE OPPOSITE EDGE TONATION

Right edge: R 1 O 2 Y 3 L 4 G 5 T 6 B 7 I 8 V 9 P 10 M 11 S 12 13 14 15 16 17 13 19 20 21 22 — Systemic Front Back Local Once or Twice a Day — NEXT DAY USE OPPOSITE EDGE TONATION cap as a symbol of their allegiance. Patients, who came for rest-cures at the Institute's "Chromarium," also had to adopt Ghadiali's many prejudices: he was against high-heeled shoes, silk stockings, caffeine, tobacco, alcohol, drugs, pills, potions, furs, and enemas. Ghadiali persuaded them to assume his own eccentric habits if they were to get well; he practiced vegetarianism (and published his own cookbook of recipes), gargled with salt, bathed in coconut oil, cleaned his teeth after each meal (he sold a special toothpaste), and preferred squatting over a hole to using a lavatory. When people wrote to him seeking a cure to their ailments, they were returned a "Free Guidance Chart"—instructing them as to what colors to project where and when—which listed all these peculiar rules along with some personalized instructions. One man—who was, in fact, an FDA agent—wrote in to describe his sick son's symptoms, only to receive unsolicited advice for himself:

"THE SUFFERER MUST: CHANGE FOOD. SLEEP WITH HIS HEAD TO THE NORTH, THIS CASE WILL NEED CAREFUL WATCHING

YOU STOP SMOKING FOR LIFE. CHANGE FOOD. SLEEP IN A SEPARATE BED WITH HEAD TO NORTH. YOU NEED SPECTRO-CHROME SERVICE AS MUCH AS YOUR SON, FOR YOUR OWN BENEFIT"

Ghadiali's slogan was, "No Diagnosis, No Drugs, No Surgery." "Stop Insulin at once," he advised diabetics, "and irradiate yourself with Yellow Systemic alternated with Magenta on Areas 4 or 18 and eat plenty of Raw or Brown Sugar and all the Starches!!!." These kinds of prescriptions were to make his run-in with the medical establishment inevitable. Ghadiali had never received any medical training, though he would often appear in full military regalia in the advertising material he used to promote the Spectro-Chrome as Colonel Dinshah P. Ghadiali (Honorary) M.D., M.E., D.C., Ph.D., LL.D., N.D., D.Opt., F.F.S., D.H.T., D.M.T., D.S.T. All of these qualifications, save the ones he awarded himself as President of the Spectro-Chrome Institute, were bought from diploma mills; his M.D., for example was bought for $133.33 from Oskaloose College, a diploma mill in Iowa. He wanted to be a doctor and disguised his jealous hatred of them by claiming that it was in fact the medical profession who felt envious and threatened by his cure-all. He published a cartoon of the "Medical Octopus" straddling the "Ocean of Ignorance" and the "Bay of Bunk", each tentacle a different medical institution. "This fearful-looking monster is the dread of America," he wrote, "but, the TRUTH behind the Scientific Researches of DINSHAH makes it squirm in agony. It dares not A PUBLIC DEBATE, because, Dinshah WILL pound it into pulp."

In 1931, Ghadiali was arrested in Buffalo for second-degree grand larceny after someone who had bought a Spectro-Chrome complained to officials that it did not perform as promised. He persuaded three surgeons to testify in his defense. Dr. Kate Baldwin, Senior Surgeon at the Women's Hospital of Philadelphia, claimed that she had successfully treated glaucoma, tuberculosis, cancer, syphilis, gastric ulcers, and serious burns with Ghadiali's device. "I am perfectly honest in saying," she told the court, "that, after nearly thirty-seven years of active hospital and private practice in medicine and surgery, I can produce quicker and more accurate results with colors than with any or all other methods combined—and with less strain on the patient." As a result of such testimony, Ghadiali was acquitted (he'd already spent eighteen months in jail in 1925, accused of having sex with his secretary, who was underage, though he maintained he'd been framed by the Ku Klux Klan). The American Medical Association, feeling that the government's expert witnesses had been humiliated in the trial, began their own investigations. They concluded in 1935 that the Spectro-Chrome, which they described as "a cross between a stereopticon and an automobile heater," was worthless. Ghadiali's machine, they wrote, was reminiscent "of the marvelous gadgets illustrated by cartoonist [Rube] Goldberg," which achieve minimal results with maximum effort.

After the passage of the Food, Drug, and Cosmetic Act of 1938, which granted the FDA new powers in regulating therapeutic devices, the government once again began to assemble evidence against Ghadiali. The Spectro-Chrome was only one of the devices on the market for localized color therapy—by 1938 you could buy the Emesay, Kromayer,

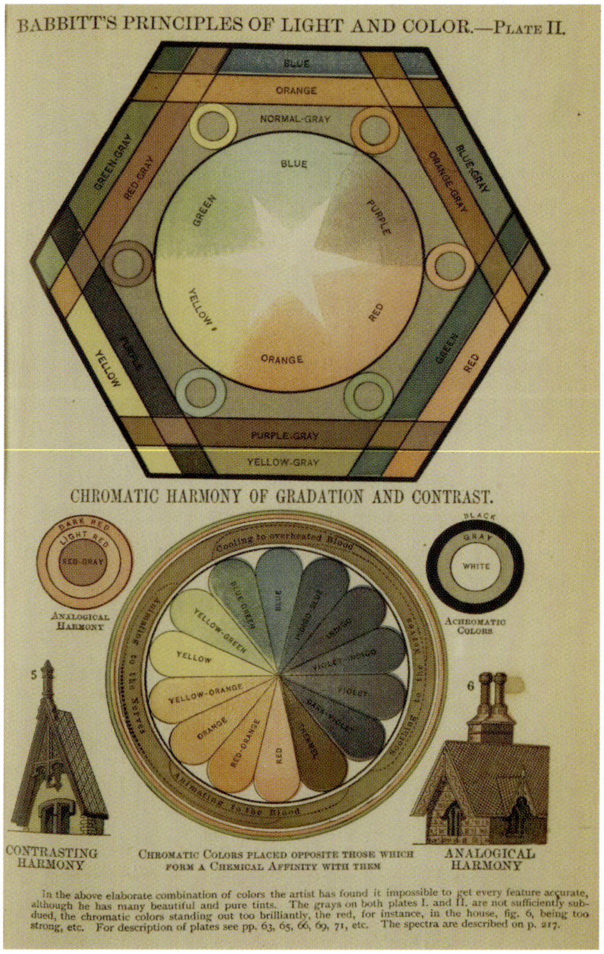

Alpine Sun, Helion, and Chromoclast lamps, all kitted out with localizing masks and color filters for chromo-therapy—but it was singled out for special investigation. FDA agents tracked down newspaper advertisements placed by people selling secondhand Spectro-Chromes, in order to try and identify dissatisfied customers. Agents posed as patients; doctors conducted independent trials. The post office provided the addresses of every Spectro-Chrome consignee, whom FDA agents then visited and interviewed (their names, collected in the McCarthy era, read something like a blacklist: Walter Chandler, Anna Cabaj, Dorothy Westphol, Stella Hitkowosk).

Finally, in October 1946, Ghadiali appeared in court charged with introducing a misbranded article into interstate commerce, a violation of the criminal code. "The use of colored lights would have no effect on health," the FDA concluded, "and when used as directed, or in any manner whatsoever, may delay appropriate treatment of serious diseases, resulting in serious or permanent injury or death to the user." Lawyers for the prosecution called seventy-six witnesses, including several of the experts in diabetes, heart disease, tuberculosis and cancer from whom they'd commissioned independent clinical trials and animal tests. They had found the Spectro-Chrome to be "of no value at all in any of their specialties." Any cures that had been made were attributed to auto-suggestion or to the diseases and fevers having run their natural course.

The government attacked five of the case histories in Ghadiali's *Encyclopedia* in particular, proving that his claims to have cured these patients were false—three had in fact died from their conditions. The burn victim Dr. Kate Baldwin claimed to have healed died a few months after leaving the hospital, her body one open sore. A blind girl who supposedly had had her sight restored by Spectro-Chrome Metry was still blind and always had been. The paralytic, treated from age three to seven with the machine and photographed in the book to prove she was able to walk after her color therapy, was pushed to the witness box in a wheel chair. She explained that she had been held upright until the camera was focused, wobbled for a fraction of a second while a picture was snapped, and was caught as she tumbled to the floor.

Ghadiali called 112 satisfied Spectro-Chrome users in his defense (fifty-seven of whom merely suffered from constipation) and the trial lasted two months as a result. Some of them had become quite dependent on their machines—one woman claimed she patted and talked to hers. But Ghadiali's case effectively crumbled when a patient he claimed to have cured of epilepsy with "tonations of Orange Systemic," went into seizures on the stand, slumped to the floor, vomited, and swallowed his tongue. A real doctor rushed over to him and stopped him from choking to death by holding his tongue down with a pencil. "The jury was sent out and the court was recessed," read the FDA's notes on the trial, "Dinshah P. Ghadiali stood coldly by and neglected to offer Spectro-Chrome treatment." After seven and a half hours' deliberation, the jury returned to declare Ghadiali guilty. His dream of having a "SPECTRO-CHROME IN EVERY HOME" ended when he was given a three-year prison sentence and fined $20,000; all his promotional literature was ordered to be burnt, and further production of Spectro-Chromes outlawed.

On his release in 1953, Ghadiali simply changed the name of his organization to the Visible Spectrum Research Institute; in 1958, the FDA obtained a permanent injunction through a federal judge and closed him down. He died in 1966, aged ninety-two. His son, Darius Ghadiali, is now seventy-seven and runs the latest incarnation of the Spectro-Chrome Institute, the Dinshah Health Society, still based in Malaga, New Jersey. He sells his father's books and pamphlets, but not his devices (the injunction still stands); however, he has published "Inexpensive Projector Plans" in his book *Let There Be Light* (1985), illustrating how to build a makeshift Spectro-Chrome out of cardboard, theatrical filters, and a reflector lamp: "Tonate with confidence," Darius Ghadiali writes, "using a 25 or 40 watt bulb" (after all, his father started out with a kerosene lamp and a pickle bottle).

During a recent telephone conversation, Darius Ghadiali described his father to me as "stoic, charismatic, short-tempered, autocratic," and told me that he was known as the "Kingpin of Fakers" because of the million dollars he made. "My father did tend to not necessarily quite stick to facts," he admitted, "he was a little bit flowery, which in the 1931 Buffalo case—the only major case he won—the judge called 'puffery,' but he also said that that in itself did not make fraud." The Institute made 500 Spectro-Chromes a year in its heyday, and Darius and his six brothers spent their childhood casting, assembling, and painting boxes. Though their father made a fortune selling Spectro-Chromes, he died $14,000 in debt. "It was made and spent," Darius explained, "on development, lectures, advertising, building, lawyers; very little for personal use—we lived on shoe strings almost."

The Society now boasts three to four thousand members, many of whom meet in Malaga for an annual conference. Darius Ghadiali considers himself to be living proof of his father's theories: he has only taken antibiotics once in his life, and told me that his current regimen includes drinking water charged with Lemon Systemic. "The time for universal use of Spectro-Chrome has not yet arrived, but it will come eventually," he concluded optimistically. "It has to: Spectro-Chrome is just too useful. There is nothing more powerful than an idea whose time has come."

---

opposite: Edwin Babbitt's color system, showing the spectrum's different physiological effects. From Babbitt, *The Principles of Light and Color* (1878).

C.V.—A WORK IN PROGRESS

PATRICK POUND

C.V.—a work in progress is a sort of covert operation.

In the early 1990s, as an artist with a taste for little deceits and art crimes, I decided to "infiltrate" the worldwide vanity press system. This was to be an artwork, or a "home project," undertaken as if by a character in a novel. I also liked the idea of an international project, undertaken at my little desk, that produced a vast range of artworks. Artworks I didn't have to make. I had noticed that there were plenty of good artworks out there if only artists were prepared to buy them.

C.V.—a work in progress began as a parody of the growing artists' mania for *curricula vitae* and the art world's literal obsession with identity. Over a decade or so, the project evolved into a collection of awards that beggar belief. Each new addition was a new piece of evidence, a new piece in the puzzle. Slowly I was putting together a thoroughly false, and amusing, picture.

By continuing the project for so long, and at such expense, I was aiming for a saturation of stories; for a fiction convincing in its thoroughness, if not its facts. Gradually I inserted a variety of half truths and outright fabrications into this vanity system. I began carefully, with the inclusion of a false hobby or two (lepidoptera, rugby) and went on to credit myself with invented projects, such as the editing of a book of letters of a nonexistent author, or the setting up of F.A.F.—a society dedicated to the uncovering of Fakes and Forgeries.

By paying to become a Fellow of the International Biographical Association, I was "awarded the right" to adopt the letters F.I.B.A. after my name. Letters from the vanity press companies were then addressed to Patrick Pound F.I.B.A. With this award came a stamped, embossed identity booklet. The fictional wheel had come full circle.

The sales pitches for these awards are now themselves a vast collection. I have dossiers of thousands of pages of offers, an archive awaiting display as "Pitches at an Exhibition." While the solicitations keep coming, late last year I called a halt to any further purchases from the procession of possible accolades. I closed the collection with a final sash and plaque when I became the International Artist of the Year for 2004.

My interest in fictional identities began in the early 1980s, when I faked a series of letters to the editor of a New Zealand newspaper. On one occasion, I succeeded in having 14 published in just two days; they were all regarding a music review and took all sides. Since 1989 I have written on and around my artwork under a collection of pseudonyms. Beginning with an ersatz interview in my first catalogue, *Fragments and Fakes*, I have affectionately parodied critical mannerisms, while saving money on author's fees.

My pseudonyms include Monica Smith (Monica being a pun on moniker), Dr. Gerry Ford (Ford, Gerry—forgery), the curator Ian Smith Jr. (Ian Smith Jr. being the son of Ian Smith, that is, Smith's son Ian, curator; that is, Smithsonian curator). Ray Fox is an allusion to Reynard the fox, that trickster of medieval marginalia. Under the name Simon Dermott, I have written several reviews of books, from Ralph Rugoff's *Scene of the Crime* catalogue to a crime scene photographer's guide. Simon Dermott was the specialist in museum security and the detecting, tracing, and exposing of forgeries from the film *How to Steal a Million*.

I am an artist working at the categories of things. Whether categorizing thousands of newspaper cuttings in albums by subject, or photographing people taking photographs, I am an artist who reads the world as an endless series of overlapping lists. From a collection of Lost Bird posters culled from the streets to a collection of early postcards of a single street I am copying the world in the form of the index. These works call into play the limits of description and the description of limits. From the collection of 365 unremarkable brown things, to twenty-six pieces of evidence lifted from my street and placed in bags, my work has the look of being made by someone who upon trying to explain the world, and having failed, has been reduced to collecting it.

If collection is consumption lived, then *C.V.—a work in progress* is a limit case. I have bought my way onto this ridiculous list and ended up with yet another collection for display.

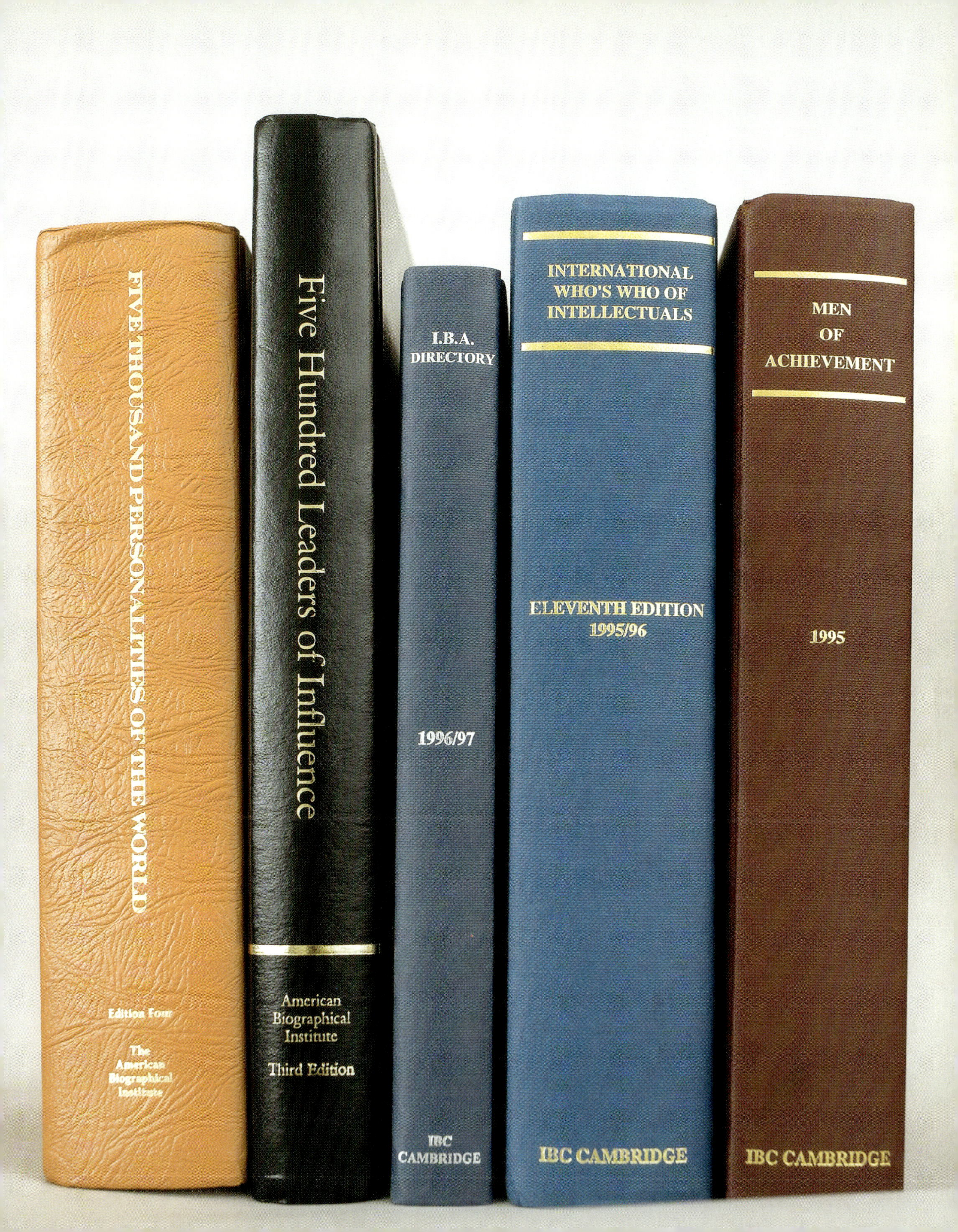
FIVE THOUSAND PERSONALITIES OF THE WORLD
Edition Four
The American Biographical Institute
Five Hundred Leaders of Influence
American Biographical Institute
Third Edition
I.B.A. DIRECTORY
1996/97
IBC CAMBRIDGE
INTERNATIONAL WHO'S WHO OF INTELLECTUALS
ELEVENTH EDITION 1995/96
IBC CAMBRIDGE
MEN OF ACHIEVEMENT
1995
IBC CAMBRIDGE

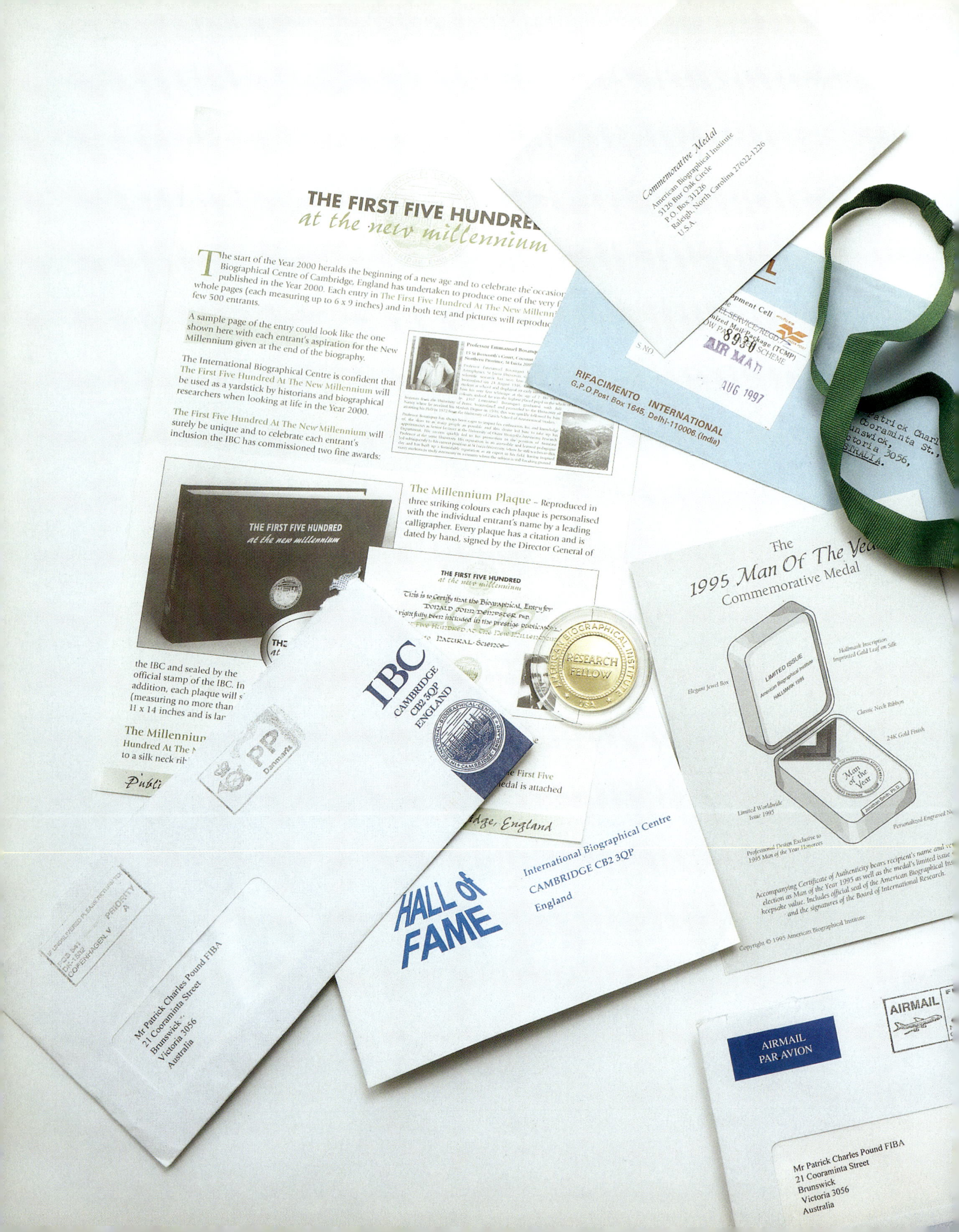
THE FIRST FIVE HUNDRED
at the new millennium
The start of the Year 2000 heralds the beginning of a new age and to celebrate the occasion
Biographical Centre of Cambridge, England has undertaken to produce one of the very
published in the Year 2000. Each entry in The First Five Hundred At The New Millenni
whole pages (each measuring up to 6 x 9 inches) and in both text and pictures will reproduc
few 500 entrants.
A sample page of the entry could look like the one shown here with each entrant's aspiration for the New Millennium given at the end of the biography.
The International Biographical Centre is confident that The First Five Hundred At The New Millennium will be used as a yardstick by historians and biographical researchers when looking at life in the Year 2000.
The First Five Hundred At The New Millennium will surely be unique and to celebrate each entrant's inclusion the IBC has commissioned two fine awards:
The Millennium Plaque – Reproduced in three striking colours each plaque is personalised with the individual entrant's name by a leading calligrapher. Every plaque has a citation and is dated by hand, signed by the Director General of
the IBC and sealed by the official stamp of the IBC. In addition, each plaque will s (measuring no more than 11 x 14 inches and is lar
The Millenniur
Hundred At The N
to a silk neck rib
THE FIRST FIVE HUNDRED
at the new millennium
e First Five
edal is attached
dge, England
Commemorative Medal
American Biographical Institute
5126 Bur Oak Circle
P.O. Box 31226
Raleigh, North Carolina 27622-1226
U.S.A.
RIFACIMENTO INTERNATIONAL
G.P.O Post Box 1645, Delhi-110006.(India)
AIR MAIL
AUG 1997
RESEARCH FELLOW
AMERICAN BIOGRAPHICAL INSTITUTE
The
1995 Man Of The Yea
Commemorative Medal
LIMITED ISSUE
Copyright © 1995 American Biographical Institute
IBC
CAMBRIDGE
CB2 3QP
ENGLAND
PP
Danmark
HALL of FAME
International Biographical Centre
CAMBRIDGE CB2 3QP
England
PRIORITY
COPENHAGEN V
Mr Patrick Charles Pound FIBA
21 Cooraminta Street
Brunswick
Victoria 3056
Australia
AIRMAIL
PAR AVION
AIRMAIL
Mr Patrick Charles Pound FIBA
21 Cooraminta Street
Brunswick
Victoria 3056
Australia

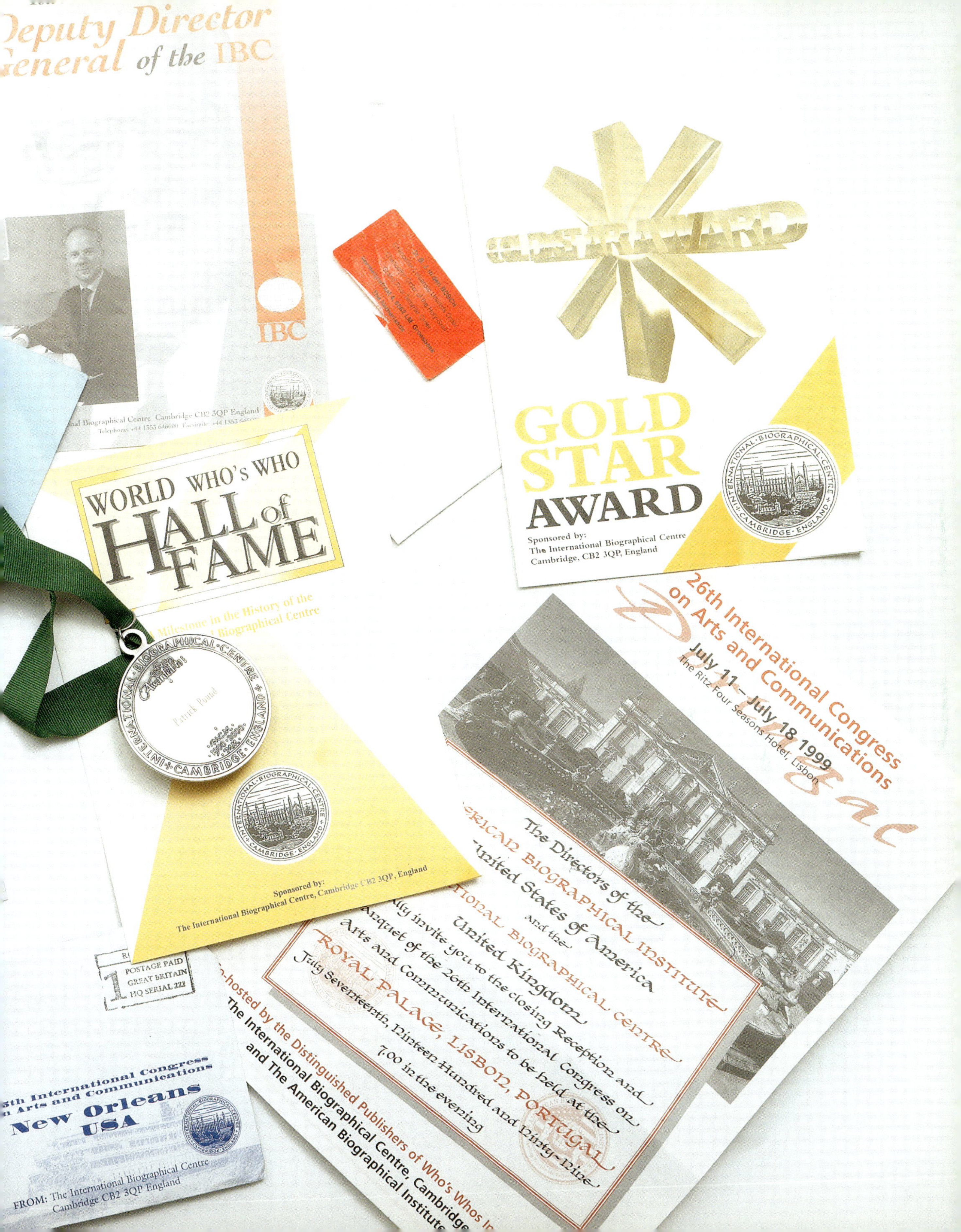
Deputy Director General of the IBC
IBC
GOLD STAR AWARD
Sponsored by:
The International Biographical Centre
Cambridge, CB2 3QP, England
WORLD WHO's WHO
HALL of FAME
INTERNATIONAL BIOGRAPHICAL CENTRE
CAMBRIDGE ENGLAND
Sponsored by:
The International Biographical Centre, Cambridge CB2 3QP, England
26th International Congress
on Arts and Communications
July 11 – July 18 1999
The Ritz Four Seasons Hotel, Lisbon
The Directors of the
United States of America
and the
United Kingdom
Royal Palace, Lisbon, Portugal
July Seventeenth, Nineteen Hundred and Ninety-Nine
7.00 in the evening
POSTAGE PAID
GREAT BRITAIN
HQ SERIAL 222
New Orleans
USA
FROM: The International Biographical Centre
Cambridge CB2 3QP England
The International Biographical Centre, Cambridge
and The American Biographical Institute

A MATTER OF DEGREES

ALLEN EZELL & JOHN BEAR

"In spite...of all precautions, it was not very difficult for medieval scribes to forge diplomas well enough to deceive rivals...So there are many bogus diplomas from that era."

—J.M. Wallace-Hadrill, *The Barbarian West: The Early Middle Ages, A.D 400-1000* (1952)

In 1986, a congressional committee found that over half a million Americans held fake degrees. Since then, fueled by the Internet, the situation has gotten a lot worse. Hundreds of degree mills now sell worthless diplomas, including medical and law degrees. Their total sales exceed $500 million a year.

Having spent many years investigating degree mills for the FBI, we can safely say that the University Degree Program (UDP) is the largest, most sophisticated, worldwide degree mill ever known. From 1998 to 2003, UDP marketed and sold degrees from over eighteen fictional universities (each with their own website). These institutions were supposedly located in four different European countries, and it was claimed that they were "recognized" by several non-existent, but academic sounding, entities. However, many of their campuses were no bigger than a mailbox.

Americans and Canadians represented about 85% of UDP's sales, and degrees were telemarketed for $2,900, with a $500 discount if you signed up immediately for an instant scholarship. Degrees were sold in all majors, including the medical field, and UDP provided letters of verification and recommendation to accompany them. They did all this from two round-the-clock "boiler rooms," located in Jerusalem and Bucharest, where ninety people, working for just over $1 an hour, manned the phones over two shifts. Degrees were printed in Jerusalem and wire transfers directed to Cypress and London, while credit-card payments were processed in Romania. The "degree package" you were sent bore a return address in Beverly Hills, and the degree verification fax was sent from Chino, California.

We estimate that the American who ran and owned UDP made $150,000 a day selling fake degrees. He was, in fact, a rabbi from Boston, Massachusetts. In 2003, after a lengthy FBI investigation, the Federal Trade Commission closed down his operation (though clones soon sprang up). The Boston Rabbi extorted $450 million through UDP but was fined only $57,000—roughly eight hours' revenue. The degrees and transcripts he sold, and probably continues to sell, will haunt the business and academic community for decades.

---

opposite: an extract from the telemarketing script given to University Degree Program employees. (The instructions to the caller are highlighted in bold and bracketed.) Note that the caller was instructed to say that the school was a "non-accredited diploma mill," but this was to be said quickly and softly. Not all of them did so and, in the authors' experience, if the person being called noticed and said, "What did you just say?" the phone usually went dead.

overleaf: fake diplomas

Hi, this is **[say your name]**.

I'm a registrar with the University Degree Program. I apologize for my European accent. We just wanted to contact you to tell you that, because we have some spaces left in our program, we reduced our registration fee by more than $2,000. What I am going to tell you is very important, so if you don't understand everything I say, just let me know. If now is a good time for you, I'll explain our new program and answer any questions that you might have.

[Wait—Continue only if you are not interrupting and he is not in a rush!]

That's great! The name of our institution is Thornewood University. We have no central campus. Our campus is in the homes and offices of our students. We are not affiliated with or located in any country, but we do have a mailing address in the United Kingdom. We are fully recognized members of distance-learning organizations in Europe. Our original founders got together in 1933 and now we are a part of a multinational group.

First of all, let me be honest with you. If you're looking for an accredited university, I suggest that you register at Harvard or Yale, pay the several hundred thousand dollars tuition, and study the many years required. Is this what you want?

[Wait—If "Yes," hang up!]

Or, would you rather have the benefits of an Ivy League education immediately with very little cost? **[Wait!]** Of course you would, so listen carefully! We don't give a damn about other universities, employers, professors, or anyone else. We only care about YOU! We will do anything legal, moral, and reasonable on your behalf. As your **[speak softly and fast]** nonaccredited "diploma mill," **[normal speech]** our job is to take care of your needs and wants by backing up your credentials. For example, we supply you with documents because of your work, private study, and life experience. Are we what you're looking for?

[Wait—if "No," hang up!]

Before I tell you more about our program, I want to tell you that I'm on your side 100 percent, and I am listening to everything you tell me. So that I can recommend the best program for you, please tell me, career wise, what you want out of your future.

[Wait!—listen closely to him, showing interest.]

In which field of study do you want your degrees?

[Wait—You can recommend a field of study here if needed.]

Good choice! Now, let me ask two brief questions. Do you feel that you have the potential to be a qualified professional in your field? **[Wait!]**

Do you feel that you only lack documentation of your accomplishments? **[Wait!]** With your background, I feel that you can take advantage of a PhD in **[state the name of his field]** or an MBA—the price is the same so, which do you prefer, a PhD, MBA, or both? **[Wait!]**

Of course, we'll give you a bachelor's and master's for background, right, **[say his name]**? **[Wait!]** You can comfortably use these diplomas to supply the documentation you lack.

These nonaccredited diplomas should reflect your credentials so that you can use them for business, employment, and personal purposes. However, this program will be successful only if the degrees are in a field for which you are qualified.

In fact, the initial diplomas and transcripts that you receive are sample documents that we tailor make according to your instructions. These documents are free when you pay to register for the program. Of course, you cannot use sample diplomas for licensing or transferring credits.

Now, before I tell you the low price of registration in our program, let's custom design your diplomas so that you know exactly what you are getting. Your diplomas will look exactly like those diplomas you've seen many times hanging on the walls of doctors, lawyers, and other professionals. Actually, most university diplomas look very much alike, but let's select a university and make your diplomas look like theirs. Of course, the diplomas will bear our university's name. What's your favorite university? **[Wait!]**

That's a good choice because they have a very impressive diploma. What name do you want printed on the diplomas? **[Wait!]** Can we put on your diplomas that you graduated with top honors? **[Wait!]** As to the graduation dates, we want them to correspond to your age. What year were you born? **[Wait!]** We'll date the diplomas to (dates—bachelor's, 2 years after DOS; master's, 4; MBA and PhD, 6.)

You can assume any titles that come with your diplomas. For instance, when you get the PhD, or MBA, you can legally call yourself doctor, or put "PhD" after your name. Do you plan to call yourself doctor? **[Wait!]**

In addition, to show what good students receive, there are custom-made transcripts and recommendation letters from professors at the university. Isn't this a great idea? **[Wait!]** We'll also issue laminated wallet-sized replicas of your diplomas so you can carry your credentials in your wallet to impress your friends. Do you understand? **[Wait!]**

Along with your materials, you'll receive our e-mail address, our UK mailing address, and our fax number for you to give to your prospective employers or anyone checking your credentials. Naturally, when we receive an inquiry concerning your qualifications, we verify that you received your diplomas. We even send certified copies when requested. You do want us to back you up when someone checks, don't you? **[Wait!]**

You have one full year to make any changes on your diplomas free of charge. The rest is up to you. You receive optional correspondence course lists and evaluation examinations so you can take the courses and get recognized degrees whenever you have time. Once your diplomas arrive along with their supporting materials, you're set for life. That's all there is to it. Isn't this perfect—**[use his name]**? **[Wait!]**

Excellent! Where do you want your diplomas and materials shipped? **[Wait!]** What is your daytime phone number? **[Wait!]** What is your evening/weekend telephone number? **[Wait!]** What is your fax number? **[Wait!]** What is your e-mail address? **[Wait!]**

Now, [use his name], our program is perfect because you designed it yourself but, if I were you, I'd only be concerned about one thing.

[Wait for him to say "What's that?"] Will your friends and relatives be jealous of your newfound success? **[Wait!]**

Let me ask you this—If I were to give you $250,000 in cash right now, would you give me $10,000? **[Wait!]** Of course you would. Do you know that a person with a college degree can earn $25,000 more per year? **[Wait!]** That means over ten years, a degree can be worth more than $250,000 in extra earnings. In other words, I'm offering you the equivalent of maybe a quarter of a million dollars, right [use his name]? **[Wait!]**

Moreover, we both know that I'm not going to ask you for $10,000. So now, how much are you willing to pay for $250,000 in cash? **[Wait!]**

<If he says $3,400 or more> Well, **[his name]**, I have an additional surprise for you. If you can invest just **[the price he said minus $500]** in your future for the program—for signing up right now, on this call—I'll mark your account "Paid in Full." It can't get any better than that. Which is easiest way for you to pay—cash, check, or credit card? **[Wait!]**

<Go to "Wire," "Check," or "Credit Card">

<If "Negative">

I'm a little confused, [his name]. You told me that you are willing to pay [the price he said], and I say the registration fee is only (the price he said minus $500.) What would you suggest? **[Wait!]**

<If anything else>

Well, I'll tell you what. If you can invest just twenty-nine hundred dollars ($2,900) in your future for the program—for signing up right now, on this call—I'll mark your account "Paid in Full." It can't get any better than that. Which is easiest way for you to pay—cash, check, or credit card? **[Wait!]**

SEQUOIA UNIVERSITY

CHARTERED UNDER INTERNATIONAL LAWS AND INCORPORATED
IN THE STATE OF OKLAHOMA, 8 JULY, 1952

College of Homœopathic Medicine

To all to whom these Letters shall come Greetings:

The Trustees of the College on recommendation of the faculty and
by virtue of the authority in them vested have conferred on

who has satisfactorily pursued the studies required for graduation as a
Physician and Surgeon
and passed the Examination therefor

THE DEGREE OF

Doctor of Medicine

With all Rights privileges and Honors
thereunto appertaining.

Given on the day of 19

SEQUOIA UNIVERSITY

J W Hough, MD. Ph. D.
PRESIDENT

N. C. Bourassa, BSc
SECRETARY

Florida State Christian College

To all whom these presents shall come, Greetings
The faculty and officers of Florida State Christian College
hereby confer on

who has satisfactorily and honorably completed the required course
of study and training, the degree of

In Testimony Hereof, *and by virtue of the authority in us vested by the State of Florida, this Degree is this day conferred. Signed and sealed at Fort Lauderdale, Florida, this day of 19 .*

QUAERERE et LIBERARE

Dr. Herman Keck, Jr.
Chancellor of the Florida State College

Millicent C. Rawitz
President of the Board of Trustees

Judith Rivera
Dean and Registrar

Dr. A. Richard Segran
Chairman of the Board of Regents

K H Kirkconnell
President

Dr. N E Stephenson
President of the Board of Education

Certificate Number:

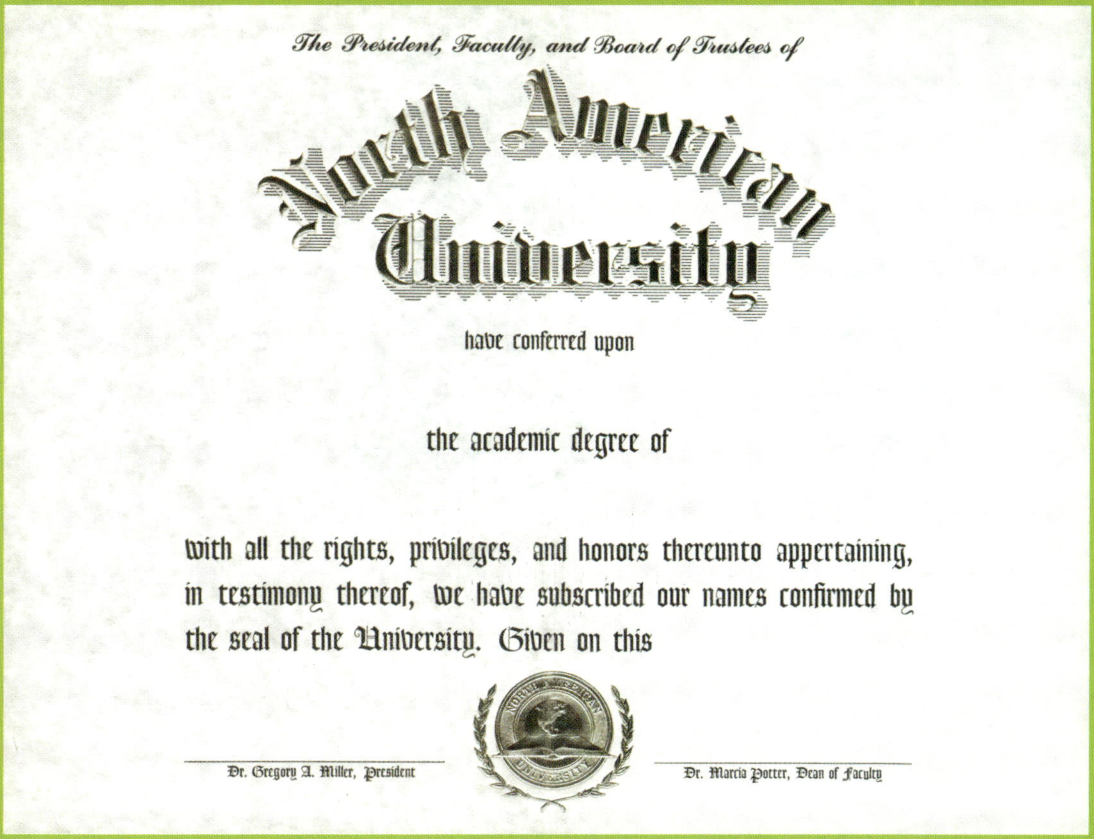

The President, Faculty, and Board of Trustees of

North American University

have conferred upon

the academic degree of

with all the rights, privileges, and honors thereunto appertaining, in testimony thereof, we have subscribed our names confirmed by the seal of the University. Given on this

Dr. Gregory A. Miller, President

Dr. Marcia Potter, Dean of Faculty

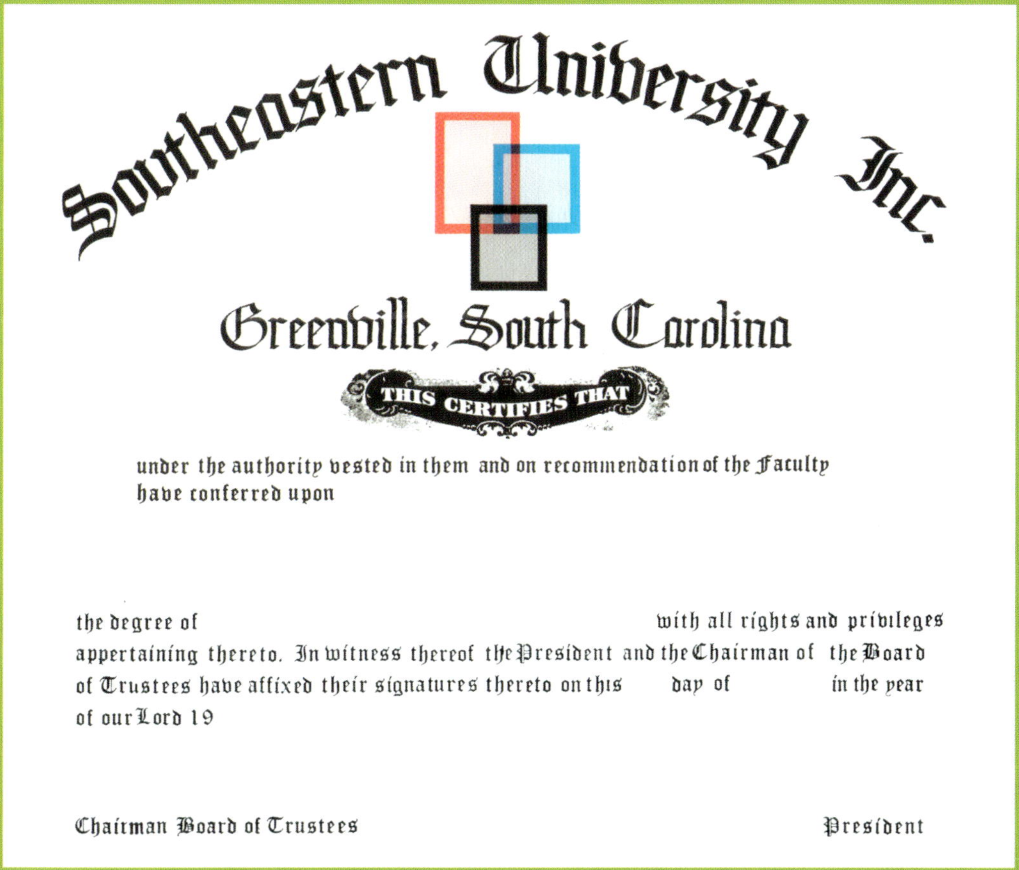

Southeastern University Inc.

Greenville, South Carolina

THIS CERTIFIES THAT

under the authority vested in them and on recommendation of the Faculty have conferred upon

the degree of with all rights and privileges appertaining thereto. In witness thereof the President and the Chairman of the Board of Trustees have affixed their signatures thereto on this day of in the year of our Lord 19

Chairman Board of Trustees

President

NEW FOUNDLANDS

GEORGE PENDLE

On 21 June 1972, the world's heaviest monarch, King Taufa'ahau Tupou IV of Tonga, accompanied by members of the Tonga Defense Force, a convict work detail and a four-piece brass band, set sail from his archipelago kingdom aboard the royal yacht *Olovaba*. On the king's stately mind was one thought—the invasion of the Republic of Minerva, located 270 miles to the west of his country's capital, Nuku'alofa.

The Republic of Minerva had done little to warrant the 400-pound sovereign's considerable wrath. It lay outside of Tongan territorial waters; it had been in existence for less than six months and, other than crustaceans and limpets, it had no inhabitants. Indeed, seeing as the Republic was situated upon the hazardous Minerva reefs, whose surface was completely submerged at high tide, it hardly seemed conducive to sustaining any human population whatsoever.

Yet the Republic was not entirely lacking the impress of humanity. Some of the reefs had been piled high with sand, and a small stone platform jutted through the waves. From this edifice flew the flag of the Republic of Minerva—a white torch on a blue background—clearly signaling dominion over the amphibious territory. But while this lone construction had survived the attentions of the tides, it could not hold out against the attentions of its new visitors. As the brass band played the Tongan national anthem (rough translation: "Hear our prayer, for though unseen / We know that Thou hast blessed our land. / Grant our earnest supplication, / and save Tupou our King"), King Tupou himself tore the scurrilous flag down and read a proclamation of sovereignty over the reefs. Within a few hours the platform had been dismantled, and the Republic of Minerva had been annexed without so much as a whimper.

Well, almost without a whimper. One curious footnote to this incident states that as the convict work detail set about removing all trace of Minerva from existence, a fight broke out between two of its members. By the time it could be stopped, one man lay slain on the reef. So it was that when the Tongan forces finally sailed for home, back to their presidential palace and prison cells, they left the former Minervan Republic with the remarkable statistic of having a murder rate higher than that of its population.

* * *

How many countries are there in the world? The question is not as simple as it seems. The United Nations claims 191 members; the United States Department of State supposes 192 independent countries, while the CIA *World Factbook* spreads its net even further by suggesting 268 nations, dependent areas, and other entities. But leaving aside whether territories or colonies such as Puerto Rico or Bermuda should be included (not to mention the political status of such "non-countries" as Palestine, Tibet, and Taiwan) there are a vast number of claims from other, less well-known nations asserting their independent status.

Call them micronations, model countries, ephemeral states, or new country projects, the world is surprisingly full of entities that display all the trappings of established independent states, yet garner none of the respect. The Republic of Counani, Furstentum Castellania, Palmyra, the Hutt River Province, and the Empire of Randania may sound fantastical, but they are a far cry from authorial inventions, like C.S. Lewis's Narnia or Swift's Laputa. For while uncertain territories like the Realm of Redonda might not be locatable in your atlas, they do claim a genuine existence in reality, maintaining geographical boundaries, flaunting governmental structures, and displaying the ultimate necessity for any new nation: flags. Admittedly, they may be little more than loose threads on the patchwork of nations, but these micronations offer their founders a much sought-after prize—sovereignty.

Such idiosyncratic nation-building can trace its roots to the early nineteenth century, when even the mightiest empire had yet to consolidate its grip on the more far-flung regions of the world. The swampland of the Mosquito Coast was just such an untouched area, and it was here that the Scottish adventurer Gregor MacGregor decided to found his new kingdom—the Territory of Poyais. The Scot might never have been heard from again had he chosen to live out his life in his small and inhospitable nation, but MacGregor was keen to transmute sovereignty into sovereigns.

Granting himself the title "His Highness Gregor, Cazique of Poyais," MacGregor traveled to Britain in 1821 and was received with all the hoopla that accompanies a visiting head of state. With the aid of a fictitious guidebook and hundreds of doctored maps, he proceeded to amaze the general public with tales of Poyais's European-style capital city and enlightened government (for a fuller appreciation of the scam, read David Sinclair's *The Land That Never Was*). Poyais land offices were set up in London, Edinburgh, and Glasgow, and he even managed to charm the London Stock exchange into advancing him a £200,000 loan for investment in the new state.

The hoax was exposed only when 250 Scottish investors who had been won over by tales of the bucolic and resource-rich country chartered a boat to take them to Poyais. They were greeted by the untamed jungle. Those who tried to eke out a living on the inhospitable coast swiftly died from disease. Others managed to escape to more temperate climes. MacGregor, however, grew rich from the scheme and lived out the rest of his days in Venezuela where, upon his death, he was accorded a state funeral fit for a monarch.

The Territory of Poyais displayed many of the themes that would appear in micronations for the next century-and-a-half: Firstly, that the love of money is usually a significant incentive in a micronation's foundation. Secondly, that a micro-nation's founders will always bestow upon themselves thoroughly dramatic titles. Thirdly, that since all the world's good spots have been taken, micronations are usually gifted with dire and hazardous geography. And finally, should any other country enquire into the status of a micronation, it is liable to collapse.

For example, take the Republic of Indian Stream, a self-declared republic in North America that existed from 1832 to 1835. An ambiguous border treaty between Britain and the US had created a 500-square-mile legal loophole between Canada and the state of New Hampshire. Three hundred enterprising American citizens, all hoping to avoid federal taxes, quickly established a government and constitution and declared Indian Stream a sovereign state. The Republic went unchallenged, but when one of its members was arrested for unpaid debts and taken to serve time in a debtors' prison in Canada, the Republic of Indian Stream swiftly planned a counterstrike. Crossing the border into Canada, they shot up a local judge's house, broke their fellow "Streamer" out of prison, and returned triumphantly home. This bravado did not last for long. By the next morning, doubts about the attack were mustering; British retaliation was feared, and before long the Republic voted to be annexed by the New Hampshire militia. Indian Stream was soon incorporated into the state, where its libertarian longing would continue to be nurtured for years to come.

There have, of course, been some exceptions to the avaricious underpinnings of micronations. In 1860 a French lawyer named Orelie-Antoine de Tounens traveled to South America to live among the Mapuche Indians. Horrified by their treatment at the hands of the Chilean and Argentine authorities, de Tounens argued that the Mapuche's lands did not automatically belong to either Chile or Argentina. With the apparent consent of his Indian hosts, he immediately declared himself King Orelie-Antonie of the Kingdom of Araucania and Patagonia, wrote a national hymn, designed a flag, and posted notices in the Chilean newspapers telling of the foundation of the new Araucanian kingdom. Despite his best efforts, he was roundly ignored.

In an effort to be taken seriously, de Tounens began to formulate plans for the Mapuche to attack the Chilean army. However, before he could send his subjects into glorious combat, he was betrayed to the Chilean authorities, declared insane, and deported. He would return to his realm on numerous occasions over the following years, traveling under false identities and bringing arms and ammunition to aid the Indians in their struggle. Each time, he would be captured or turned over to the authorities. He eventually died in France in 1878, penniless and thousands of miles from his kingdom. (The Kingdom of Araucania and Patagonia was briefly revived in the 1880s, when it was claimed as a real country in an import/export scam perpetrated in Morocco. Thus, despite de Tounen's idealism, his country never totally escaped the micropatrological lust for money.)

Micronations rose and fell over the next sixty years. But by 1945, it seemed as if the consolidation of boundaries following the two world wars would somewhat stem their growth. Occasional micronations were still being formed, but they seemed a little more frivolous than those of the previous century. In 1948, the Principality of Outer Baldonia was founded on a four-acre rocky island sixteen miles off the coast of Nova Scotia by Russell Arundel, self-proclaimed "Prince of Princes" and president of the Pepsi-Cola Bottling Company. With its governmental charter and sixty-nine admirals of the Baldonian Navy (fishermen who harvested tuna in the surrounding ocean), Outer Baldonia bore all the hallmarks of what would become an increasingly common type of micronation—the whimsical state. Its governmental charter insisted that citizens swear, drink, and lie about the size of fish they had caught, yet Outer Baldonia showed that even a joke country could punch above its weight when Arundel declared war on the Soviet Union. It took some time for this news to reach the USSR—diplomatic channels had yet to be formed between the two nations—but when it did, a coruscating article in a state-controlled Soviet publication condemned Baldonia's war-mad "fuehrer" and declared that Outer Baldonia's constitution had the aim of "turning his subjects into savages."

It was not until the 1960s and 1970s that a true renaissance of the ephemeral state took place. As Erwin Strauss recounts in his seminal *How To Start Your Own Country*, these seemed inspired most dramatically by the writings of Ayn Rand. The nineteenth-century adventurer had transformed into the twentieth-century libertarian. Filled with the prickly passion of libertarianism, many of these new nation-builders seemed edgier and more fanatical than their predecessors, as if the ever-increasing spread of legitimate nations had made their quest all the more desperate. Although charlatans, jokers, and a few idealists could still be found setting up new nations, they were now joined by survivalists and neo-Nazis wanting to start their own countries (such as Aryana and the Aryan Nation). Many of this new breed were thinking of more rigorous ways to ensure their sovereign rights.

One of the major problems in founding a new country, second only to being ignored, is the threat of invasion by a more legitimate nation. As a result, when a group of Ayn Rand disciples tried, in 1969, to set up a new country named Oceana, defense of the realm was paramount. Even though the exact location for Oceana had not been definitely fixed, boot camps were organized for all those who wanted to live there. Most ominously of all, plans were made to steal a nuclear missile, the ultimate deterrent should another country come knocking on their door. Fortunately, the group was disorganized and lacking in funds, and when the ringleaders decided to rob a bar to fund their project, the hapless group was promptly arrested and their startling story discovered.

Perhaps the most persistent character to emerge from this era of ephemeral states is Michael J. Oliver. A concentration camp survivor, coin dealer, and land developer, Oliver wrote the treatise *A New Constitution for a New Country* (1968) in which he created a model constitution for a nation whose extremely limited government could be financed voluntarily. Along with his sinister-sounding group, the Phoenix Foundation—whose members included John Hospers, the Libertarian Party's first presidential candidate—Oliver would spend the next decade in an emphatic quest for his tax-free independent state.

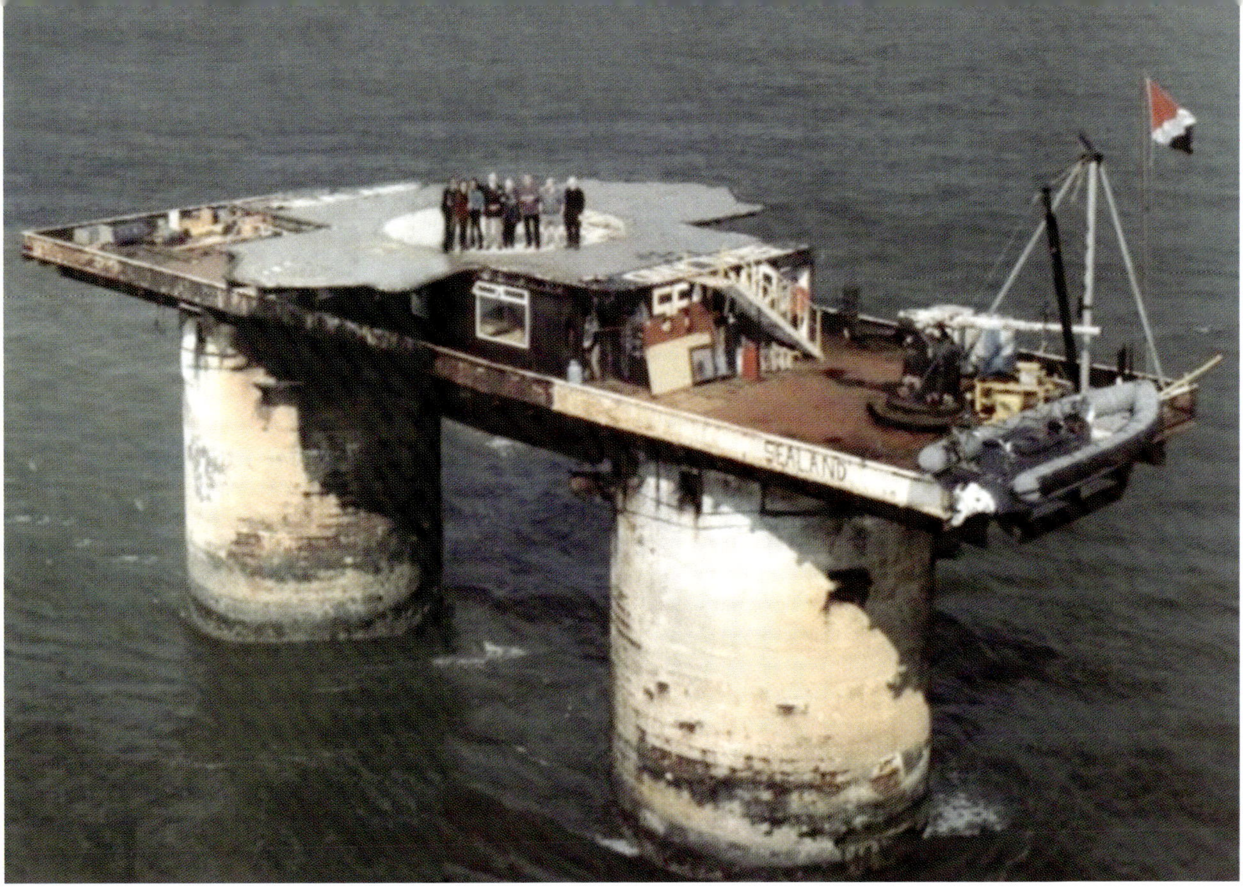

It was Oliver who, in 1972, had hired a dredging ship to deliver tons of sand to the Minerva reefs as part of a plan to build a resort there named Sea City. Before the Tongan intervention, he had hoped that Minerva would one day attract a population of 30,000, who would have "no taxation, welfare, subsidies, or any form of economic interventionism." A few years after the Minervan debacle, Oliver was at it again, this time aiding separatist movements on both the Bahamian island of Abac and the South Pacific Island of Vanuatu, in the hopes that the new governments would be sympathetic to his libertarian cause. But Oliver had overreached himself. Despite having provided financial support to 800 separatists on Vanuatu, his revolt was quickly crushed by the arrival of troops from Australia and Papua New Guinea. Oliver denied any wrongdoing, but by now the Phoenix Foundation had caught the eye of the FBI. With charges threatened against him for violating the Logan Act, which prohibits private citizens from interfering in US relations with foreign powers, the Phoenix Foundation slowly melted away. Oliver, unfortunately for those interested in his monomaniacal quest, has not been heard from since.

* * *

above: Sealand, a sovereign micronation founded on a North Sea anti-aircraft platform abandoned by the British after WWII. Image taken from a forthcoming film about Sealand by Framed Nation Films.

The United States Office of the Geographer stresses that five factors are needed to become a country: space, population, economic activity, government structure, and recognition from other countries. Of these, it is the last that has always been the hardest to attain. However, one micronation has perhaps come closer to fulfilling these requirements than any other. Founded by a former "pirate" radio operator, Paddy Roy Bates, Sealand is situated on an abandoned World War II anti-aircraft tower, seven miles off the British coast. Consisting of 550 square meters of solid steel, it was declared independent by "Prince" Roy in 1967. (The country's initial economic activity consisted largely of selling passports and minted coins—both common practices amongst modern micronations out to make a quick buck).

The first step in gaining international recognition came in 1968, when Roy's son, the Prince Regent Michael, was ordered to a British court for firing his rifle at a Royal Navy vessel that had come too close to the platform (he claimed they were planning an invasion). However, the court decreed that since the incident occurred outside British territorial waters, it had no jurisdiction in the matter. The second step came in 1978, when Alexander G. Achenbach, a German professor whom Prince Roy had named as prime minister of Sealand, staged a coup d'etat and invaded the platform with the help of some Dutch heavies. A furious Prince Roy hired a helicopter and retook the platform within a day, holding his invaders captive. Although he released the Dutch miscre-

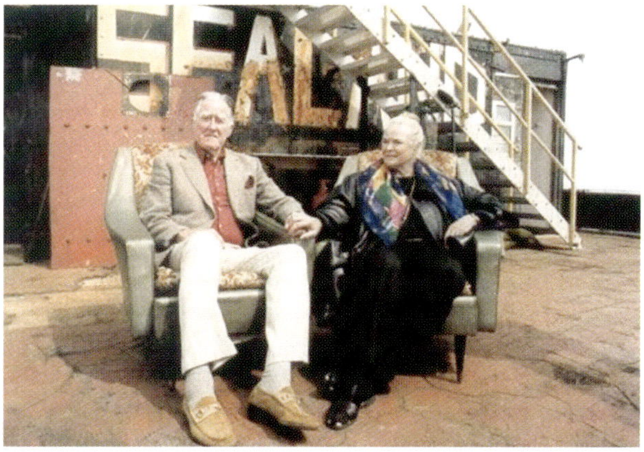

ants, he claimed Achenbach was guilty of high treason and imprisoned him indefinitely on the island.

Hearing of this strange event, the German authorities petitioned the British government for Achenbach's release. But the British government, citing the court decision of 1968, disavowed all responsibility for Prince Roy. Eventually, Germany was forced to send a diplomat to Sealand to negotiate with the monarch, allowing a delighted Prince Roy to claim that this official visit amounted to de facto recognition by the German government (the German government strongly denied this). Sealand's status remains uncertain, but it still exists to this day. Its latest guise has it acting as an offshore data haven, hosting secure web servers that are free from all international registration requirements.

Just as Sealand now plays host to the Internet, it is the Internet that has revealed itself as the host for a whole new generation of fictional state projects. As the libertarian fetish for micronations weakens, the virtual geography of the Internet grants a modicum of affordable tangibility to new micronations, without any of the traditional perils associated with abandoned anti-aircraft platforms or disputed South Pacific atolls. The Institut Français de Micropatrologie (<www.geocities.com/CapitolHill/5829>) does its best to keep track of them all, but these new micronations can be formed in little more than a day of battering at the keyboard. This new breed of countries does not try and make any actual claims on statehood, preferring instead to act as vehicles of whimsy and wonder.

Take the website for the Republic of Howland, Baker and Jarvis, (<users.metro2000.net/~stabbott/RHBJ.htm>). It claims to comprise a group of small islands that do actually exist (they can be found about 600 miles north of Tuvalu). Yet read the Republic's official history and you soon find that all is not as it seems. On 2 July 1937, Amelia Earhart is reported to have landed on Howland Island on her famed around-the-world trip. However, this was the leg of Earhart's journey on which she went missing, never to be heard from again. The founders of the Republic take this one fantastic moment as the starting point for a wonderfully convincing alternate history that shows how Earhart's brief visit to the island led to the growth of a modern nation-state.

In comparison, the Royal Kingdom of Elgaland-Vargaland (KREV) has no pull on believability. Although it claims physical territory, it insanely suggests that this consists of all the border frontier areas between all countries on earth. In doing so, the joint kings of KREV (for even these postmodern micronations can rarely resist the traditional attraction of a royal title) seem to be taking the artist Gordon Matta-Clark's *Fake Estates* project—in which Matta-Clark bought small, inaccessible, and unusable lots of land, situated between buildings—to its furthest logical extension. KREV is a country made up of the intersections between real countries, a nation of negative space—a micronation that is best to debate rather than to visit.

While these new nations rarely dare to enforce their claims to nationhood, it seems to be their unspoken hope that they will, one day, break out into the real world. In Jorge Luis Borges's short story "Tlön, Uqbar, Orbis Tertius," the author describes finding an entry in an encyclopedia for a country named Uqbar. No such country exists, but the author slowly comes to see it as the first indication of a massive conspiracy of intellectuals to imagine a whole new world named Tlön. Slowly but surely, the world of Tlön begins to seep into the real world, first in mentions in encyclopedias, then with the appearance of actual objects from Tlön, until the world of the narrator slowly and inexorably becomes Tlön itself. How long before a micronation makes this fateful leap into actuality?

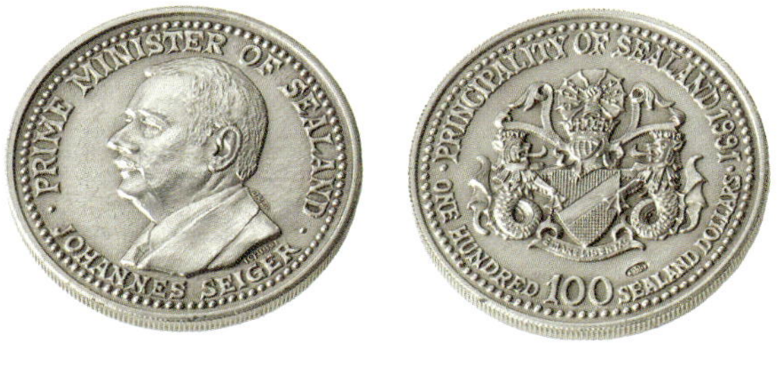

top: Prince Roy and Princess Joan of Sealand. Still taken from a forthcoming film about Sealand by Framed Nation Films.
above: Unauthorized Sealand coin minted by the "exile government" of Sealand based in Germany and headed by Johannes Seiger, successor to Alexander Achenbach, leader of the rebels in the attempted coup of 1978. Photo Ryann Cooley

HATING YOUR COUNTRY

CECILIA SJÖHOLM

A work of art such as Leif Elggren's and Michael von Hausswolff's Royal Kingdom of Elgaland-Vargaland plays on the allegorical and fictional character of the modern state, working with seemingly arbitrarily implemented systems that make up its machinery and creating fictional techniques for approval of citizenship, laws, money, institutions, and so on.[1] Revealing the modern, democratic state as a mere formality surrounded by the functioning machinery of such techniques, independent of any territorial weight, a work of art such as this shows the kernel of the community as an empty space, lacking in substance and flesh. The modern nation-state appears to be a fictional creation, rather than a community of substance, in terms of its territory, language, and culture. The reason for this is that territorial concerns and the religious, ethnic, and historical issues they tend to carry are never raised in the context of a project like Elgaland-Vargaland. One may, perhaps, interpret this imaginary state as a commentary on the dispassionate machinery of a Scandinavian, bureaucratic, social democratic state, appointing its citizens through formal application rather than hearty allegiance.

It is difficult, however, to relate the comic relevance of such fictions to more passionate manifestations of the nation-state where territory *is* at stake—in war, in the face of destruction by a foreign power, or perhaps in the promise of independence from former occupants. The territorial conflict between the Israelis and Palestinians would refute any allegorical modeling of the state as empty of substance. Rather than allow its citizens to be appointed through application to a state that already exists in a finite form, Israel has tried to expand its borders according to the placement of its citizens. The territorial claims of the conflict have their background in diverse considerations—ethnic, religious, historical, or simply strategic. This is, naturally, typical in cases of disputes: when former Yugoslavia disintegrated, one of the main problems was the entangled web of considerations motivating those that pulled the strings in the conflict. What either side will have in common in such conflicts, however, is a passionate investment that appears to refuse the dismantling of the nation-state or its representation as empty or allegorical. Such passionate investment can be called nationalism. The passionate investment will be spiritual rather than territorial, but the two cannot be separated. Only in a fully settled national context will issues of territory evaporate and be made invisible, allowing for national substance to disintegrate or reveal itself as technique, ideology, and symbolism. In cases where borders are in dispute, however, the fictional character of the nation-state has yet to emerge in a finite form: the state will claim its identity through territory rather than rely on symbols. In other words, the symbols of the state will be identified with territorial claims and little else. This means, of course, that critique of national technique, ideology, and symbolism will appear to threaten the existence of the state itself. It also means that artists and intellectuals will be unable to criticize the idea of the nation-state in order not to appear as traitors.

Does this mean, then, that "safe" states, where border disputes have been resolved, will enjoy a higher level of sophistication when it comes to artistic and intellectual critique of their identities? Does it mean that passionate investment in the state as a religious, historical, or ethnic idea is the fanatic and barbaric consequence of states of war and repression, whereas the artistic and intellectual critique of nationalism is the outcome of peace and democracy? Ever since the Enlightenment, progressive European intellectuals have been raised in a spirit of cosmopolitanism. The contemporary inheritors of Montesquieu are numerous—Julia Kristeva, Jacques Derrida, and Giorgio Agamben have all adhered to this tradition, to mention only a few. And since the disintegration of the Third Reich, it is not only intellectuals who have learnt to shun political nationalism as an exaggerated love for the homeland, as a perverted form of fixation to which only extreme groups on the right will be dedicated. While cherished in the United States, the political value of "patriotism" is very low in Europe and never brought into election campaigns.

Strangely, however, only a loving relation to the nation-state has been made taboo. Love, however, is rarely isolated from its counterpart, hatred, and intense investments such as love or hatred are never far apart when it comes to the nation-state. Overall, the powerful effect of a negative investment in one's homeland is an underestimated force in the life of intellectuals. There is a fine tradition of hating one's country in European cultural life; where loving your country is considered chauvinist, hating it has been regarded a healthy critical force in progressive circles. However, both the political left and right have shown tendencies to rationalize affective investments, and looked at more closely, such investments bring them closer to one another than they may like to think. Emotional investments in a nation, whether loving or hateful, are simply too excessive to be rationalized as critique, however much leftist intellectuals wish to cover their abjection as political criticism. The hatred of a nation may be as powerful as love, and as confused about its motives and sources. The nation is an object of identification releasing an array of desires and drives. Never a neutral concept, it is a symbolic body that is as politically and culturally charged in rejection as in adulation. When the nation becomes an object of exaggerated investment, whether the terms of that identification are positive or negative, the relation to the nation-state becomes based on an economy of what psychoanalysis calls *the drive*. The nation becomes a fleeting, imaginary object through which narcissistic forces of introjection and projection are released. Neither an object in the proper sense of the term, nor a fantasy, the nation becomes that non-objectal entity that may catapult the full power of the drive.

Such a relationship has forced writers, artists, and intellectuals into excessively rejective modes of writing, rationalized as social criticism, ever since the beginning of the twentieth century: Friedrich Nietzsche, August Strindberg, and Knut Hamsun are examples of such excessive rejection, as are Ferdinand Céline and Ezra Pound. Nietzsche despised the incapacity of his fellow countrymen to rise above the banal discourses that defined them. Martin Heidegger, arguably, did the same as Nietzsche in his definition of *das Mann*, dreaming of the emergence of works of art that would truly capture the grains of Germanic being that he sowed through his philosophy. Strindberg and Hamsun both hated the social environment of their contemporaries, blaming its shortcomings on an ingrained provincialism. Céline incarnates a position where an exaggerated *hatred* of the nation is reversible in relation to an exaggerated *love*, as incarnated in the dream of a strong, potent nation. Céline's extreme and fascist form of subversion is less interesting than the logic of his abjection: all his judgments relate to his identity being determined by an authority into which he projects the capacity to recognize him in the fullness of his being. The dream of a "mystic positivity," as Céline has put it, that would save us from suffering is not only a symptom of fascism but an illusion that has proved common through the investment in the nation-state. It is produced by ideologies reinforcing nationalism through propagating the erroneous belief that identities may become strong through a direct identification with a strong symbolic order such as the nation. The promise made out by such beliefs, however, may easily end in disappointment and, thus, in the kind of rejective excesses that is exemplified by Céline. Hatred or love of the nation are reversible afflictions, resulting in similar symptoms: exaggerated affectations and deluded beliefs concerning the role that the nation can play in the core of one's very being.

Hating one's country is in no way isolated to the beginning of the last century, however. There is only one thing that makes me get up and sit down at my writing desk in the morning, the late Austrian writer Thomas Bernhard said: my intense hatred of Austria. His colleague, Elfriede Jelinek, has continued to slaughter Austria's "culture of death" in novel after novel, play after play, as intensely disgusted by it as Bernhard ever was. Numerous writers and artists in voluntary exile will testify to a highly ambivalent relation to their home country. The other side of cosmopolitanism is that it may well be fueled by a perhaps unacknowledged hatred of one's country. Indeed, the nation itself can be defined as a fictional space in a sense much broader than that of borders or bureaucratic machinery. The nation is also a fictional object. Although it is not an object in the full psychoanalytic sense of the word; i.e. not an object of desire, it has been fictionalized as a fantasmatic space of libidinal investment. We only need to think of the Oedipalization of national belonging that occurs when we speak of the nation as the "fatherland" or maternal soil of our being. Investment in one's home country will be motivated not only by a sense of belonging, as the ideology of nationalism will pretend, but also by unconscious motivations of desires and drives. It is widely recognized that the nation-state is a creation of modernity. The ideology of it being a necessary creation is refuted by the many nations whose borders are mainly contingent in character, rather than the necessary product of history, religion, and the development of an ethnic and linguistic community. It is also recognized that the rise of nationalism has contributed to the spread of racism and the systematic repression of ethnic groups that lack national definition. The extent to which the nation may be part of the unconscious formations of fantasy and desire, however, are rarely brought up and discussed, not even in by intellectuals and artists who may well be feeding off such investments in their work.

Julia Kristeva, in her cosmopolitan ethics, has argued for an objectal understanding of the fiction of the nation. If the nation is to serve any function in the formation of the individual's capacity of identification at all, then that function must be compared to that of a transitional object. Just as the transitional object paves the way for full and loving relations for the child, and prepares it for encounters with the outside world in a mode of safety and self-assurance, so the nation should prepare its citizens for a wider sense of being. Identification with the nation must, however, be brought to a point where it is lost and replaced with an acceptance of identities as split and faulty—thus the insistence on the nation as transitional rather than a final goal. The nation is, in the best-case scenario, a good image of identification only to be traversed in the same way that a loving mother must be given up as object of desire. Its reversal into a bad object can have disastrous adverse effects through that same logic. At best, the nation is an instance in a greater international context, offering its citizens a reassurance of belonging which they can use for the benefit of a contemporary cosmopolitanism: "[T]he transitional nation [...] offers its identifying (therefore reassuring) space, as transitive as it is transitory (therefore open, uninhibiting and creative), for the benefit of contemporary subjects: indomitable, individuals, touchy citizens, and touchy cosmopolitans." There is a decisive difference between a cultural nationalism advocating a universalist ideal, and a romantic nationalism which augments the drive of identification rather than offering transitory possibilities of sublimation. As a transitional object of identification, the nation is to be likened to Montesquieu's *esprit general*, offering a historical identity that can serve as a foundation for wider and more generous processes of identification. A wider possibility of identification offers its embrace and inclusive welcome also to the private sphere. One is not to feel alienated for being in one's own world, and the specific cultural, sexual, and religious differences of individuals are to be respected through the law. Such an esprit general would counteract the regressive drives of nationalism, without effacing the value of possibilities of identification.

The modern nation threatens to catapult its subject into an exaggerated discourse of love or rejection, all directed toward an imaginary object that may seem to offer everything but gives little in return. The modern democratic nation may present us with the extraordinary promise of a strong, symbolic order, but this is also what releases the possibilities of its own undermining as a space of democratic ideals. The collapse of an imaginary space of unity, the space of protection and guardianship, into an imaginary space of projective identification, may be historically contingent and require many factors to be realized, but there is no doubt that the threat of an intolerant nationalism is built into the construction of the nation-state as such. When the promise of the nation is made too strong, or may seem too weak, the threat of a freefall beyond that promise arises. When the fiction of a strong nation begins to appear transparent and faulty, it may well produce rejection and hatred by subjects who demand a powerful fiction to identify with, and with such rejection the threat of fascist tendencies that claim to rebuild the strength of the nation will begin to appear politically viable. It is therefore understandable that cosmopolitanism will appear as a solution to many intellectuals, offering a disinvestment in the anti-democratic developments of national identification. The problem is, however, that cosmopolitanism may too easily do away with that which Heidegger has told us belongs to our state of "thrownness": our belonging to a nation (or a people, as he puts it) which will define us precisely through that which escapes identification—pointing to that which will remain foreign through any kind of "technical" definitions of belonging that we may use. Paradoxically, Heidegger in his seemingly nationalist discussions of the poeticizing of the "earth" in *The Origins of the Work of Art*, shows that poetry (the epitome of art, according to Heidegger) will carry with it an excess in relation to any kind of world it will unravel, an excess that will point to the foundation of a people and the history that makes the definition of a people possible. The search for foundation, however, opens a lack of ground, and the need to establish a foundation elsewhere than in the values one has become used to apply. Thus the idea of the nation as foundation of the community must give way for the realization that the nation is nothing but the history of its origin, and thus the product of a kind of creation that can be seen in a work of art: uncanny, foreign, and excessive. It is no longer the nation that defines the work of art, but the work of art that defines the nation. The nation, therefore, cannot be anything but the investment in uncanny cultural products that will define and redefine its origin. If cosmopolitanism, therefore, is useless as a remedy against nationalism because it fails to acknowledge the passionate investments in the nation that the fiction of the nation itself seems to propel — in terms of love or hatred — then Heidegger is right at least in acknowledging that the nation will continue to haunt us because it is part of our state of thrownness. And if cosmopolitanism has failed to create a worldwide movement of solidarity, a collective sense of undoing the investment in national identity and nationalism, it may well be because the nation belongs to the conditions that will continue to determine the way we define ourselves through that which is foreign to us. Hating your country may well be better than pretending you do not live there.

1 See pages 96-97 for more information on Elgaland-Vargaland.

BORDERVILLE

INVERTEBRATE

Invertebrate posted a request to the online film community for the titles of movies featuring border crossings. *Borderville* is assembled out of objects ripped from these movies.

Pages 73-78, left to right: rain clouds, *Salvador*, 1986; mountains, *The Great Escape*, 1963; soldier with binoculars, *Three Kings*, 1999; customs building, *Touch of Evil*, 1958; Sweet & Low upholstery van, *Up in Smoke*, 1978; helicopters, *Three Kings*, 1999; moustached customs officer, *The Day of The Jackal*, 1973; customs officer with detector dog, Traffic, 2000; road and herd of goats, *Blackboards*, 2000; Mexico border point, *Traffic*, 2000; French customs official, *The Day of The Jackal*, 1973; Swiss borderline, *Shining Through*, 1992; Alpine mountains, *The Living Daylights*, 1987; halt sign, *Shining Through*, 1992; warning sign, *The Long Goodbye*, 1973; danger sign, *Bad Boys II*, 2003; barbed wire, *Blackboards*, 2000; lookout tower, *Salvador*, 1986; blue sky, *The Wild Bunch*, 1969; rocks, *Blackboards*, 2000; helmet, *Europa*, 1991; road, *From Dusk Till Dawn*, 1996; traffic cone, *Traffic*, 2000; access control barrier, *The Living Daylights*, 1987; checkpoint, *Three Kings*, 1999; luggage on trolley, *Not Without My Daughter*, 1991; customs booths with barriers, *In America*, 2002; searchlight, *Bad Boys II*, 2003; floodlight, *Traffic*, 2000; barren mountain, *Blackboards*, 2000; three guards, *Kundun*, 1997; clear blue sky, *The Sound of Music*, 1965; parcel, *Blackboards*, 2000; flaming buckets, *Not Without My Daughter*, 1991; muddy rivers and trees, *The Wild Bunch*, 1969; watchtower, *Bad Boys II*, 2003; car, *Salvador*, 1986; lookout post, *Three Kings* 1999; Department of Justice sign, *In America*, 2002; desert, *In This World*, 2002; El Salvador coat of Arms, *Salvador*, 1986; hazy sky, *Gandhi*, 1982; walking stick, *Blackboards*, 2000; cello, *The Living Daylights*, 1987; customs and immigration facia, *Touch of Evil*, 1958; dead dog, *Up in Smoke*, 1978; border post No A/102 sign, *Kundun*, 1997; traffic queue, *Traffic*, 2000; jeep, *Not Without My Daughter*, 1991; desert hill, *Three Kings*, 1999; traffic cones, *From Dusk Till Dawn*, 1996; green sky, *In This World*, 2002; dog, *Up In Smoke*, 1978; queue, *Salvador*, 1986; Italian flag, *The Day of the Jackal*, 1973; wooden fence, *The Great Escape*, 1963; shoe, *Blackboards*, 2000; Welcome To Austria sign, *The Living Daylights*, 1987; Welcome To France sign, *The Day of The Jackal*, 1973; yellow sky, *In This World*, 2002; You Are Leaving The United States sign; *The Wild Bunch*, 1969; check point sign, *Not Without My Daughter*, 1991; dry grass with flag, *Refugee*, 2000; soldiers, *Three Kings*, 1999; tent, *In This World*, 2002; exploding bridge, *The Wild Bunch*, 1969; hands and passport, *Europa*, 1991

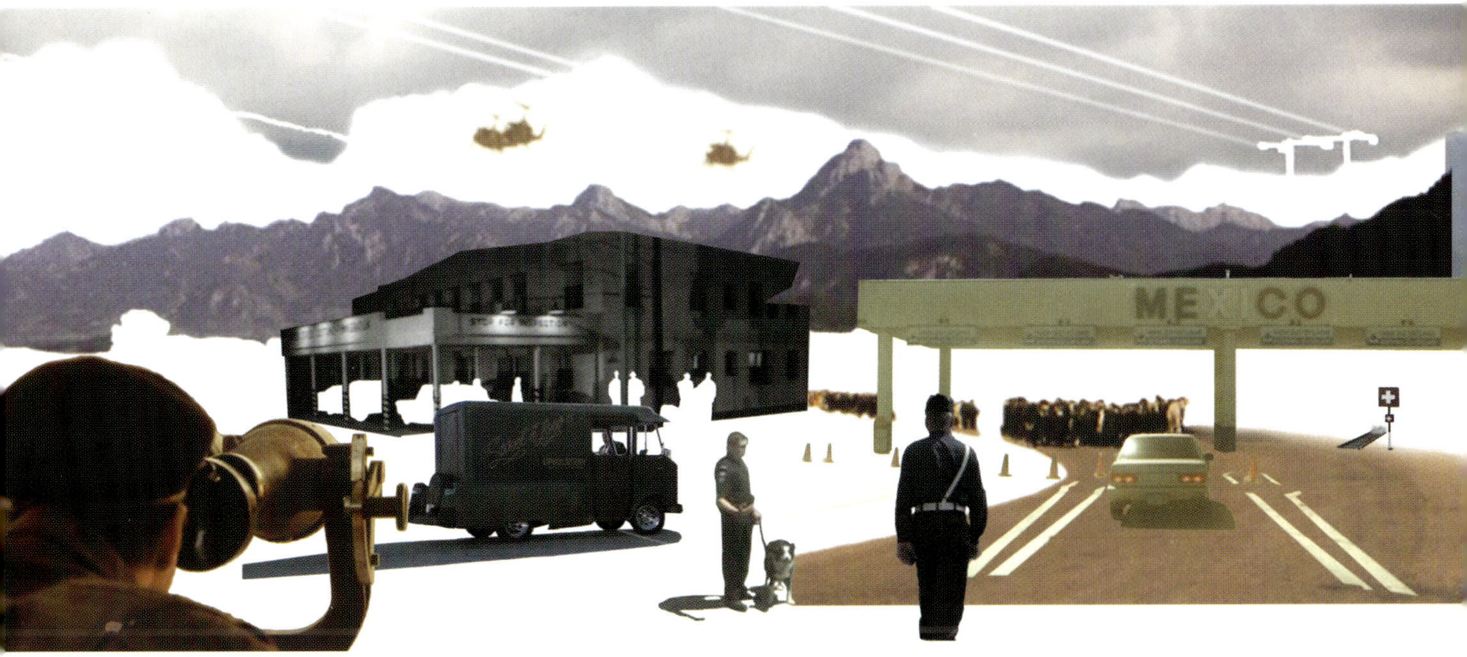
MEXICO

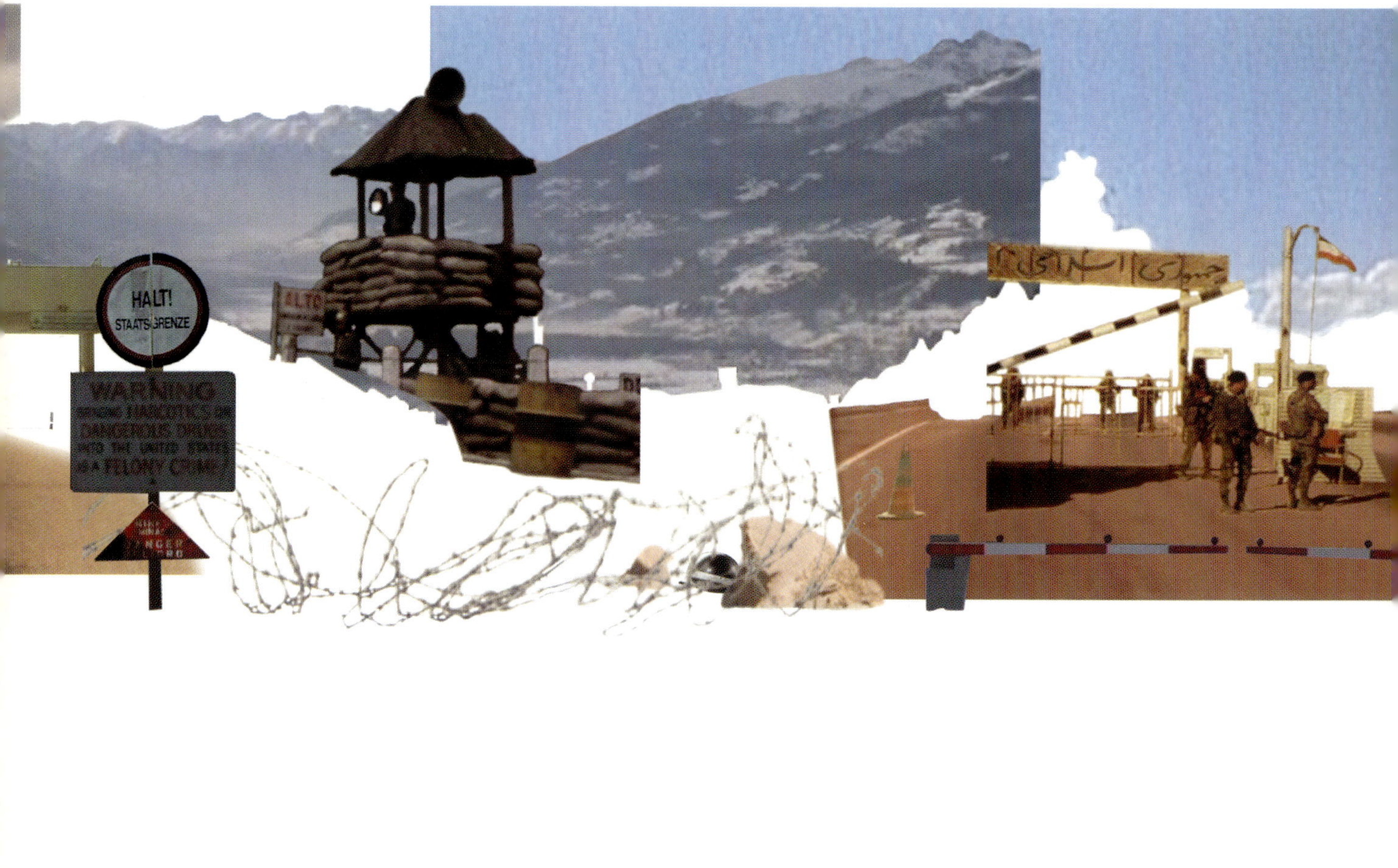
HALT!
STAATSGRENZE
WARNING
BRINGING NARCOTICS OR
DANGEROUS DRUGS
INTO THE UNITED STATES
IS A FELONY CRIME

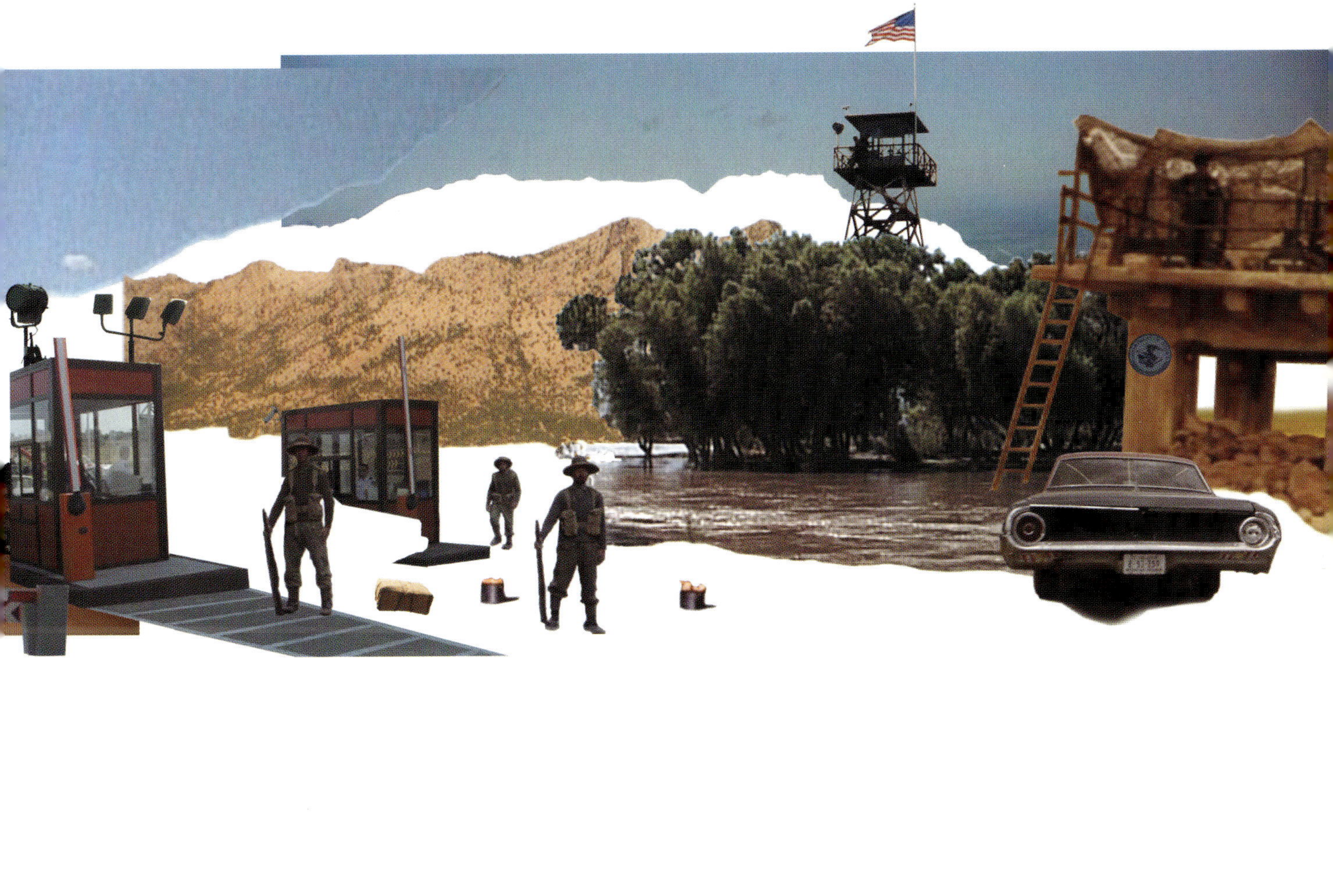

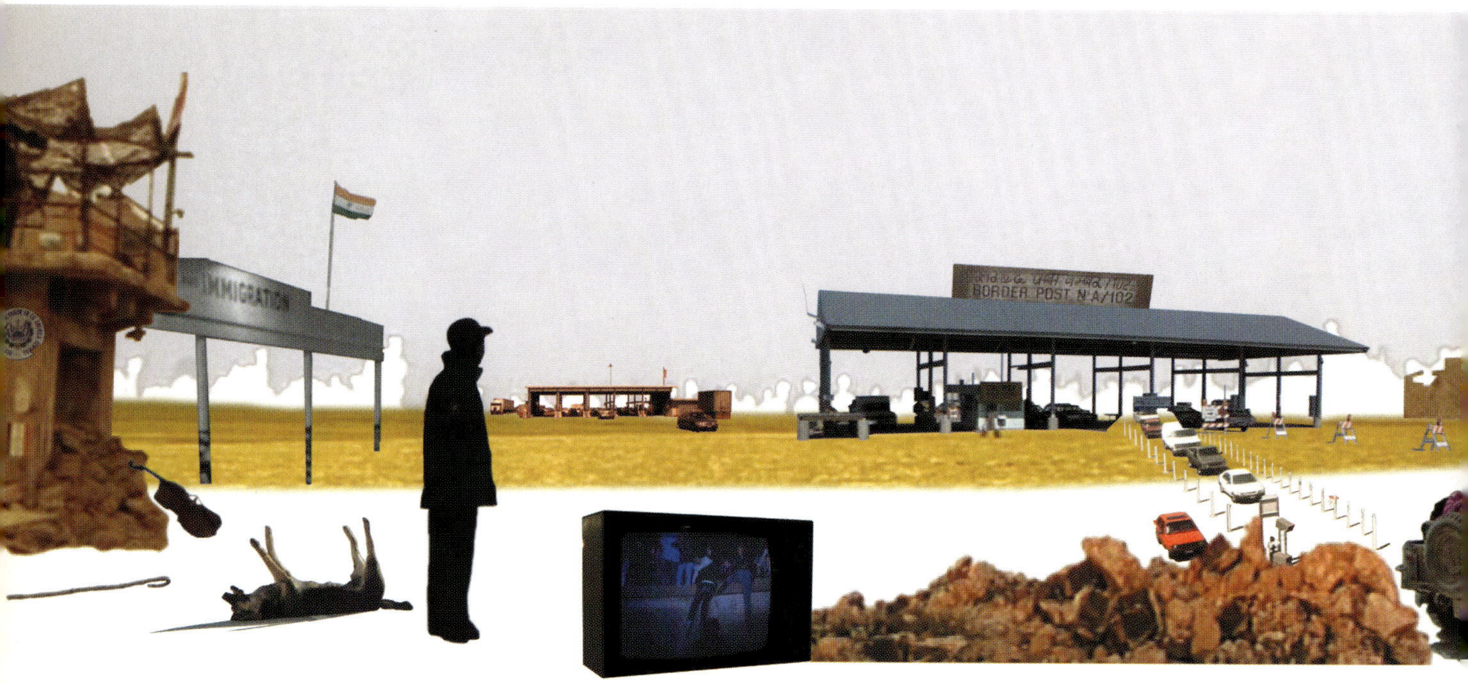
IMMIGRATION
BORDER POST N°A/102

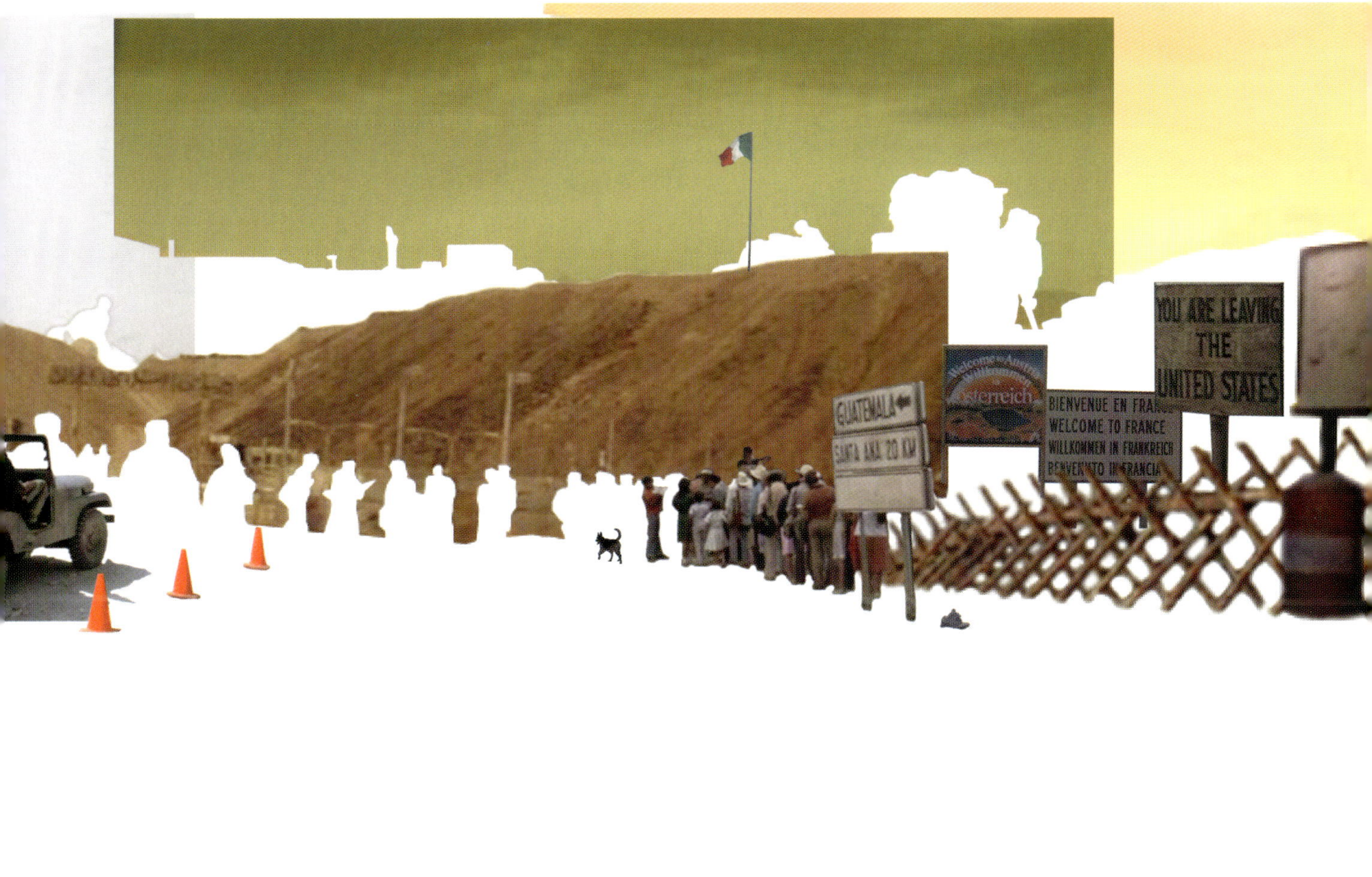
GUATEMALA
SANTA ANA 20 KM
Österreich
BIENVENUE EN FRANC
WELCOME TO FRANCE
WILLKOMMEN IN FRANKREICH
BENVENUTO IN FRANCIA
YOU ARE LEAVING
THE
UNITED STATES

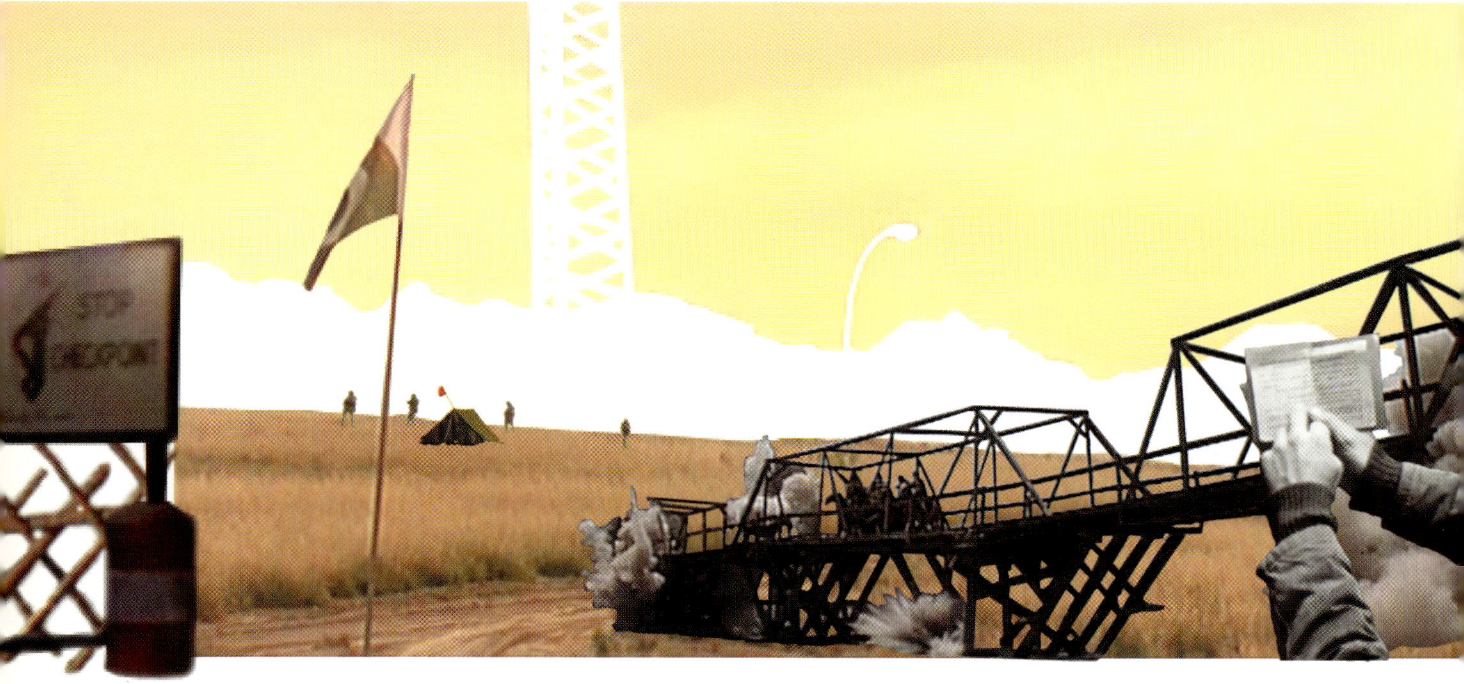
STOP
CHECKPOINT

CONFECTIONS OF ZENO

TONY WOOD

For centuries, the Atlantic formed a forbidding outer limit to the European imagination. Arab geographers referred to it as the "Great Green Sea of Gloom," while cultures from Ireland to Greece entertained beliefs in mythical lands yet to be located on its vast, ceaselessly roiling surface—or beneath it, as in the case of Atlantis. The logic of these legends—St. Brendan, Hy-Brazil, Antillia, Ultima Thule—seems to be that only fantastical or paradisiacal places could lie on the other side of what is known, as if the only safe routes across this sea lay through magical redemption.

The discovery of the New World did not explode these myths; after all, Columbus, Vespucci, Erikson, and the rest had merely made it to the other side of the Atlantic, and several centuries would pass before it had been comprehensively charted. The descriptions Europeans made of the West Indies, Mexico, or Brazil exponentially increased the catalogue of wonders: strange plants and animals, unclothed and occasionally hostile natives, vast pyramids and statues, enormous quantities of treasure. But the old marvels remained beguilingly intact, and maps of the fifteenth and sixteenth centuries show not only ragged, partial versions of the continents we now inhabit, but also a scattering of places that have since faded into oblivion, their hypothetical existence disproved or increasingly disregarded.

There are, however, a few curious exceptions to this pattern—places that were never the stuff of legend, which were discovered, named, mapped and described, and then were gradually erased from atlases and from history. Atlantis sank; Hy-Brazil was never found; but Frisland, Drogeo, Icaria, Estotiland—all these were authoritatively marked onto charts, most notably by Gerardus Mercator, whose conical projection of the globe is still the standard representation of our world. The *Weltkarte* he published in Duisburg in 1569 was a key source for subsequent mapmakers, and because it included Frisland and its conjectural companions, their physical presence was simply assumed. At least a century would pass before a steady tide of doubts and counterproofs washed them away.

Their disappearance is all the more surprising given that the existence of one of these places was at one point even physically corroborated. In the late 1570s, Martin Frobisher made a series of voyages in search of the North-West Passage—the Holy Grail of Elizabethan navigators, since it would give England access to the riches of Cathay without having to pass through Spanish territory. Frobisher fought his way through storms and across icy seas to present-day Canada and, believing he had found a clear route to Asia at the third attempt, decided to return to England in triumph—with a shipful of black rock that was thought to contain gold, but turned out to be worthless. In 1578, he landed on an island he had sighted on previous journeys, and claimed it on behalf of Queen Elizabeth. According to his maps, the place was known as Frisland, but with a patriotic flourish he renamed it Anglia Occidentalis.

Frobisher was not alone in his endeavors. John Dee, a mathematician, philosopher, and alchemist who was a prominent figure at court, was at precisely this time writing treatises justifying the expansion of British power—he was the first to use the term "British Empire," in 1577, and the same year had declared Queen Elizabeth's title to "Greenland, Estotiland and Friseland" on the basis of King Arthur's supposed previous conquest of these northerly isles. Both Dee and Frobisher had based their calculations—geopolitical and positional—on the maps in Abraham Ortelius's *Theatrum Orbis Terrarum*, published in Antwerp in 1570, which itself owed a great deal to Mercator's *Weltkarte*. (A copy of Ortelius's atlas remains in the library of Middle Temple in London, together with a globe featuring Frisland; now the haunt of lawyers, Middle Temple was where Elizabethan explorers gathered to discuss their voyages, past and projected, and presumably where Frobisher got his information.) Though few of them lived to find out about it, all of these men—and many more sailors, mapmakers, writers, and politicians—had fallen victim to a sly, understated hoax.

The source for much of Mercator's representation of the north Atlantic was a book published in Venice in 1558, described as an account of the fourteenth-century voyages of the brothers Antonio and Nicolò Zeno, and accompanied by a woodcut map. The book was compiled from family papers by Antonio Zeno's great-great-great grandson, also called Nicolò, a respected writer, mathematician, and geographer, and member of the city-state's Council of Ten. Around 1380, so the story goes, Nicolò Zeno left Venice on a trip to England and Flanders, but was blown wildly off course by a storm, and shipwrecked on an island which, he subsequently discovered, was called Frisland. Attacked by the natives, he was rescued by Zichmni, prince of nearby Porlanda; the two formed an alliance, Zichmni becoming lord of Frisland and the neighboring islands of Ledovo, Ilofe, and Sanestol with the help of Nicolò's naval know-how.

This information is said to come from letters Nicolò wrote to Antonio Zeno, who then joined his brother in Frisland, and continued in Zichmni's service for ten years after Nicolò's death. Together, Antonio and Zichmni led expeditions to Grislanda, Engroueland, and Icaria, meeting hostile natives, stunted cave-dwellers and practically-minded monks who fashioned all manner of things from volcanic rocks. Further discoveries are mentioned in material supposedly drawn from another letter, this time from Antonio Zeno to another brother, Carlo. These were not made by Antonio himself, but were narrated to him by a Frisland fisherman who, blown off course, found himself among the savages of Drogeo, where he lived for many years before escaping to Estotiland. Here the fisherman found the king's library stocked with books in Latin—evidence of some earlier European contact—and heard tell of more civilized peoples, of cities and great wealth lying to the south, seemingly a reference to the settled tribes of North America or perhaps Mexico.

All of these places appear on the "Carta da Navegar" which accompanied the book. The tip of Scotland can be glimpsed at the bottom of the map's centre, and Denmark, Sweden, and Norway are recognizable and duly labelled; above Norway is a gulf, with Europe's landmass looping across the top of the map to "Engronelant"—as Greenland was often then known. Iceland, too, appears, though it has acquired seven unfamiliar extra islands to the east. Indeed, apart from the slightly misplaced Shetland islands—here "Estland"—everything else on the map, though scrupulously labeled, is entirely fictional.

Within only a few years of their publication, however, these details had all been incorporated into standard cartography—starting with the 1561 edition of *Ptolemy* published in Venice, which was widely reproduced thereafter and used as the basis for subsequent maps. Sailors navigated the North Atlantic assuming the existence of Frisland, Estotiland, and Drogeo—Frobisher had actually landed on Greenland when he thought he was planting the English flag on Frisland—and around a hundred years passed before enough journeys were made and reports filed to confirm that where Zeno had carefully mapped out islands, there was nothing but sea.

Had Zeno simply made it all up, and if so, why? If it had been genuine, his map would have been well in advance of European knowledge in 1380. Greenland appears more clearly defined than on any other maps before the mid-sixteenth century, and the tip of Estotiland seems to match the location of Labrador, long before John Cabot's voyages. Indeed in 1898, the British geographer Frederick Lucas wrote a meticulous, schoolmasterish demolition of Zeno's account, in which he observed that the antedating of the map could be seen as an indirect claim for the discovery of America by a Venetian—scoring a point or two against rival Genoa, Columbus's city of origin. It seems likely that Zeno mingled what was known of the north Atlantic in the mid-sixteenth century with a handful of inventions and transpositions—moving the Faroe Islands next to Iceland, planting Faroese place-names on Frisland. Even Frisland was not entirely his invention—Catalan maps and Italian *portolanos* of the fifteenth century contain islands variously called Fisland, Fixlanda, and Frislanda, widely thought to be versions of "Fishland," and to refer to Iceland or the Faroes, both known for their plentiful supplies of fish.

Zeno's account itself is not wildly fanciful or fantastic—no giants or many-headed beasts, no gravity-defying cities or talking horses; there is no sense of satire or deeper political or moral purpose, as with More's *Utopia* or Montaigne's cannibals, no agenda other than the transmission of information. In fact, there are relatively few details: a fuller description of Frisland is promised by Antonio Zeno for another volume, and that of other places is laconic enough to seem sober and unembellished. Some of what appeared on the map was either correct or commonly conjectured, and this seems to have been enough for the rest simply to be accepted. And after all, Nicolò Zeno was a man of some reputation, in a city whose wealth was built on trade and intelligent navigation; he was also, crucially, the editor of the northern section of the 1561 *Ptolemy*, and was thus uniquely placed to insert his imaginary countries into an authoritative context, from which they drew life for years to come.

Many geographers continued, even into the last century, to place their trust in Zeno's map and the account of his ancestors' travels, carrying out mind-bending contortions of Faroese place-names or Icelandic topography to demonstrate Zeno's good intentions. Some have argued that Frisland simply sank, or else its size and solidity were overstated, and it was some sort of sandbank. (Many of the same arguments are made for Frisland's fellow north Atlantic phantom, Buss Island, reportedly discovered in 1578, and mapped in some detail by Captain Thomas Shepherd in 1671, but rapidly forgotten, and conclusively erased from maps by the end of the eighteenth century; Shepherd, meanwhile, was kicked out of the Hudson Bay Company "on account of bad behaviour.") Like other hoaxes, the annals of Zeno acquired a coterie of true believers—though a current website devoted to the Kingdom of Frisland has its tongue firmly lodged in its cheek, what with its images of the island's priestesses carrying ceremonial Frisbees.

Why would Zeno lie? Perhaps the question is misconceived, and the issue of his motivation misplaced. Frederick Lucas, for one, believed he was on the trail of "a contemptible literary fraud—one of the most successful and obnoxious on record." No special reason was needed, he notes, for Thomas Chatterton and William Henry Ireland to pen their forgeries of fifteenth-century songs or Shakespeare plays—success was its own reward. At several centuries' remove, though, the question seems to be rather why anyone would have taken either text or map at face value. Both contain many clues as to their own spuriousness, with the map merely the most literal part of the hoax—and ultimately the most successful. Some of these signs are relatively subtle—the monastery of St Thomas in Greenland labeled not with the Latin *cenobium*, but Zenobium—while others parade the text's inauthenticity before the reader's eyes. Not only is the oral narrative of Drogeo and Estotiland embedded in a letter whose content has in turn been conveyed by the compiler; not only are these letters not fully reproduced, but merely excerpted; at the book's conclusion, the compiler confesses that none of the original documents exist, and that he has reconstructed them from memory.

The admission which should unravel the whole story—and with it the claims to existence of Frisland, Drogeo, Icaria, Estotiland, Porlanda, Neome—is curiously moving in its contrition and contradictoriness. "I grieve that the book and many other writings... have come, I know not how, unhappily to harm; because, being still a boy when they came into my hands, and not understanding what they were, I tore them in pieces and destroyed them, as boys will do." There is something at work here that goes beyond any subconscious desire of the criminal to be caught. Perhaps Zeno's fiction is designed to stand in belatedly for a

opposite: Mercator's map of the Arctic, 1606. The upper-left corner prominently features Frisland.

childhood wonder on which he missed out—the boy who destroyed the maps of distant lands instead of poring over them—or perhaps to atone for some more obscure crime of the imagination.

The motto of Zeno's publisher, Francesco Marcolini, appears on the book's frontispiece: *Veritas Filia Temporis*, "truth is the daughter of time." Perhaps we should think of falsehood not as the opposite of truth, but rather as her wayward twin brother—a little like the figure we glimpse in Zeno's confession, the uncomprehending, destructive child growing into a trickster whose inventions led countless ships astray.

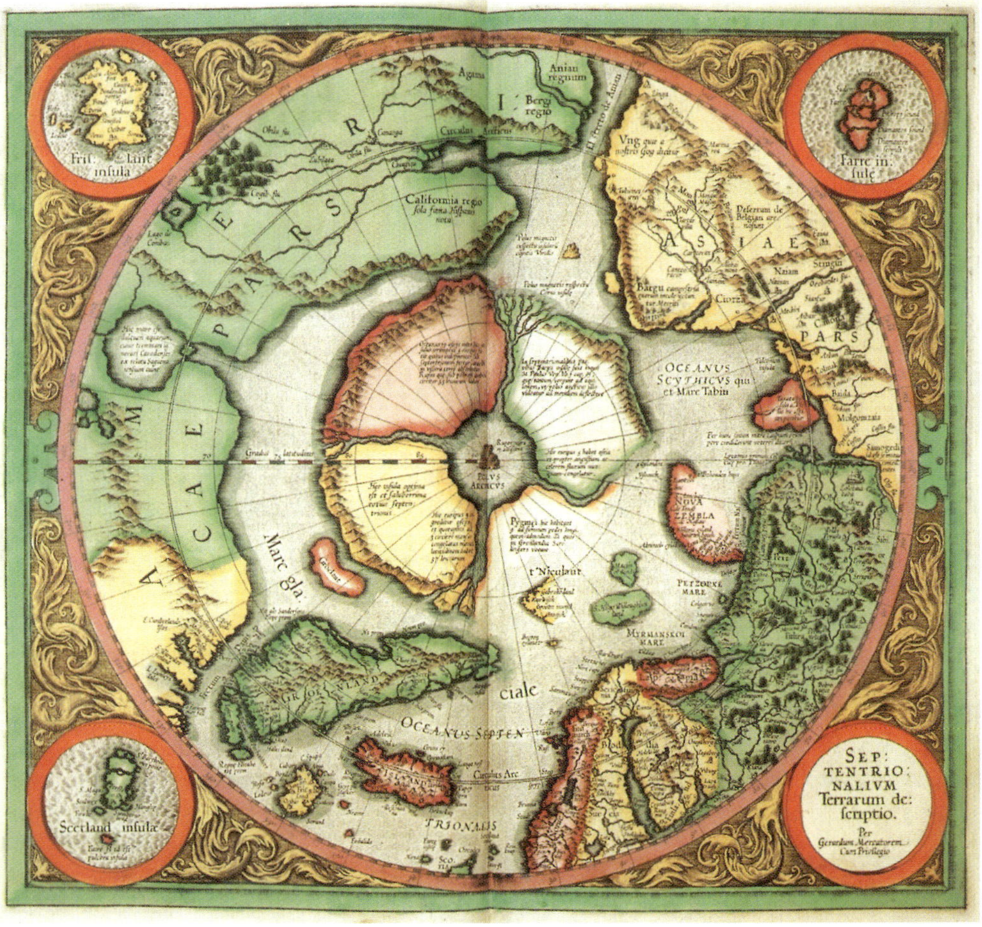

THE EPHEMERA OF FICTIONAL STATES

WILLIAM BRYK

Fictional and ephemeral states are works of art. Few were more purely so than the creations of American watercolorist Donald Evans. He drew on childhood memories of stamp collecting to commemorate, as biographer Willy Eisenhart wrote, "everything that was special to him, disguised in a code of stamps from his own imaginary countries, each detailed with its own history, geography, climate, currency and customs..." Thus Evans created thousands of stamps for Achterdijk, Nadorp, and Sabot, bearing wooden shoes, fruit, windmills, and landscapes; the Italianate Lo Stato di Mangiare, celebrating food and drink and its giant dirigible Cetriolo, the Cucumber; the Near Eastern Adjudani, with exotic pictorials of dhows, minarets, and falcons; and newly independent ex-colonies such as Amis and Amants, which commemorated friendship and the *coup de foudre*, love at first sight.

But Evans's countries existed only on his tiny watercolors. States exist in reality: they are sovereign, free from external control and wielding supreme power within their jurisdictions. Many persons weary of the state under which they live, desiring sovereignty over their own lives, have at least fantasized about creating their own countries to redefine their relationship to the outer world. This is close to anarchism, which rejects the state as intrinsically evil in favor of individual sovereignty against all the world.

Some dreamers hope their new states will be the lands in which they can be (or might have been in some previous age) their own kings and queens and heroes, in which they can play with dreams of power and glory without fear of failure, as the Brontë sisters did in composing their childhood epics of the kingdoms of Angria and Gondal. Indeed, Bruno Fuligni, in his study of ephemeral states and micronations, *L'Etat, c'est Moi*, calls such entities private monarchies or, perhaps more accurately, cryptarchies.

But the actual state can't be set aside at will. One can't merely nail a declaration of independence to one's front door and bid the state farewell. Failing to pay taxes, for instance, will soon make one's true sovereign, the non-fictional state supported by lawyers and policemen, exercise its power to collect.

Some try squaring the circle. Over thirty years ago, when Australian wheat farmer Leonard Casley—objecting to government-imposed wheat production quotas—declared the independence of his 18,500 acre farm as the Hutt River Province Principality, his defiance of the state extended to stamps, coins, paper money, decorations, robes of state, a crown, and tourism, but not to taxes. He continued paying them, rationalizing them as "an international courtesy." Of course, no true sovereign pays taxes to another: Australia merely tolerates Prince Leonard's idiosyncrasies, as it does those of the Emperor of Atlantium, the Grand Duke of Avram, the Prince of Aeterna Lucina, and a surprising number of other microstates. Nonetheless, the Hutt River Province Principality, which claims sovereignty without possessing it, creates its simulacrum through tokens. Its coins, postage stamps, flags, and paper money are to all appearances as real, as solid, as those issued by non-fictional states.

The least expensive ephemera of this kind are postage stamps. Fictional states have been producing postage stamps for nearly 150 years: they are now so common that philatelists have classified them as "Cinderellas." Thus Nova Potuca, supposedly a new African republic proclaimed in 1893, was merely a fiction invented to sell bogus stamps to collectors. Belgian philatelic publisher Ernest Moens devised Capacua, supposedly located in Bolivia, as a joke for April Fool's Day, 1883: he printed stamps for it, too. Clipperton Island, an atoll 1,630 miles south-southeast of San Diego, 700 miles southwest of Acapulco, awarded to France by arbitration in 1935, has no inhabitants, arable land, or commercially exploitable natural resources. Nonetheless, imaginative printers produced Clipperton postage stamps before the turn of the twentieth century. Indeed, Clipperton supposedly has a self-proclaimed emperor, last heard from in Seattle.

Whether Clipperton's emperor has been to the island of his dreams is unlikely. That's a pity: the oldest stunt for creating one's own country is claiming an uninhabited island by right of occupation. Thus, on 27 December 1810, Jonathan Lambert, mariner and adventurer of Salem, Massachusetts, and two companions landed on Tristan da Cunha, an uninhabited island 2,800 miles west of the Cape of Good Hope. They had apparently sailed from Rio de Janeiro some weeks before, and Lambert's ambition to rule the island had reportedly been the gossip of the town.

On 4 February 1811, he renamed Tristan—and the neighboring Inaccessible and Nightingale Islands—the Isles of Refreshment, proclaimed himself their proprietor in terms asserting absolute sovereignty (indeed, Fuligni says he proclaimed himself their "sovereign" or "emperor"), adopted a flag, and sent a copy of his proclamation by passing ship to the *Boston Gazette*, which published it on 18 July 1811.

Ships stopped every few weeks to water. Their logs record the islanders harvesting sealskins and planting vegetables. But Lambert and most of his companions perished on 17 May 1812, perhaps in an accident while fishing from a boat off the island, leaving an Italian drunkard, Tomaso Curri, alone "as a Robinson Crusoe on the island." Curri ruled as absolute king of all he surveyed until his death in 1816, after which the British began an occupation of Tristan that continues to the present day. Lambert is not forgotten: in 1985, the island issued a ten-penny stamp commemorating him and his flag, a white square bearing blue and red diamonds and half-diamonds, which is now reportedly in London's Public Record Office Museum.

James Aloysius Harden-Hickey, man of letters, swordsman, and adventurer, used a variant on that method to become James I, Prince of Trinidad. Born in San Francisco, California, on 8 December 1854, Hickey was raised and educated in France, where he graduated with honors from Saint-Cyr, the French military academy. Having inherited an income and secured a reputation as a master swordsman (he could easily pick the buttons off your waistcoat with a foil), Harden-Hickey took up literature, publishing eleven novels and receiving the title of Baron of the Holy Roman Empire for his polemics in defense of the Church.

During the late 1870s, Royalists unleashed a media blitz against the new French Republic by financing newspapers, most edited in the spirit of Hyppolite August Jean de Villemessant of *Le Figaro*, who observed, "If a story doesn't cause a duel or a lawsuit, it isn't any good." Harden-Hickey's swordsmanship and polemical skills made him the perfect editor for *Triboulet*, a weekly named for King Louis XII's jester. The cover of the first issue on 10 November 1878 showed *Triboulet* clubbing Marianne, symbol of the Republic. With writing as vigorous as its artwork, *Triboulet* soon had a circulation of 25,000. Within the year, its staff had served among them some six months in jail; the paper had been fined 3,000 francs; and Harden-Hickey had fought forty-two libel suits and at least twelve duels. The fun lasted until the money gave out in 1887.

Then Harden-Hickey traveled the world. While crossing the South Atlantic, his ship stopped at the deserted island of Trinidad, some 700 miles off Brazil (not to be confused with the Caribbean islands of Trinidad and Tobago, just off Venezuela). As American journalist Richard Harding Davis wrote in *Real Soldiers of Fortune*, "Trinidad is...but a spot upon the ocean. On most maps it is not even a spot." Harden-Hickey went ashore and claimed it in his own name. Sir Edmund Halley, the astronomer, had landed in 1698; some Brazilian Portuguese had briefly colonized it in 1700; but mariners landing in 1803 and 1822 had found only birds and turtles. This strengthened Harden-Hickey's claim: the English never settled the island; the Portuguese abandoned it. Trinidad was there for the taking.

On Sunday, 5 November 1893, the New York *Tribune* gave front-page publicity to his scheme for Trinidadian independence. Harden-Hickey argued the island was "...rich with luxuriant vegetation... surrounding seas swarm with fish...the exportation of guano alone should make my little country prosperous..." In January 1894, he proclaimed himself James I, Prince of Trinidad. He purchased a schooner to ferry colonists, supplies, and mail, hired an agent to negotiate the construction of docks, wharves, and houses, and contracted for Chinese coolies to provide an instant proletariat. He commissioned a jeweler to make a golden crown and issued postage stamps.

A Parisian friend, the Count de la Boissiere, became foreign secretary, opening a chancellery at 217 West 36th Street, a brownstone just west of Seventh Avenue. Richard Harding Davis visited it in 1894. Children were playing on the stoop. A street vendor was peddling vegetables. On the front door was a handwritten note: Chancellerie de la Principaute de Trinidad.

But in July 1895, the British, then constructing a submarine cable to Brazil, took possession of Trinidad, based on Halley's discovery in 1698. The Brazilians asserted a claim based upon the Portuguese occupation of 1700. Boissiere protested to Secretary of State Richard Olney, asking the United States to recognize Trinidad and guarantee its neutrality. Olney gave copies of the protest to the press corps, who then poked fun at Prince James and at Boissiere, his broken English, and his formal manners. The exception was *The Evening Sun*, where Davis, finding the Count "courteous, gentle, and...distinguished," gave Harden-Hickey a straight treatment.

Without his island, Harden-Hickey spiraled into depression, as much of the world mocked him for trying to make his dream come true. Various attempts to raise money for an invasion of England from Ireland fell through. In early February 1898, Harden-Hickey registered at a hotel in El Paso, Texas. On 10 February 1898, the maids found him on the bed. A half-emptied morphine bottle was on the nightstand and a letter to his wife pinned to a chair. In his trunk was the crown of Trinidad.

Yet a third, and perhaps the most ephemeral, of these kingdoms is that of Redonda, whose King and court have never ruled in their own country. In London's Soho and Fitzrovia in the 1960s, John Gawsworth—the man of letters who reigned over Redonda in absentia as the slightly derelict King Juan I—was known to jot patents of nobility on paper bar napkins in exchange for drinks. Juan had inherited the crown from Matthew Phipps Shiel, a prolific and nearly forgotten author of fantastic tales of adventure, who claimed he had been crowned King of Redonda at fifteen. In July 1865, his father Matthew D. Shiel, an Irish-born entrepreneur based in Montserrat in the British West Indies, had claimed the uninhabited island of Nuestra Senora de la Redonda—one of the smaller Leeward Islands—and, as one commentator has suggested, "with certain influence of the abundance of alcohol," proclaimed himself King Matthew I.

Nonetheless, in 1872, Great Britain annexed Redonda, apparently over King Matthew's objection. He eventually abdicated in favor of his son and, on 21 July 1880, his fifteenth birthday, Matthew Phipps Shiel was supposedly crowned Felipe I, King of Redonda by the Anglican bishop of Antigua, in a ceremony on Redonda itself. King Felipe soon moved to London, never to return, where his enormous, wildly uneven output of novels and short stories became known for bizarre imagery evoked in increasingly florid, even grotesque, prose. His only novel to come to Hollywood's attention was *The Purple Cloud*, a surprisingly readable and superbly constructed tale of the last man on earth published in 1901. Nearly half a century after it was first optioned, the novel became the basis for a 1959 vehicle for Harry Belafonte, Inger Stevens, and Mel Ferrer, *The World, The Flesh, and the Devil*.

Whether Shiel's claim had any foundation is a question of faith. Arthur Machen, himself a writer of fantasy and horror, who knew both Shiel and Gawsworth, described "...a short life of Shiel, written by himself..." as "a mass of the most infernal & extraordinary lies," and later summed up King Felipe as "an inveterate liar." Even Jon Wynne-Tyson, Shiel and Gawsworth's literary executor, who reigned as King Juan II, wrote that "The legend is and should remain a pleasing and eccentric fairy tale; a piece of literary mythology to be taken with salt, romantic sighs, appropriate perplexity, some amusement, but without great seriousness. It is, after all, a fantasy."

Nonetheless, Shiel never completely stopped corresponding with the Colonial Office over his right to the kingship. Lawrence Durrell, one of Gawsworth's occasional drinking buddies, wrote that King Felipe had created a number of dukes to help him carry on the battle—an appropriate title, as dukes were originally Roman military commanders. When Shiel died on 17 February 1947 after a reign of sixty-seven years, Gawsworth, whom a childless Shiel had nominated as his successor, became Juan I.

Born Terence Ian Fytton Armstrong in London in 1912, Gawsworth had won early fame as a poet, critic, editor, and anthologist. When Lawrence Durrell first met him in 1931, Gawsworth was barely surviving as a writer, inhabiting a rotten-floored attic above a jazz band's rehearsal space in Soho. Nonetheless, as Durrell noted, Gawsworth already possessed "an enviable collection of treasures in the way of first editions, manuscripts and letters of famous poets, and also a number of literary curiosities which he had picked up in the sale rooms which he regularly frequented; he had a skull-cap of Dickens', a pen of Thackeray's and so on."

Gawsworth rose quickly in the literary world. He was elected to the Royal Society of Literature at twenty-five and awarded the Society's Benson Medal "for meritorious works in poetry, fiction, history, and belles-lettres" at twenty-seven. He had a passion for literature itself, editing several magazines, including the *English Digest*, *Literary Digest*, and *Poetry Review*, and frequently soliciting financial assistance for aging writers down on their luck, including Shiel, for whom he obtained a pension from the King's Civil List. This convivial eccentric was a kind of institutional memory of literature, from knowing friends of Oscar Wilde to giving hospitality to a drunken Dylan Thomas, who stole his shirts.

But after serving in the Royal Air Force during World War II, Gawsworth found his talents as poet and man of letters insufficient to sustain him and gradually fell on hard times, becoming a self-described "inveterate old diabetic bookman, slipper-padding around my shelves and files." He largely survived through his skills as bibliophile: Durrell recounted how Gawsworth daily rifled boxes of three-penny second-hand books in Charing Cross Road, invariably finding something others had overlooked, and selling it to a rare book dealer for breakfast money. But increasingly, Gawsworth merely held court in the bar of the Alma tavern in Westbourne Grove, where knowledgeable tourists to West London frequently tracked down the somewhat seedy King. As one of Gawsworth's successors to the Redondan throne later sniffed, "In return for buying His Majesty a drink, it was sometimes possible to receive a Dukedom, inscribed on the back of a beermat."

Thus Redonda became a burned-out minor poet's means of getting by, and his name survives largely through his ephemeral Kingdom. Naturally, as a writer, Juan I showered his honors upon writers whom he admired. He thus granted Durrell the title of Duke of Cervantes Pequeña, although he never got around to having the title engrossed on parchment. Others admitted to Redonda's "intellectual aristocracy" were such literary and theatrical figures as Arthur Machen, Henry Miller, and Dirk Bogarde, who all became Dukes of the Realm.

Juan's last years were a nightmare, marked by disillusionment, ill health, and alcoholism. By the late 1950s, when Durrell ran into him wheeling a pram loaded with empty beer bottles that he was on his way to sell, he had fallen on very hard times indeed. Nonetheless, when Durrell bought him a few drinks, the King "solemnly created my brother a duke as we stood at the bar." By the late 1960s, his friends learned he had been reduced to homelessness when a reporter found him sleeping in Hyde Park. They tried to rescue him, but following a heroic binge, Juan I died after emergency surgery for bleeding ulcers in September 1970. He was not yet sixty.

The kingdom's motto, *Floreat Redonda!* then took on new meaning as some nine claimants contested the succession. As early as 1960 Gawsworth may have passed the right of succession to Dominic Behan, brother of Irish playwright Brendan Behan. But other candidates also claimed Gawsworth had nominated them, and apparently no one who knew Gawsworth could argue with the idea that he might have passed the right of inheritance several times to whoever was picking up the tab on any given night.

Today, Redonda, like a strong poker hand, has three kings. One, history teacher William Leonard Gates, who reigns as Leo V, holds court in London's Fitzroy Tavern. A rival, King Robert I the Bald, maintains a website offering honorary commissions in the Royal Redondan Navy; Kingdom of Redonda Rum (a "rare and fortifying rum... perfect for punches, served neat or for cleaning automotive parts!"); and cigar boxes ("which once contained the actual cigars smoked by His Majesty himself, King Robert the Bald! These handy and exceptionally durable metal boxes are the perfect container for all those personal hygiene and prophylactic products best left from general view!").

Juan II, whose claim arose from his appointment as Gawsworth's literary executor, was unique among the island's modern kings because he actually went there, landing on Good Friday of 1979. In 1997, he abdicated in favor of Spanish novelist Javier Marias, who reigns as Xavier I, energetically renewing the Redondan peerage by creating Francis Ford Coppola the Duke of Megalopolis, Pedro Almodóvar the Duke of Trémula, belletrist A.S. Byatt the Duchess of Morpho Eugenia, and the late German novelist W.G. Sebald the Duke of Vertigo.

Far from these virtual courts, the Redonda of reality is a nature preserve, part of Antigua & Barbuda, over which Queen Elizabeth II reigns. Redonda has no permanent human population and no post office building (or any other building, for that matter). Nonetheless, since 1979, Antigua and Barbuda have issued numerous stamps for Redonda—including a commemorative illustrating Goofy, the Disney cartoon character, dressed as Sherlock Holmes, searching for Easter eggs. These are valid for postage, though Redonda has no mailboxes.

opposite: Donald Evans, *Sabot, 1917, Postes maritimes*, 1975. Watercolor on paper mounted in philatelic sheets. Courtesy Spanierman Gallery, LLC.

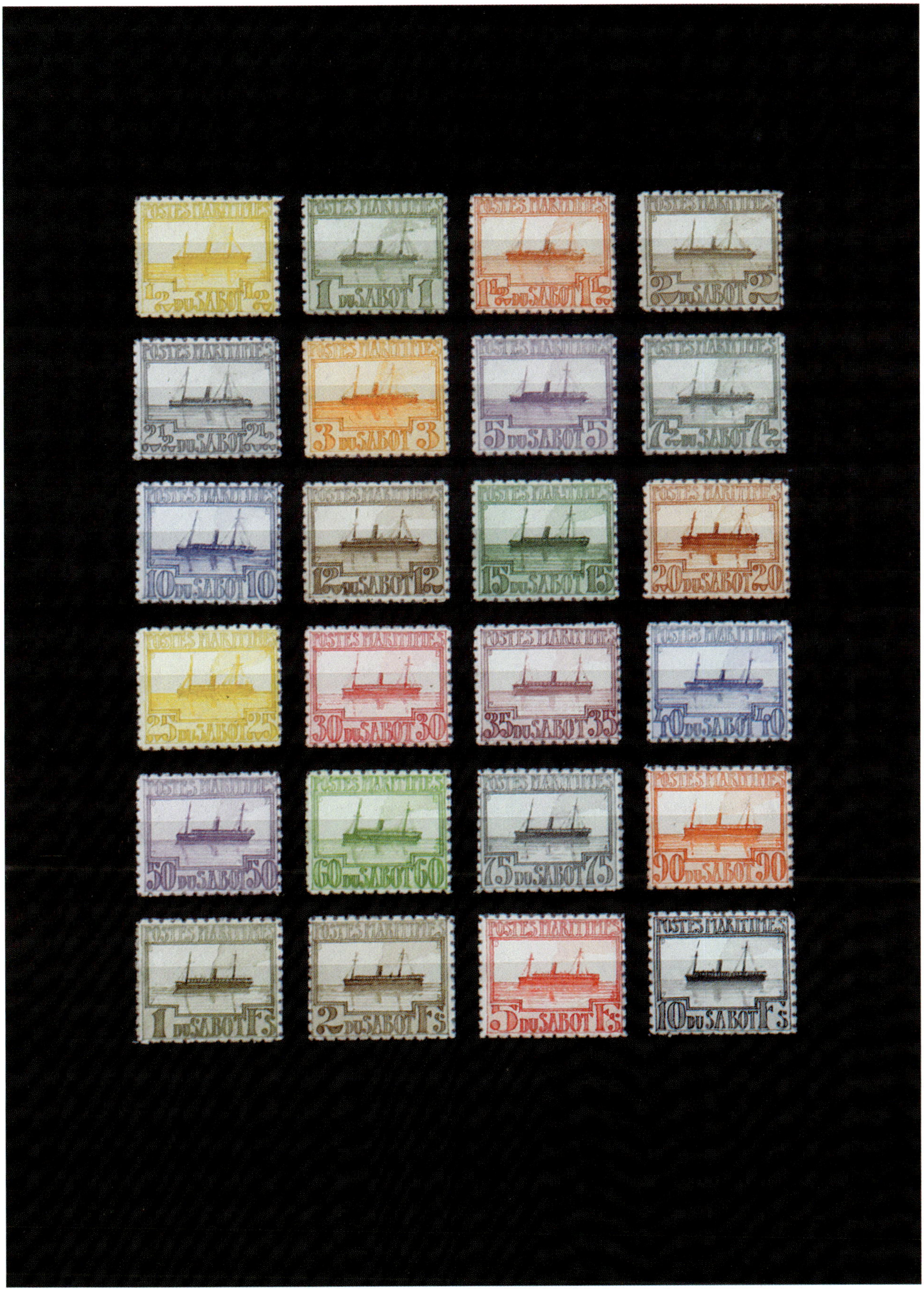
POSTES MARITIMES
1 DU SABOT 1
2 DU SABOT 2
3 DU SABOT 3
5 DU SABOT 5
10 DU SABOT 10
12 DU SABOT 12
15 DU SABOT 15
20 DU SABOT 20
25 DU SABOT 25
30 DU SABOT 30
35 DU SABOT 35
40 DU SABOT 40
50 DU SABOT 50
60 DU SABOT 60
75 DU SABOT 75
90 DU SABOT 90
1 DU SABOT Fs
2 DU SABOT Fs
5 DU SABOT Fs
10 DU SABOT Fs

Geophysical processes make land, but geopolitical machinations make governments. Bedrock conditions—the placement of a river or mountain range, the dimensions of an island—may help to demarcate a country's borders. But a state is also bounded by its history, by the collective beliefs of its inhabitants, and by its relations with tourists, interlopers, regional authorities, and global patterns of information circulation. As regards ideological and symbolic character, then, the sui generis republic or principality might have as strong a claim to statehood as any other. In this selective portfolio of self-declared nations, the jurisdiction of international bodies such as the United Nations and the World Court, along with the self-interest of well-established countries like Australia and Norway, intersect with the private prerogatives of citizens and subjects whose allegiance is, first and foremost, to their own imaginations.

Protesting unfair tax and quota systems; colonizing virgin territory and reclaiming lands disdained by other countries; exploring new models of governance; asserting the right to practice one's own brand of authority: the nations presented here have been founded for reasons that will be familiar to any student of history. And, as with grander nations, the problems encountered by the Hutt River Province Principality, Kymaerica, the Kingdom of Fusa, the NSK State in Time, The Royal Kingdom of Elgaland-Vargaland (KREV), and the New Free State of Caroline (a.k.a. Millennium Island) are no different from those that mark the large-scale history books. Newly discovered traces of indigenous civilizations might tip the balance in a struggle for sovereignty; a rugged individualist might hold out—with the help of a devoted band of followers—against the onslaught of far more powerful adversaries. A fledgling state might swell its population by offering harbor to those in flight from their countries of origin; or a civil experiment might peaceably transform the definition of citizenship and the frontiers of no-man's-land. And, as with any other place whose national culture has been shaped by the artists who conceive of themselves as sons and daughters of the soil, the fictions attached to these states are often indistinguishable from their facts.

Special thanks to Robert Blackson and Peter Coffin for their help in assembling this portfolio. Thanks also to His Imperial Majesty George II of Atlantium for graciously loaning us materials related to Atlantium, Sealand, and Hutt River Province Principality.

For more information on the range of self-declared nations see <www.cabinetmagazine.org/issues/18>.

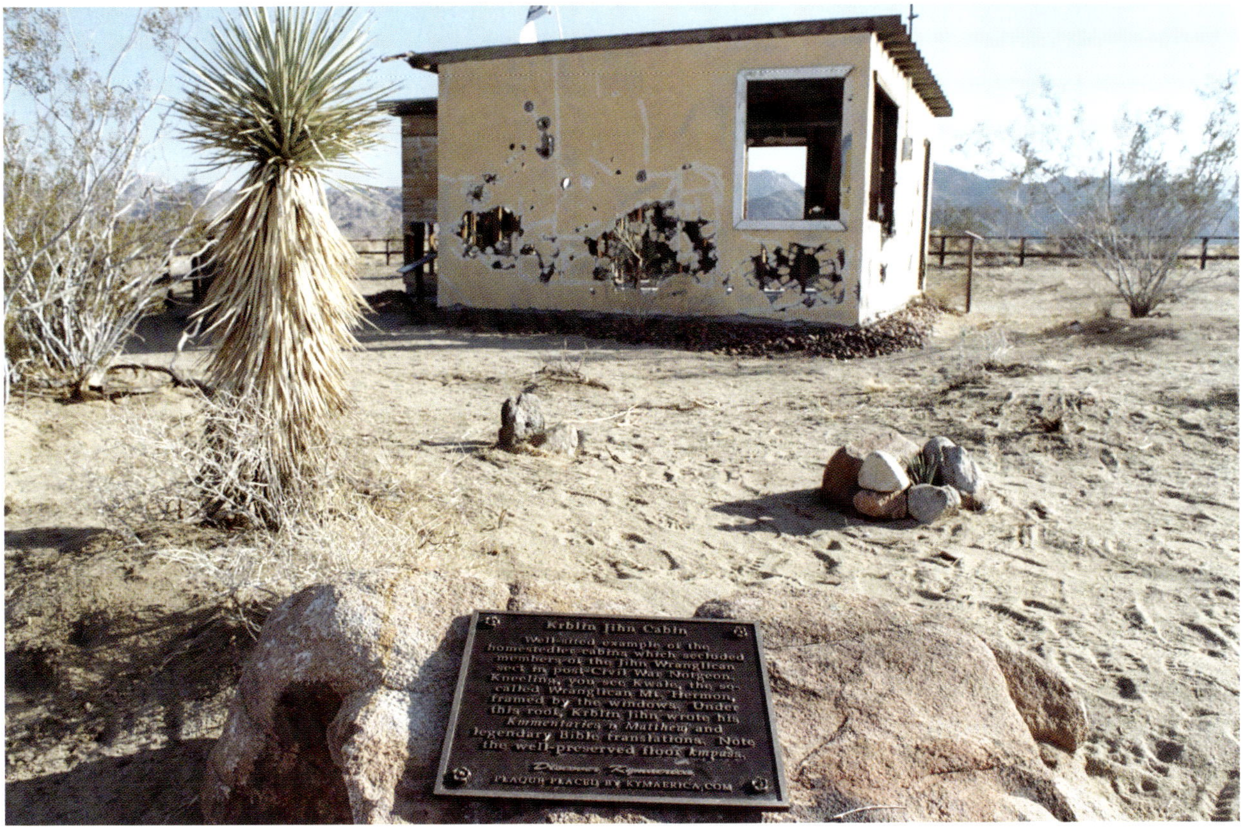

KYMAERICA

"Kymaerica is a land (and some waters)," writes its creator and Geographer-at-Large Eames Demetrios, "somewhat co-existent with our linear world and a general landscape quite similar to large parts of what we would call North America. There are about 80-90 districts, containing over 4,000 gwomes. A *gwome* is cognate word meaning "footprint of (the) nation." Usually it refers to a nation (so the terms are often used interchangably), but it is actually a term for a physical area within a district which has a unified political structure. Kymaerican influences and stories are everywhere in our linear world and likely vice versa. But there also many wonders in Kymaerica not easily found here."

As Demetrios explained in a recent interview, "the easiest way to describe it is that it is a reinterpretation of the North American landscape. It tries to give people an alternate experience when they are in this linear world. We take so much for granted from the way this country was settled and from the way buildings are there, and Kymaerica is trying to present a largely different reality. Some of it is magical, some of it is humorous, some of it is textural. It's another way to look at our space. That includes some pretty unusual things. I've written one book based on it and created many limited edition prints. I've done historical landmark plaques—one in Chinatown, one in Houston, and one in Athens, Georgia. It is trying to create a psychological environment in these places."

There are over 5,000 zones or quasi-nations in Kymaerica. Each one has its own story. For example, there is the Tehachapi, which is the great road building culture in Kymaerica, and they built most of what we now think of as the interstate highways. There are the people who were the original Samurai who were blown off course and settled what we now call Santa Barbara (which they named Hizuro-koro). There are the People of the Wind who make buildings totally out of air and who believe that what we call hills are actually depressions in the sky, and what we call valleys are actually hills in the sky. In the area that is present day linear San Diego there is something called the Sandafuegan Fire Cult which puts out valuable possessions and then sets fire to them."

above: Krblin Jihn Kabin, a Kymaerica historical site in the nation of Notgeon (near Joshua Tree, California). The historical marker in the foreground reads "Well-sited example of the homestedler cabins which secluded members of the Jihn Wranglican sect in post-Civil War Notgeon. Kneeling, you see Kwale, the so-called Wranglican Mt. Hermon, framed by the windows.Under this roof, Krblin Jihn wrote his Kmmentaries n Matthew and legendary Bible translations. Note the well-preserved floor kmpass." Photo Eames Demetrios.

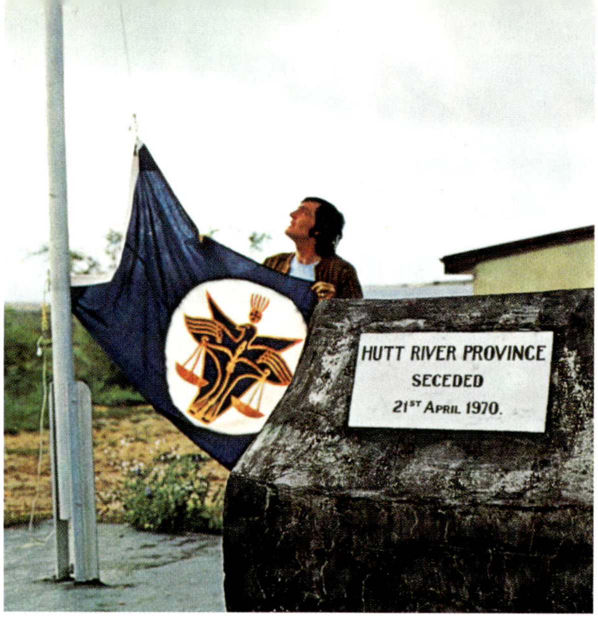

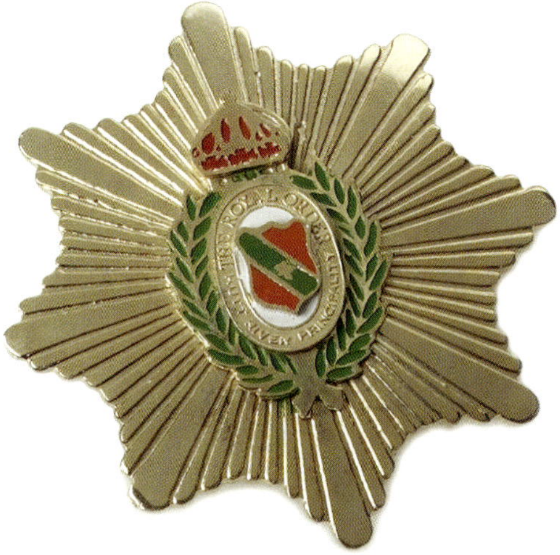

HUTT RIVER PROVINCE PRINCIPALITY

A micronation occupying some seventy-five square miles of pasture and farmland roughly twenty miles inland from the Indian Ocean in Western Australia, Hutt River Province Principality was founded in 1970 when, in response to agricultural quotas imposed on his family's lands by the state government, wheat farmer Leonard George Casley seceded from Australia.

The Hutt River Province secession grew out of a series of legal maneuvers seeking to overturn the quota ruling, which demanded a huge reduction in crop production, along with a commensurate loss of revenue, from the 18,500 acres of land Casley farmed. When Sir Douglas Kendrew, then-Governor of Western Australia, refused to increase the farming quota, Casley applied for independence, claiming that the legal principle of "unjust enrichment" demanded some form of compensation, in this case, territorial in nature. The Parliament of Western Australia responded by introducing a bill that would have allowed the government to seize Casley's land—in order to place itself outside the jurisdiction of the state, Casley (along with his wife, Shirley, and seven children) delivered formal notification on 21 April 1970 of his intention to secede from the state of Western Australia, the federal government of Australia, and the commonwealth of Great Britain. Debate over the status of Casley's new country reached Australian Governor General Sir Paul Hasluck, the Commonwealth's chief administrator on the continent, who ruled that he had no constitutional authority to intervene.

There were other attempts to challenge the secession—indeed, the organization of the province as a principality was a strategy based on a British law that excepted individuals "assisting a defacto [sic] Prince attain his office" from charges of treason. But as time went on, the reign of Price Leonard and Princess Shirley became conventionally accepted. Over the course of the next three decades, the few dozen citizens of Hutt River Province (many of them the Casleys' children and grandchildren) developed an economy that comprised wheat, lupin, and barley cultivation, the raising of lamb and sheep for meat and wool, and the export of fresh and dried wildflowers. In April of this year, the Principality held a series of public celebrations to celebrate its 35th Anniversary (as well as the Prince and Princess's 58th wedding anniversary) featuring an exhibition of Chinese art, a dinner dance, and a "sports challenge" sponsored by The Hutt River Petanque Federation, as well as a ceremony of Royal Investitures and Awards presided over by Prince Leonard himself.

above left: Raising the flag of the Hutt River Province Principality.

above right: Breast Star of the Order of the Unicorn, 1980s. This chivalric order was created and run by Kevin Gale, the Prince Regent, without the authority of Prince Leonard and is not recognized by the Principality. Photo Ryann Cooley.

opposite: Hutt River Province Principality is one of many micronations that produces commemorative postage stamps (and coins) for the collector market. These materials are not legal tender, and the subjects they commemorate rarely have anything to do with the actual state.

HUTT RIVER PROVINCE KINGDOM

DATE OF ISSUE 31ST JULY, 1981

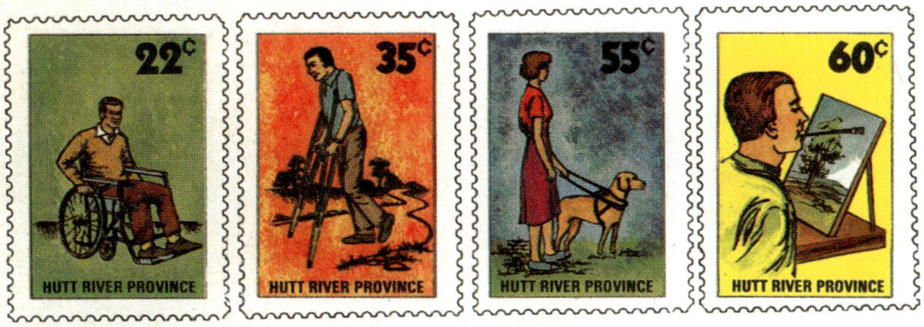

The year 1981 has been internationally selected as "The International Year of Disabled Persons".

The Postal Services of Hutt River Province has joined in the international spirit with the issue of these stamps.

Paraplegic in a wheelchair — 22¢

A cripple with crutches — 35¢

Blindwomen with guide-dog — 55¢

Quadriplegic painting by mouth — 60¢

Artwork done by Jean Mulligan. Printed by Lithography Offset. Colour separations by Gibbneys Graphics 1980. Paper used — Glopaque Super Tropical Gummed. The adhesive — synthetic P.V.A. Seventy perforations around the stamps.

This brochure and postage stamps were printed by Multi Graphics Pty. Ltd.
83 Nanson Street, Wembley, Western Australia. Phone (09) 3874450.

POSTAGE STAMP ISSUE POLICY OF THE EMPIRE OF ATLANTIUM

TOPICS TO BE DEPICTED

XI) The Subject matter depicted on postage stamps shall be relevant only to the Empire, its history, its aims, and its associations with foreign nations, except in the case of events or commemorations which are of universal significance.

XII) Commonly over-exploited, and solely revenue raising subjects such as the Olympics, foreign (especially British) Royal occasions, exotic birds and animals, and cars/ locomotives etc shall not be depicted, except where there is a specific relevance to the Empire of Atlantium.

XIII) All low-value definitive postage stamps issued by the Empire of Atlantium shall feature a likeness of the ruling Emperor.

NUMBER, AND TYPE OF ISSUES

VIII) Commemorative postage stamps shall be made each year for the occasions of :

- **a)** The Birthday of His Imperial Majesty, the Emperor
- **b)** The National Day of the Empire of Atlantium
- **c)** Christmas

XIV) No more than two additional commemorative postage stamp issues shall be made per year.

XV) No more than one definitive set shall be issued each year.

XVI) At least one, and at most two miniature sheets shall be produced to accompany each issue.

XVII) No miniature sheet shall consist of more than four stamps.

XVIII) No miniature sheet shall be produced as a separate issue.

XIX) First day covers shall be produced for each issue.

XX) Specimen overprints shall be applied only to high value definitive issues, to enable their purchase, at cheaper rates, by collectors.

AMOUNTS PRODUCED

XXI) No postage stamp issue shall exceed three thousand sheets, including miniature sheets.

XXII) The number of miniature sheets produced for a single issue shall not exceed one half of the total number of sheets produced.

XXIII) The number of first day covers produced for a single issue shall not exceed one half of the total number of sheets produced.

XXIV) The number of high value definitives of a particular denomination, which are specimen overprinted, shall not exceed one half of the total number of sheets produced, of that denomination.

XXV) The actual quantities produced of the stamps of a particular issue shall be available of direct enquiry to the Imperial Postmaster-General, at least two months after the expiry of the period of postal validity of that issue.

XXVI) With the exception of definitive sets, no postage stamp issue shall consist of more than four stamps.

XXVII) No definitive postage stamp set shall consist of more than six stamps.

PERIOD OF POSTAL VALIDITY

XXVIII) With the exception of definitive sets and Christmas commemoratives, postage stamps shall remain valid for postage, for nine months after the date of issue.

XXIX) Definitive postage stamp issues shall remain valid from the date of issue to one year after this date, after which they replacement or retention is subject to the discretion of the Imperial Postmaster-General.

XXX) Christmas postage stamp issues shall remain postally valid for three months after the date of issue.

POSTAL RATES AND CHARGES

V) Postal rates and charges shall be reviewed every five years.

XXXI) The denominations of commemorative issues shall not exceed the standard postage rate.

XXXII) The Christmas rate shall be three times the value of the standard postage rate.

XXXIII) One third of the funds obtained through the sale of the Christmas issue shall be donated to a worthy charity, nominated by His Imperial Majesty, the Emperor.

PREPARATION OF DESIGNS

XXXIV) All postage stamp designs for a particular year shall be prepared and approved by the thirty first day of January of that year.

VVVV) All designs for additional commemorative, or new definitive postage stamps for a particular year shall be prepared and approved by the thirtieth day of November, of the previous year.

MISCELLANEOUS

XXXVI) No complete or part sheets of postage stamps shall be cancelled to order,

XXXVII) No miniature sheets shall be sold other than in mint condition.

XXXVIII) One full sheet, one single copy, one miniature sheet, and one of each type of first day cover, of each denomination, of every issue, shall be set aside for inclusion in the Imperial Collection.

XXXIX) Temporary commemorative postmarks may be introduced for periods of no longer than sixty days.

ALL THE ABOVE LAWS WERE APPROVED by both Houses of the Imperial Senate of the Empire of Atlantium, on the eleventh day of November, Anno Domini Nineteen hundred and eighty four.

HIS GRACE, The Duke Imperiator.

PRIME MINISTER of the Empire of Atlantium.

IMPERIAL APPROVAL granted on the eleventh day of November, Anno Domini Nineteen hundred and eighty four.

GEORGIVS II, Imperiator

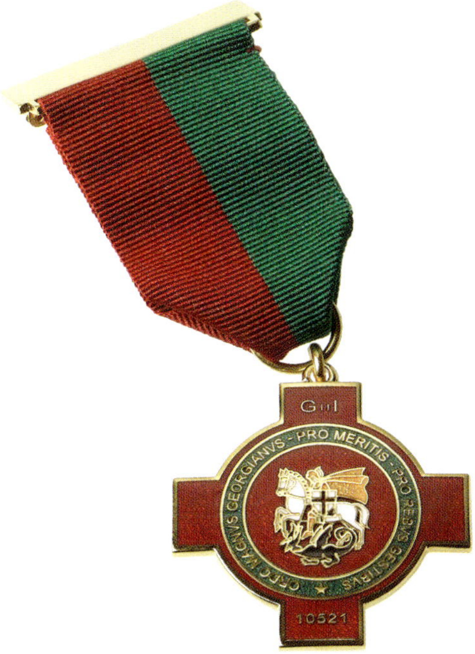

THE EMPIRE OF ATLANTIUM

His Imperial Majesty George II, ruling over the Empire of Atlantium, has stated that nations whose identities are determined by their geographic boundaries or ethnic majority are gradually forcing themselves into a state of extinction. The Empire of Atlantium provides an alternative to the conventional terms of nationhood by offering a secular, democratic, republican monarchy that welcomes global, economic, and political union.

To start fresh with a nondenominational foundation, the Empire of Atlantium's Acting Minister of Communications invented the Annus Novus Decimal Calendar System, which begins with the end of the last Ice Age. Each year in this calendar is divided into ten months that alternate between thirty-six and thirty-seven days in length. The names of each month and day are determined by Latin ordinal numbers. Latin is one of the two official languages of Atlantium (the other is English). His Imperial Majesty chose Latin because "it is relatively culturally neutral by virtue of the fact that it is no longer a 'living' language."[1] The name Atlantium is derived from the Greek myth of Atalanta (just like Atlantic and Atlantis) and was chosen for its Roman heritage, from which the Empire has borrowed much of its state symbolism.

The Empire of Atlantium was founded on 3rd Decimus, 10500 (27 November 1981) by three optimistic Australian teenagers in the southern Sydney suburb of Narwee. By Sextarius 10521 (June 2002) the Empire had grown to accommodate over five hundred citizens in sixty countries. Atlantium supports numerous diplomatic representatives with Imperial legates in New Jersey, Pakistan, and Poland. Its capital in the central business district of Sydney is the world's smallest territorial state, measuring just sixty-one square meters. Regardless of this minimal territorial claim, Atlantium seeks to assert its legitimacy via the plurality of views embodied within its dispersed community of citizenship.

Unlike most other sovereign principalities and micronations, the Empire of Atlantium does not issue passports. Atlantium advocates the unrestricted movement of all peoples and therefore does not issue or recognize any form of restrictive travel documentation. "[A]nyone with the desire and motivation to forge their own destiny as a true citizen of the world is welcome to become a citizen of Atlantium."

—Charles Green

1 All quotes from <www.atlantium.org>.

above: Medal of the Great Georgian Order. Photo Ryann Cooley.

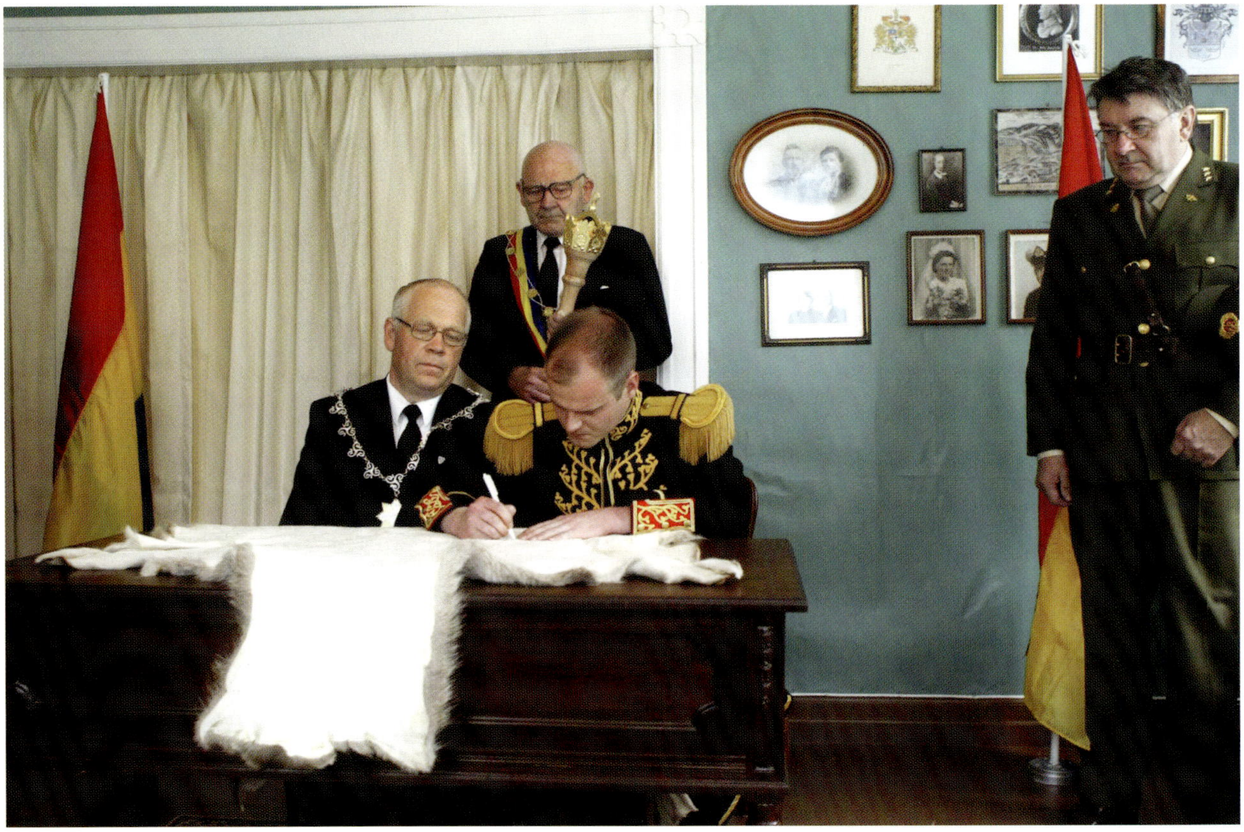

THE KINGDOM OF FUSA

On 21 June 2003, the Norwegian government declared its own Fusa County a kingdom. This regal status was legally conferred with a specific purpose: to question the function and benefits of two equally powered types of governance—that of a kingdom and that of a county. Fusa now exists as both, thus becoming a sort of self-contained control experiment.

His Excellency the Viceroy Morten Holmefjord, a leader in the arts community of Norway, rules the kingdom. Presiding over his coronation ceremony, held along the sacred banks of Gjøn Lake, were the Council of Elders and the Mayor of Fusa. Immediately after these proceedings, the Viceroy and the Norwegian government signed the Engevik Treaty, which outlines a course of peaceful relations to be maintained by the dual leadership.

As is his royal duty, the Viceroy has designated a Fusan viceregal hymn, minted a new state seal, designed a flag, and with support from the Council of Elders, penned a Fusan constitution. This document, which includes relaxed marriage and immigration laws, grants new rights to his 3,750 loyal subjects. The Viceroy has also founded a thriving new currency. The kruna's exchange rate against the standard Norwegian kroner (currently one Fusan kruna = 100 Norwegian kroner) is slowly boosting the Fusan economy and tourist industry.

On 12 September 2005 a people's election coinciding with the Norwegian national elections will decide the future of the Fusan monarchy. A majority vote in favor of the Viceroy will make him a sovereign and permanent leader of the Kingdom of Fusa. If the Viceroy loses the election, the Kingdom of Fusa will dissolve, and Mr. Holmefjord will seek political asylum in an undisclosed location in Africa.

—*Charles Green*

above and opposite: Scenes from the coronation of Viceroy Morten Holmefjord. Photos Knut Egil Wang.

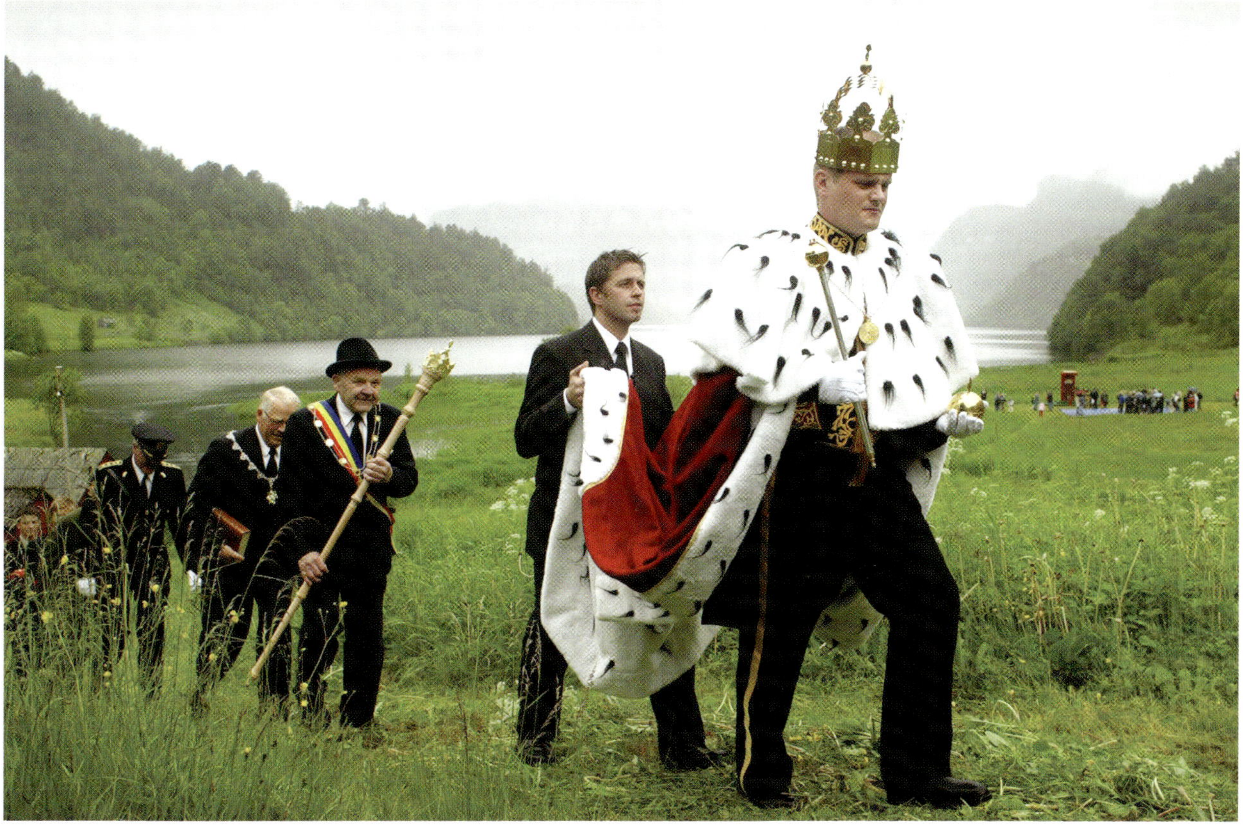

Self-dubbed "the first global state in the universe"[1] and "the Slovenia of Athens," the NSK State in Time propounds a belief that "Art is fanaticism that demands diplomacy." Issuing sober green-covered passports to anyone who "pledges to participate on a best-effort basis to support the integrity of the NSK state," the collective exists as "a state in time, a state without territory and national borders, a sort of 'spiritual, virtual state.'" (They note that "the passport can be used creatively, also as an official travel document, naturally with a certain hazard to its owner.")

NSK is a union or federation of five main groups—the twenty-year-old artist's collective IRWIN ("The future is the seed of the past"); the band Laibach ("Only God can subdue Laibach. People and things never can"); the *Novi Kolektivizem* or New Collectivism Studio, which provides graphic-design services throughout the NSK State ("Humanist Propaganda"); the Department of Pure and Applied Philosophy ("Our mission is to make Evil lose its nerves"); and the *Noordung Cosmokinetic Cabinet*—a theater company named for the Slovene space scientist Herman Potocnik Noordung—whose *One Versus One* project opened on 21 April 1995, with restagings planned every ten years until 2045, the first having taken place in 2005. ("The place of those actors who die in the meantime will be taken by a mechanical symbol, their spoken text represented by sounds—melody for women, rhythm for men. In 2045, these symbols will be shot into zero-gravity space in a capsule. This action is intended to finally abolish mimetic theatre and establish the rule of noncorporeal art.")

"To put it in a nutshell... NSK is in its structure a simple and yet complex mechanism which makes any precise explanation in a few words practically impossible....Regarding the philosophy—it may be called untranslatable, which of course means that it is understood by those who understand it....The NSK State in Time is an abstract organism, a suprematist body, installed in a real social and political space as a sculpture comprising the concrete body warmth, spirit, and work of its members. NSK confers the status of a state not to territory but to mind, whose borders are in a state of flux, in accordance with the movements and changes of its symbolic and physical collective body."

1 See <www.nskstate.com>.

opposite, clockwise from top left: Plaque of NSK embassy, Beijing, 1994; Plaque of NSK embassy, Moscow, 1992; NSK Garda Zagreb, performance in cooperation with the Croatian Army, 2000. Photo Igor Andjelic; NSK Garda Prague, performance in cooperation with the Czech Army, 2000. Photo Igor Andjelic.

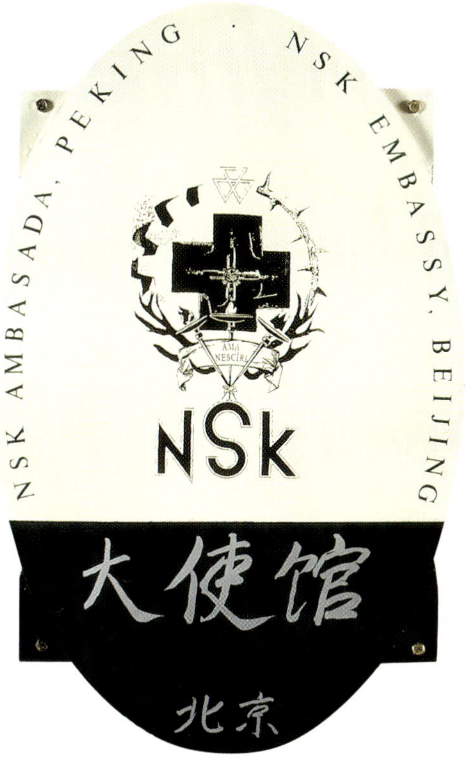
NSK AMBASADA, PEKING · NSK EMBASSY, BEIJING
NSK
大使馆
北京

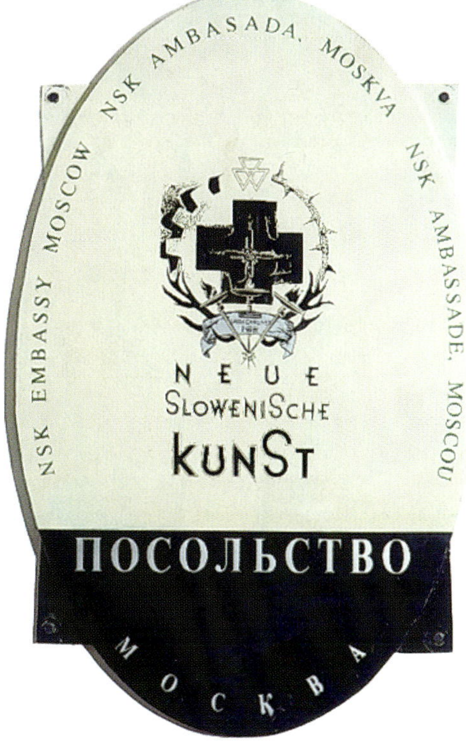
NSK EMBASSY MOSCOW NSK AMBASADA, MOSKVA NSK AMBASSADE, MOSCOU
NEUE
SLOWENISCHE
KUNST
ПОСОЛЬСТВО
МОСКВА

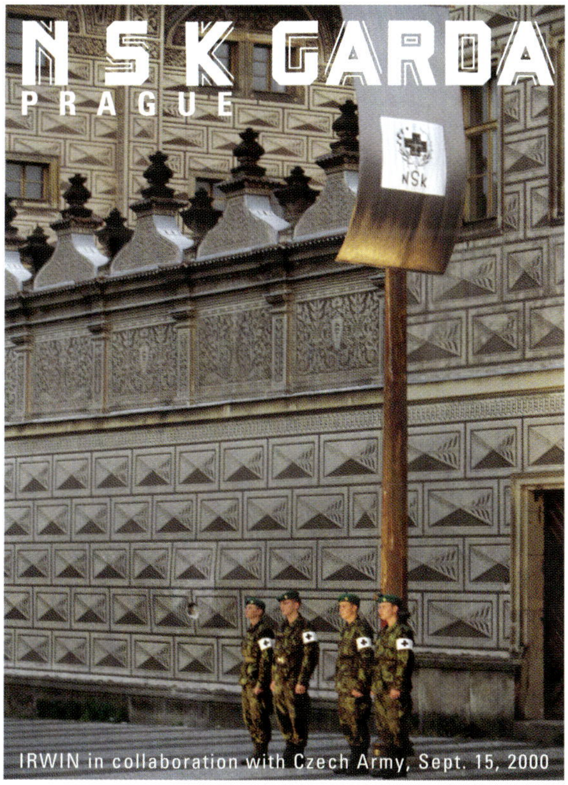
NSK GARDA
PRAGUE
IRWIN in collaboration with Czech Army, Sept. 15, 2000

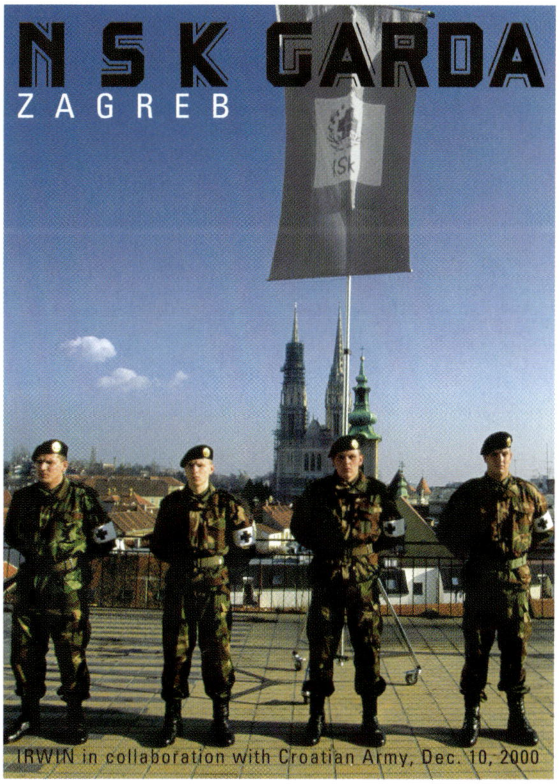
NSK GARDA
ZAGREB
IRWIN in collaboration with Croatian Army, Dec. 10, 2000

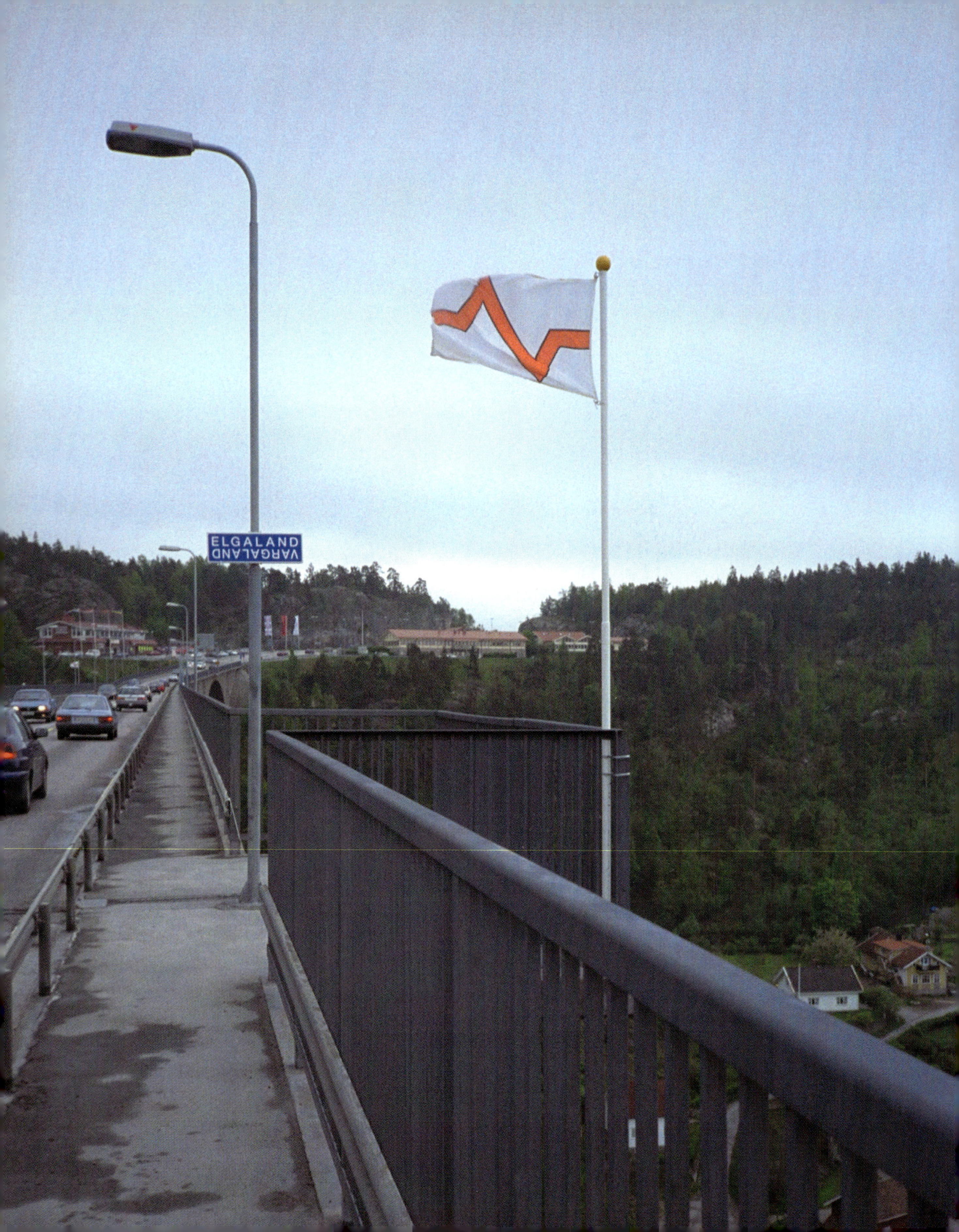
ELGALAND
VARGALAND

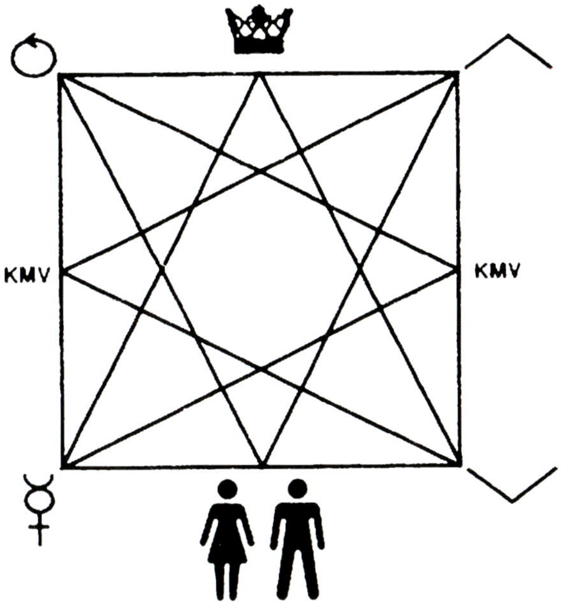

THE KINGDOM OF ELGALAND-VARGALAND

With effect from the 14th of March 1992, we are annexing and occupying the following territories:

1. All border territories between all countries on earth, and all areas (up to a width of 10 nautical miles) outside all countries' territorial waters. We designate these territories our physical territory. These territories, usually called No Man's Land or Border Crossings, are in constant flux. They change everyday, and in reports from all over the world we notice that new territories appear (e.g., the North and South Korean border), disappear (e.g., the East and West German border in 1989) and reappear (e.g., the Latvian, Estonian and Lithuanian borders). We also observe nations' fishing territories waxing and waning. There are frequent foreign violations at sea; vehicles with cargo, refugees, tourists, political and military maneuvers; animals and fishes walk and swim freely, insects and birds buzz and sing. Theoretically/practically, all past existing areas such as the borders between Texas and the USA, between England and Scotland, or between Sweden and Skåne (at the time belonging to Denmark), are annexed by the Kingdoms of Elgaland-Vargaland.

Thus begins the declaration, signed by artists Leif Elggren and Carl Michael von Hausswolff, that formed the beginning of an experiment in government that has grown in complexity ever since. The declaration goes on to announce the annexation of all other forms of interstitial territories, including the Hypnagogue State (the state between being awake and being asleep), the Escapistic Territory (conscious, mental space travel akin to daydreaming, telepathy, and so on), and the Virtual Room (a borderless digital space).

Currently with more than 600 citizens and a number of Ministries ranging from the crucial (the Ministry of Pleasure and the Ministry of Cartography) to the whimsical (the Ministry of Lamination and the Ministry of Audiology), Elgaland-Vargaland has combined political critique and mordant humor in order to undermine the pieties of traditional states and point slyly toward their array of failures. The manufactured poverty and class differences of first-world states is exposed through gestures of poetic excess, such as the printing of a million thalers (the official currency of Elgaland-Vargaland) that belong equally to all citizens. The kingdom's tenth anniversary in 2002 was marked by a group of citizens boarding a boat from Stockholm to Talinn, Estonia, carrying only their Elgaland-Vargaland passports. After being detained for a day for trying to enter Estonia with false documents, the citizens were placed on a boat and sent back to Sweden. As King Leif I states, "Our purpose was not to provoke the border police. Our purpose was to go home to Elgaland-Vargaland's physical territory: to get rejected at the Estonian border, then go back and be rejected at the Swedish border, back again to the Estonian border, etc., etc., you know, for ever. They did their job and took our passports, so we just had to go back to Sweden."

opposite: Elgaland-Vargaland physical territory, Svinesund, on the border between Sweden and Norway.

above: Schematic diagram of the political structure within Elgaland-Vargaland. The constitution guarantees every citizen's right to move freely within the hierarchy. The acronym KMV stands for "The Materialization of the King in the World."

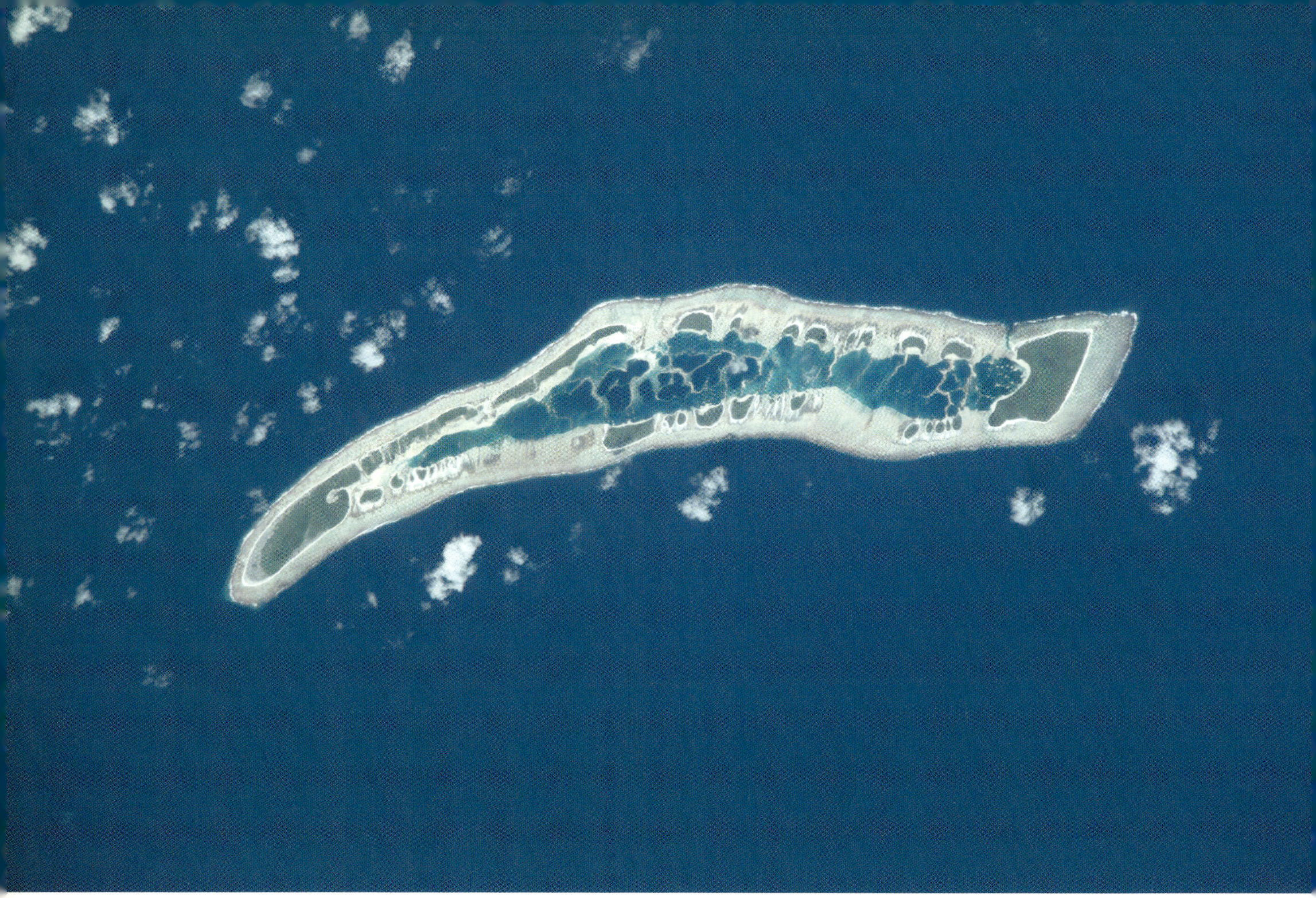

THE NEW FREE STATE OF CAROLINE

According to artist Gregory Green's account, the history of the New Free State of Caroline began in 1997 when he sent a letter to the United Nations and the World Court staking a claim on a small uninhabited island 500 miles south of Tahiti. Joining Japan, Australia, the US, and Kiribati in claiming this island only thirteen miles in perimeter, Green wanted the territory to be a haven for individuals whose beliefs are at odds with those of their current homelands. Utopian anarchist structures of government inspired by Californian feminist and anti-nuclear groups were to form the political basis of the New Free State of Caroline, and any eventual realization of the state would see Green take his place as one citizen among many.

His letter to the World Court received no response, though the United Nations wrote to advise him that it was in receipt of his claim. Two years later, in 1999, Kiribati was given sovereignty over the disputed island after archaeologists discovered Polynesian fire pits predating any of the other claimants' contact with the island, thus taking precedence over all claims not emanating from Polynesian states. The United Nations never notified Green that the case had been settled.

Green has not, however, ended his quest for a small piece of unclaimed land on which the New Free State of Caroline and its prospective nationals—some 3,000 people around the world have applied for citizenship—could find a home. He is now filing a claim on an island whose precise location he will not reveal until his claim has been processed. He will disclose, however, that it lies100 miles off Antarctica and that other claimants include Australia and the United States. Despite its inauspicious location, the serendipitous trajectory of the Gulf Stream provides the island with weather similar to San Francisco's, a meteorological coincidence that bodes well for the utopian anarchist models of government that Green will advocate if his claim is accepted.

above: Satellite image of Caroline Island, renamed Millenium Island in 1999 after Kiribati assumed sovereignty.

THE MAGIC OF THE STATE: AN INTERVIEW WITH MICHAEL TAUSSIG

DAVID LEVI STRAUSS

I first met Mick Taussig about eight years ago, as *The Magic of the State* (Routledge, 1997) was coming out. I'd read *Shamanism, Colonialism, and the Wild Man: A Study in Terror and Healing* (University of Chicago Press, 1987) when it appeared, and was especially drawn to its treatment of images and image-making in power relations. Later I was invited to participate in an informal seminar that Mick and Peter Lamborn Wilson had gathered around the subject of shamanism. The conversation among Mick, Peter, and me, on states both fictional and non, has continued since then around frequent fires and dinners, almost always within a stone's throw of the Rondout Creek, where we all live in the Hudson Valley.

After getting a medical degree from the University of Sydney, Australia in 1964 and working as a physician in the university's main teaching hospital for a year and in general practice for another six months, Mick read for a Master's degree in sociology at the London School of Economics and worked as a psychiatric resident in mental hospitals in London. He was appointed a Research Fellow at the Institute of Latin American Studies of London University in 1969, and went to Colombia in September of that year, to "join the Revolution." What he saw there intrigued him, and his fieldwork in Colombia, Putamayo, and Venezuela would continue over the next four decades. His Ph.D. dissertation (with Julian Pitt-Rivers) examining the socio-cultural impact of the commercialization of agriculture was published in Spanish in 1975. He taught in the Department of Anthropology at the University of Michigan and in Performance Studies at New York University before accepting his current position as Professor of Anthropology at Columbia University. He is the author of eight books: *The Devil and Commodity Fetishism in South America* (1980), *Shamanism, Colonialism, and the Wild Man* (1987), *The Nervous System* (1992), *Mimesis and Alterity* (1993), *The Magic of the State* (1997), *Defacement: Public Secrecy and the Labor of the Negative* (1999), *Law in a Lawless Land* (2003), and *My Cocaine Museum* (2004).

The Magic of the State is my favorite of all of Mick's books, because of its particular mixing of fiction and documentary. "This is the most 'fictional' of my writings," Mick told me. "I use the Sydney expression 'fictocriticism' to convey the hybrid sense and I clearly designate the fictional quality through a variety of devices, mainly humor and tone, camp and arch-camp. An aim of such writing is to turn the attention of the reader to the very act of writing as an 'anthropological' or cultural act which engages with the desire to succumb to authority in general, and to colonial or postcolonial tropes in particular." As the *New York Times* put it, "Over the last several decades, as the exemplars of traditional fieldwork have been toppled from their pedestals, Taussig has been developing a radical alternative. . . . Blending fact and fiction, ethnographic observation, archival history, literary theory and memoir, his books read more like beatnik novels than sober analyses of other cultures...."

In *The Magic of the State*, you write about the relation between traditional magical rites and rituals of spirit possession and the workings of the modern nation-state. You base this book on fieldwork on a "magic mountain" in the middle of Venezuela, where spirit possession is practiced, and where "there's something about spirit possession which is amicable toward hierarchy, stratification, and maybe even the State."

This book concerns spirit-possession on the mountain of Maria Lionza in central Venezuela in the 1980s and 1990s, where pilgrims in large numbers become possessed by the spirits of the dead under the rule of an imaginary spirit queen, Maria Lionza. Especially important are the spirits of the Indians who allegedly fought the Spanish in the sixteenth century and the independence soldiers of the early nineteenth century, including many black foot soldiers as well as white officers, most notably Simón Bolívar—as highlighted in the state's school textbooks, in the unending stream of state iconography from postage stamps to wall murals on bus stops and outside schools, from the standardized village, town, and city central square, the naming of mountain peaks, and of course in the physiognomy of authority wherever it be.

The dead are a great source of magical élan, grace, and power. This has been present in many cultures since the first burial. Indeed Georges Bataille (to whose ideas *The Magic of the State* is greatly indebted) argued from archaeological evidence and physical anthropology that the corpse is the origin of taboos, respect for the dead being what separates the human from the animal... Just imagine, then, the power that can accrue to the modern state, that great machine of death and war!

People today gain magical power not from the dead, but from the state's embellishment of them. And the state, authoritarian and spooky, is as much possessed by the dead as is any individual pilgrim. The current president of Venezuela, Hugo Chávez, is the embodiment of this. In a sense he was predestined by this mystical foundation of authority as writ into the post-colonial exploitation of colonial history. The success of the Patriot Act and of the current US administration owes a great deal to this, too, after 9/11.

However my argument is that such spirit possession is a dramatization not only of the Great Events but also of the more subtle imageric- and feeling-states present in the artwork of the state any and everywhere, from the traffic cop and tax clerk to the pomp and ceremony of national celebrations, from a Latin American pseudo-democracy to the US and Western European states as well. Hobbes's Leviathan is mythical yet also terribly real. This is where the rationalist analysis of the state loses ground. Foucault was amazingly short-sighted in dismissing "blood" and the figure of the Ruler.

In terms of craft and presentation, the mountain in my book is like a window opening onto the magic of the state. This is an anthropology not of the poor and powerless, but of the state as a reified entity, lusting in its spirited magnificence, hungry for soulstuff.

I love the mixing of fiction and documentary in this book. "Torn between the overlapping claims of fiction and those of documentary," you write in the preface, "I have allowed this magic of the state to settle in its awkwardness in the division of the forms.... Through something like Brecht's estrangement-effect, naming as renaming can provide insight into what we call history, its making no less than its retelling, especially history of the spirits of the dead as the mark of nation and state, but I have in mind, by renaming, something else as well—namely the evocation of a fictive nation-state in place of real ones so as to better grasp the elusive nature of stately being. After all it is not only the writer of fiction who fuses reality with dreamlike states. This privilege also belongs, as Kafka taught, to the being-in-the-world of the modern state itself." Do you think that, in casting this account in fictional terms, you were able to get closer to the "being-in-the-world" of the state?

Da mix. If you assume, as I do, that reality is really made up, then you are automatically launched into this wild project conflating fiction and non-fiction. The only choice you've got is whether to acknowledge this or not, whether you will exploit the joints and seams, or not, and whether you will allow the sheer act of writing itself to seem a self-conscious activity, drawing attention to the continuous work of make-believe in art no less than in politics and everyday life. Because they expand the notion of theater in these ways, and because they animate the magic of the state, Brecht and Kafka make congenial company for anyone working with the mix.

In *Shamanism, Colonialism, and the Wild Man*, you point out that Walter Benjamin recognized that "it was in the less conscious image realm and in the dreamworld of the popular imagination" that it was necessary to act if one wanted change. And your epigraph to *The Magic of the State* is from Nietzsche in *The Gay Science*: "How foolish it would be to suppose that one only needs to point out this origin and this misty shroud of delusion in order to destroy the world that counts for real, so-called 'reality.' We can only destroy as creators." Is this why you wrote *The Magic of the State* as essentially a work of fiction?

As you suggest, fiction allowed me to be more truthful, as when starting with the fourth chapter the narrator transforms into Captain Mission who, somewhat like a character in a play, allows me, the writer, to gain distance from what is being described. This is quite different from writing in the third person, the more usual form of non-fiction, because a note of make-believe and playfulness is injected into the work such that the reader is never quite sure what is "real" and what is not.

Mission himself is a play on the anthropologist as a man-with-a-mission, even as a latter day missionary, and also invokes the French pirate operating out of northern Madagascar in the seventeenth century whom William Burroughs made much of in his *Cities of the Red Night*. I especially liked having him and the Chief Justice—another character I made up—fight it out, spiritually, so to speak, up there on a plateau on the magic mountain. Chief was Chief Justice Rehnquist who around the time of writing the book was offering a heartfelt defense of the sanctity of the US flag in a flag burning case that reached the US Supreme Court. Flags are quite commonly used for their magic in possession ceremonies on the magic mountain. Mission and Chief get into disputes about post-modernism, about narrative and metaphor, as Chief lies on his back on the ground, his body convulsing, as he vainly tries to give birth to a demonic spirit possessing him. You can hear the wild screams as well as the knives thudding into the ground hurled from Mission's practiced hands. This was literary theory!

Reading it, I was struck by the sheer efficacy of storytelling, how it's a much more efficient way to communicate about people and concepts, because of the way it stays in the memory and the way it works on the imagination.

Yes! I love storytelling despite my reservations about the coercion of narrative. I love the fantasy of putting yourself, as reader or writer, into the shoes of the Other. But in my line of business you have to develop a type of storytelling that stands outside as much as inside the story—Brecht's issue with the fourth wall.

All the details in *The Magic and the State* are exactly what you would find on the mountain. Nothing is made up by me in that regard. Yet, by invoking these out-of-town characters, I can relieve the reader of the tedium of documentary while presenting a meta-level or second layer of consideration, namely the parallel between what is being described and what is occurring on the written page as part of the writer's craft, a series of feints, trials, bluff, and scramble of words with things—in brief, the permanently, delicately provisional nature of documentary which, instead, is usually presented as hassle-free and truth-clinching.

Right from the beginning, fiction also enters with the un-named country in which the magic mountain is set. I decided not to make this a statement about Venezuela, but instead make it an "anywhere" or at least an imaginary Latin American country. By not naming it, I committed the "crime" of decontextualization—"Where are we?"—and compounded this by giving the adjoining country (my beloved Colombia) the name of Costaguana, which is the name Joseph Conrad applies to Colombia, or at least the Santa Marta region on the Caribbean coast, in his novel *Nostromo*.

This work has tremendous relevance to my own investigations into the political uses of the magic of images. For the book on photography and belief that I'm writing now, I take permission to use "magic" first from Vilém Flusser's groundbreaking work in *Towards a Philosophy of Photography*, and move from that into the "science of images" developed in the Renaissance, especially by Giordano Bruno, to theorize the

current state of image politics. Anyone living in Bush & Co.'s United States cannot help but draw parallels between the spirit-possession politics and image magic of *The Magic of the State* and the current situation here. Do you think those parallels are relevant?

Spirit possession can be a marvelous exploration and use of images, I think, in so far as it achieves Nietzsche's mix of the Apollonian and Dionysian modes of engagement with the image. The possessed person moves into the image, which acquires a three-dimensional reality, so to speak, and does so by means of body-rhythms as with music and dance, what we might call the "bodily unconscious." Furthermore, spirit possession, like jazz music or interpretive literary criticism and social science, often allows for a free-wheeling improvisation of a role tailored to the specific problem of human relations that drives the person to either seek possession or seek guidance from someone possessed.

In an interview a few years ago with Peter Lamborn Wilson, you outlined your theory that "magic in Colombia, if not in other places, had an awful lot to do with fantasies about otherness." Do you think this is relevant to the current situation in the US?

Always. Magic, spirit possession, fast-track access of the occult, are heavily dependent on colonization and racist hierarchies as well as gendered ones (women are "intuitive," no good at science but are always the ones who find lost things...). The primitive is blessed with magic and is there as a resource to be tapped by the "civilized." This has existed, I think, since pretty much the beginnings of the human race, but was certainly boosted by the Enlightenment and modern colonialism. Crucial here is the way civilized/primitive is mapped onto metaphoric/literal.

How much of the magic of the state is manipulation by state operators, and how much is projection from the people onto those operators and operations—a popular participation?

It's a circle.

I'm fascinated by the notion of corruption and a sort of "institutionalized fraud" in magic. You write about the change in the Venezuelan "perfumeries" (bodegas, candle shops) in 1985 when magical essences were made legal as "cosmetics," and a woman tells you that the cosmetics business is "all ticket," by which she means it's all marketing (labeling, branding, advertising).

What is your working definition of "magic?" Is it different from the one used by Marcel Mauss? In *Shamanism, Colonialism, and the Wild Man*, you say, "By magic it should be here plainly understood that we are talking about *knowledge and words, words and their ability to effect things*. In effect we are talking about the marketing of a theory of signification and of rhetoric, indeed, not just of knowledge but of what is in a deeply significant sense the knowledge of knowledge that has to remain inaccessible for that knowledge to exist." How do you keep magic distinct from religion in *The Magic of the State*?

This is an artifact to some extent, because here I was using "magic" as used by Indians in the southwest of Colombia to refer to white man's books on magic as sold in the marketplaces. But there is no doubt that the "knowledge of knowledge that has to remain inaccessible" is as good a way as any of thinking of magic's knot we can't and mustn't untie if we wish to go on thinking and talking, like you need a certain speed to keep riding a bicycle.

overleaf: Glexis Novoa, *Landscape of Symbols*, 2005

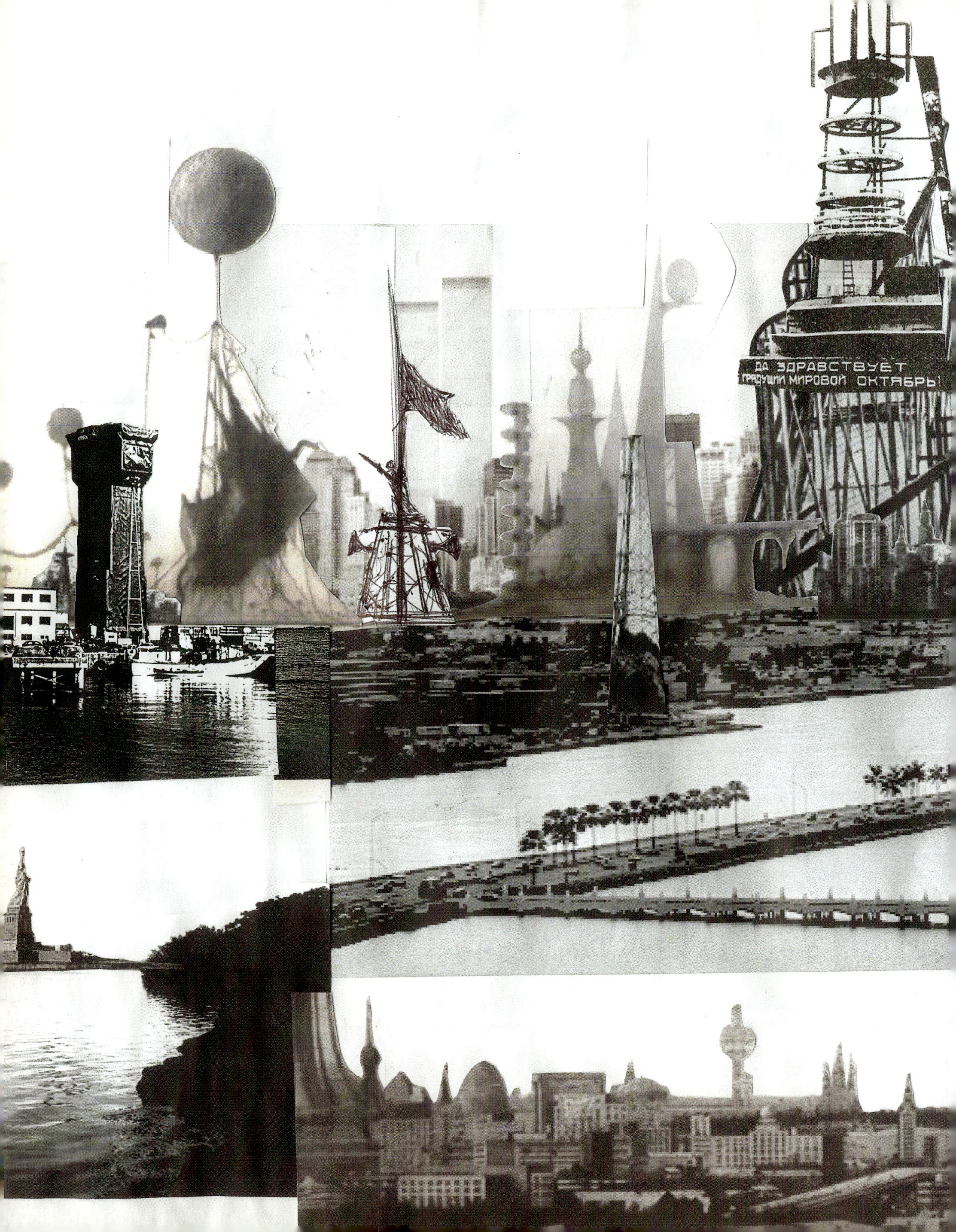
ДА ЗДРАВСТВУЕТ
ГРЯДУЩИЙ МИРОВОЙ ОКТЯБРЬ!

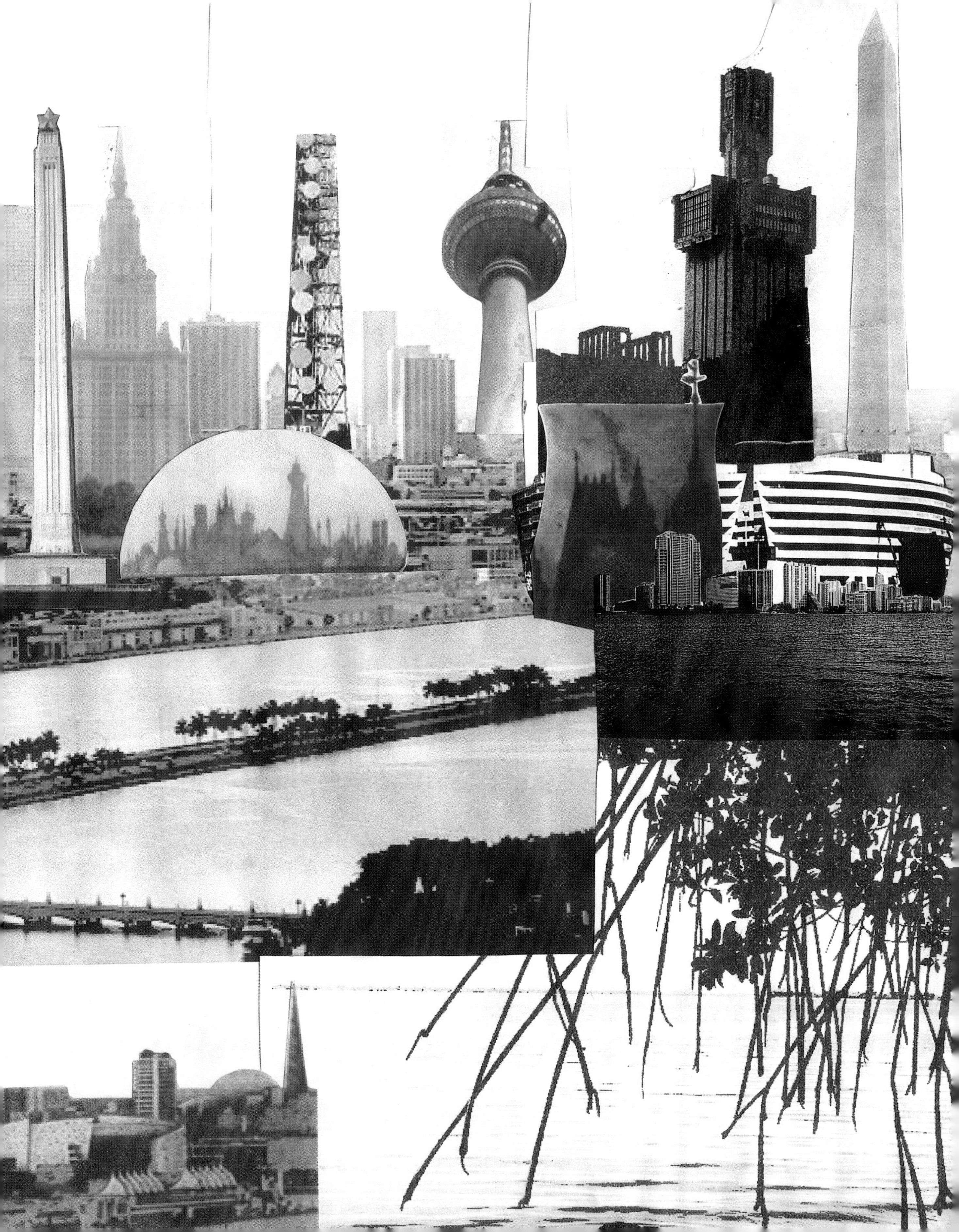

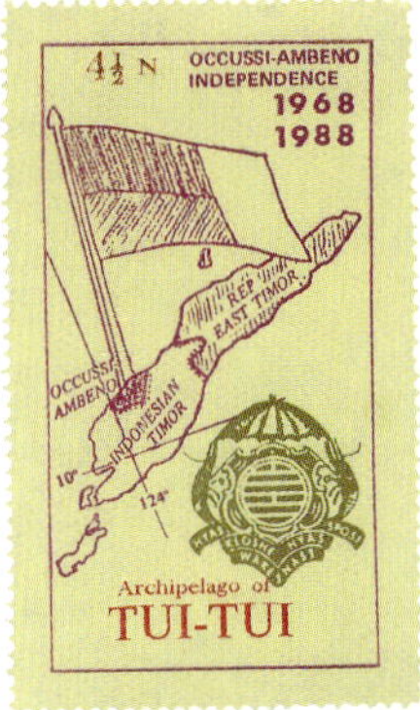

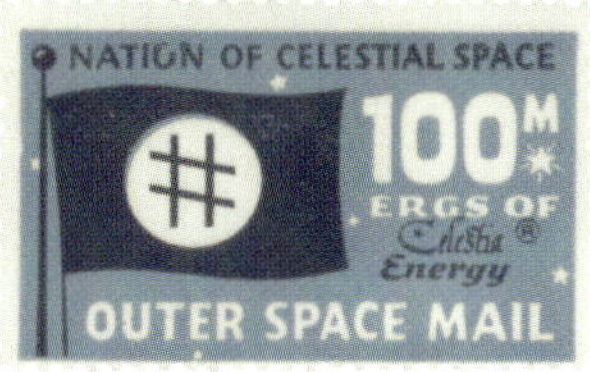

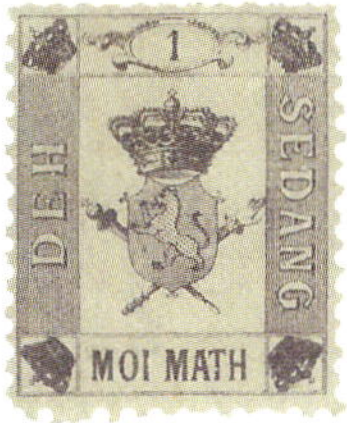

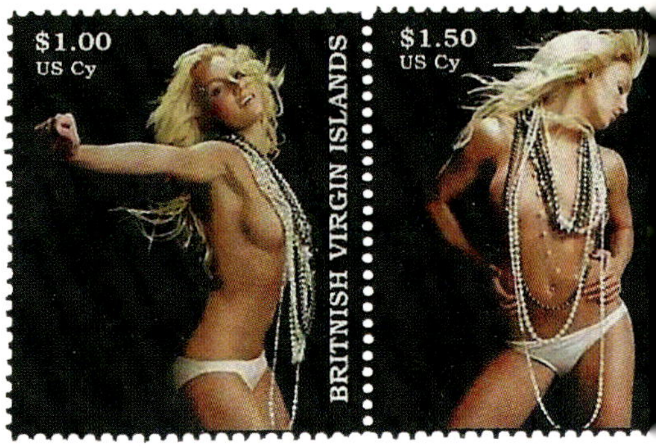

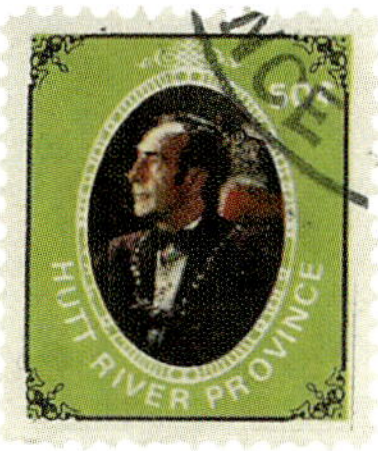

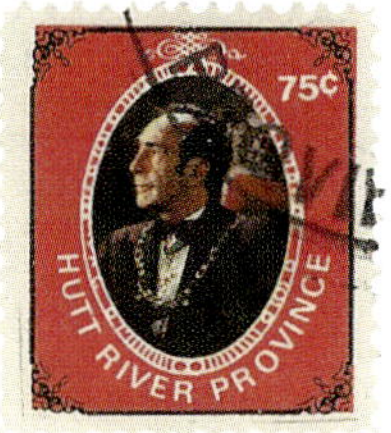

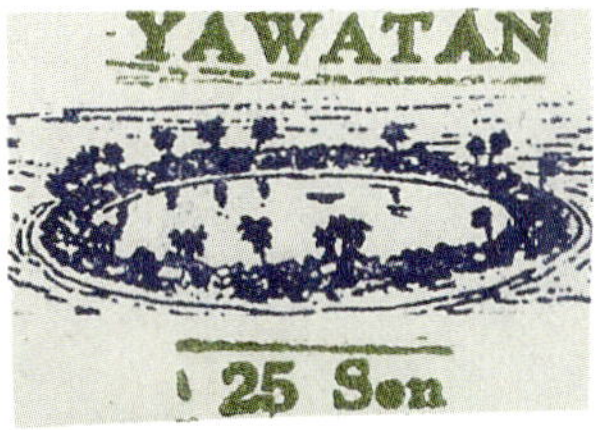

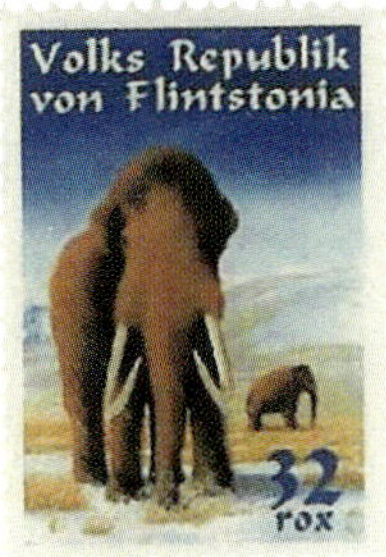

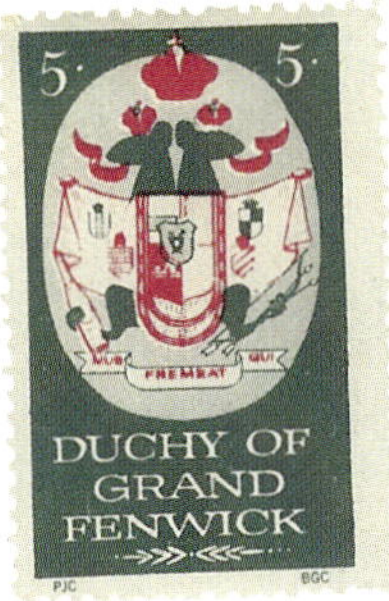

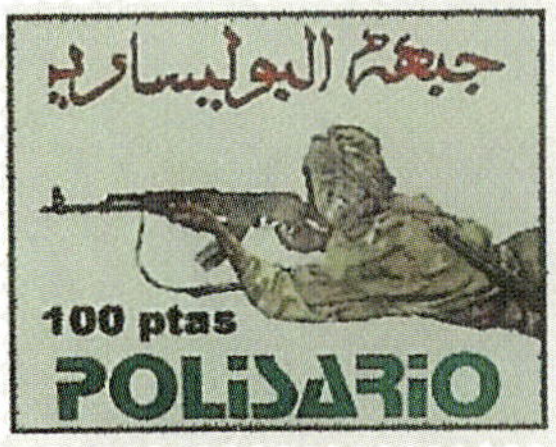

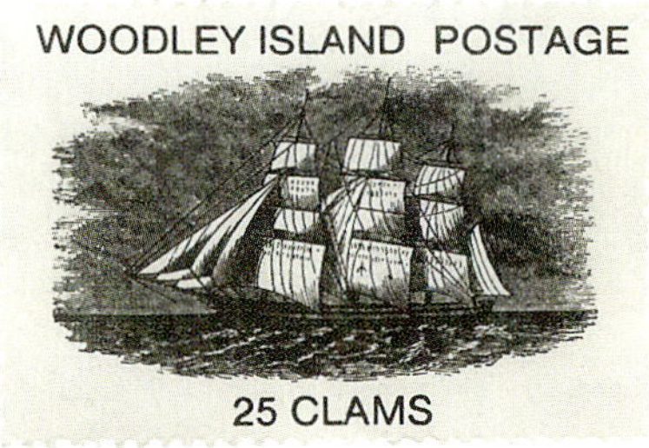

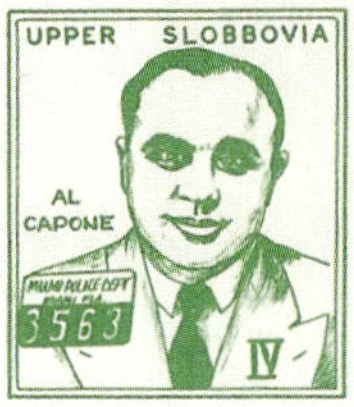

RETURN TO SENDER

BONNIE & ROGER RIGA

Ever since the first postage stamp was issued in May 1840 by Great Britain, there have been forged, bogus, and fantasy stamps. Forgeries are stamps that replicate actual postage for the purpose of defrauding the postal service or collectors; bogus stamps are fake stamps from real places, and fantasy stamps are imaginary stamps from non-existent places. These stamps, which don't appear in the otherwise definitive *Scott's Catalogue*, are collectively known as "Cinderellas"—they are the stepchildren of philately.

Fantasy stamps are most often intended as artistic, political, philosophical, or humorous statements. Advertisements for the 1959 movie *The Mouse that Roared*, in which the tiny Alpine Duchy of Grand Fenwick declares war on the US in anticipation of postwar financial aid after a hasty surrender, went out with a stamp from the fictional state. Beginning in 1961, the famous Wilkinsburg Stamp Club created Upper Slobbovia, issuing philatelic souvenir stamps for thirty years that spoofed regular US postage and current affairs. They depict unlikely American stamp subjects, such as Fidel Castro and Al Capone.

Often fantasy stamps depict satirical Utopias, such as the US Military Occupation of Sans Dinero, or the little island of Yawatan, an atoll in the South Pacific in the shape of a doughnut and perforated by a big lagoon, or Upper Bongoland. These stamps play on the notion of obscure "local posts," which were created to carry mail from a remote place where official mail delivery did not serve, to the nearest post office or vice versa. Special stamps were made to supplement the regular stamps, to show an extra fee had been paid. However, many modern "local posts" really fall under the category of fantasy, because the service does not really exist. For example, Sanda Island, that has issued a Mona Lisa stamp, is a 314-acre island located two miles southeast of the Kintyre Peninsula in Scotland which has absolutely no need for mail, being exclusively occupied by birds and sheep. However, the stamps are profitable, and they appeal to many collectors.

Some fantasy stamps are overtly political, issued by militant groups to create an air of legitimacy for their imag-

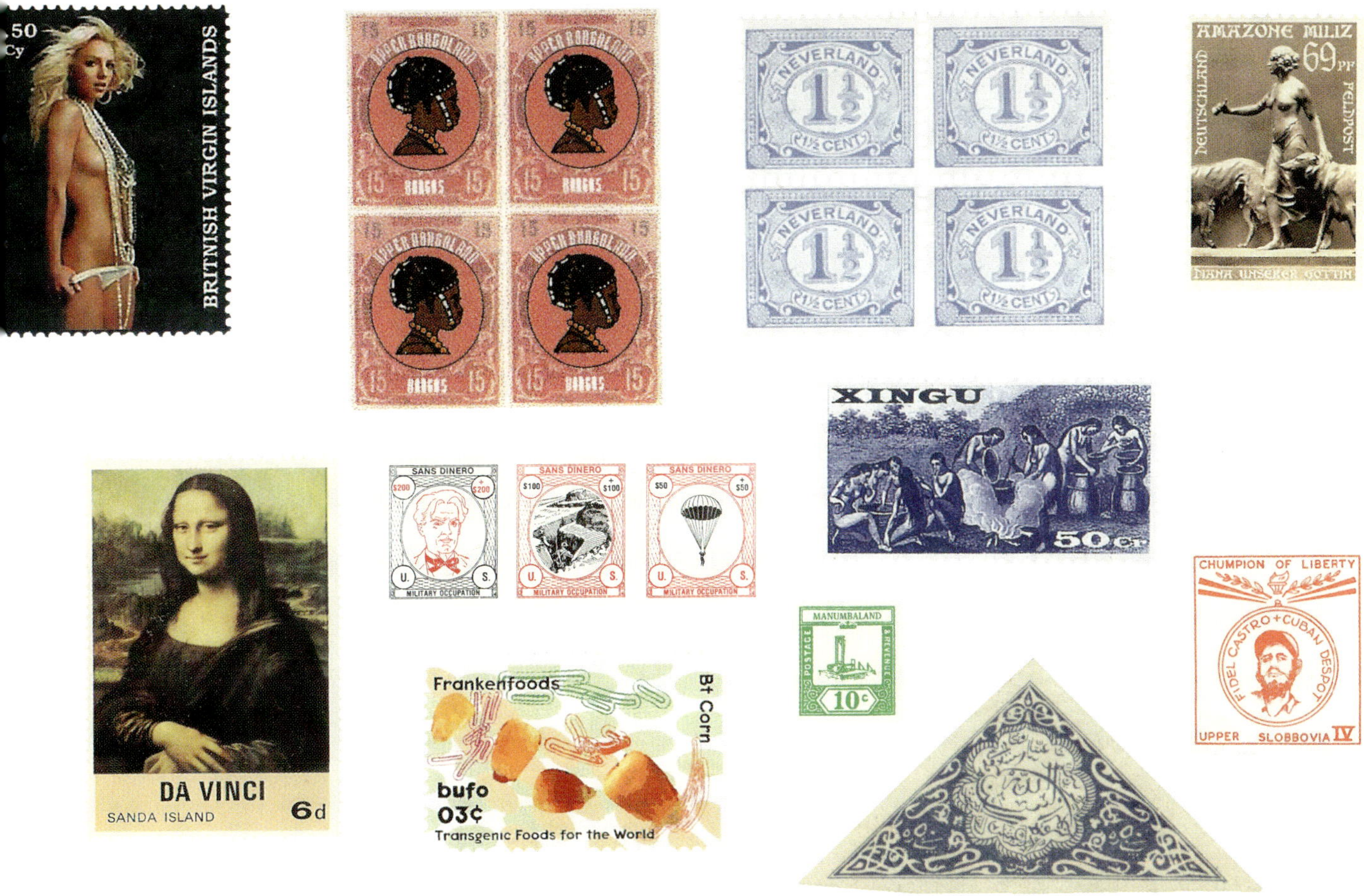

ined states. The POLISARIO stamp reproduced here refers to the *Frente Popular de Liberación de Saguía el Hamra y Río de Oro*, or the "People's Liberation Front of Saguia el Hamra and Rio de Oro," a guerilla army and political movement. Formed in 1973, and principally comprised of the Sahrawi people, the group was created to end the Spanish, Moroccan, and Mauritanian military administration of Western Sahara. In 1976, POLISARIO formally proclaimed the Sahrawi Arab Democratic Republic (SADR), a government in exile. Based in Tindouf, Algeria, it still contests the Western Sahara with Morocco, and controls the almost uninhabited part of the Western Sahara east of the "Moroccan Wall."

Similarly, a group advocating the creation of a separate Zionist State of Judea created their own stamps. The issuers claim to have the support of Rabbi Meyer Kahane, former head of the ultra-rightist Kach party, whose stated goal was to drive all Arabs out of Israel (he was assassinated in New York City in 1990, by an Egyptian militant later convicted in relation to the 1993 World Trade Center bombing).

Other fantasy stamps are more lighthearted hoaxes. One German stamp depicts Princess Diana, honorary member and patroness of the Amazonian Militia, a loosely federated organization of female freedom fighters that reputedly has branches throughout the world. The organization claims to be seeking postal recognition similar to that granted to the Sovereign Military Order of Malta (SMOM), whose stamps are now considered valid in many countries throughout the world. Another "*faux pas* fantasy" strip shows the ruler of the newly liberated Britnish Virgin Islands, a scantily clad Britney Spears, demonstrating a native ritual fertility dance.

Today, with the ready availability of computer graphics and design and printing functions, nearly anyone can produce his or her own fantasy stamps. Thanks to twenty-first century technology, there has been a resurgence of interest in the genre. Cyber stamps are also a growing area of expression. There is something attractive about the concept of a stamp that has endured email and appeals to many people, not just the stamp collector.

above: Cinderella stamps from the authors' collection.

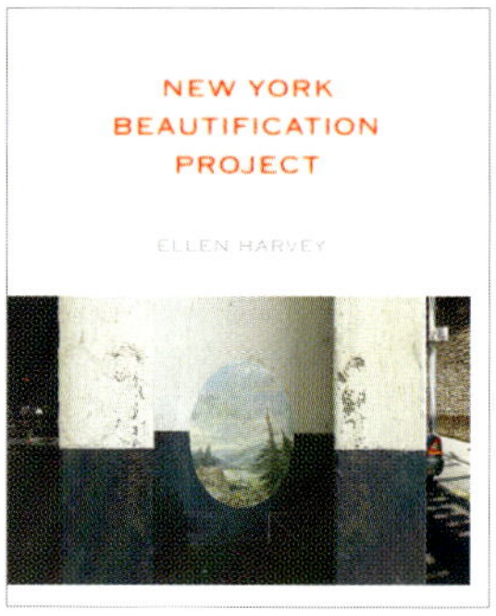

ELLEN HARVEY: NEW YORK BEAUTIFICATION PROJECT
GREGORY R. MILLER & COMPANY

Hardcover, 9 x 12 inches
94 pages / 85 color
$25 ISBN 0-9743648-1-9

Ellen Harvey's "beautification project" is both delicate and ambitious: from 1999 to 2001 she painstakingly painted small, old-fashioned landscapes on graffiti sites in New York City. Accompanying the images are the provocative and hilarious diary-like experiences that arose when her art-making went outdoors.

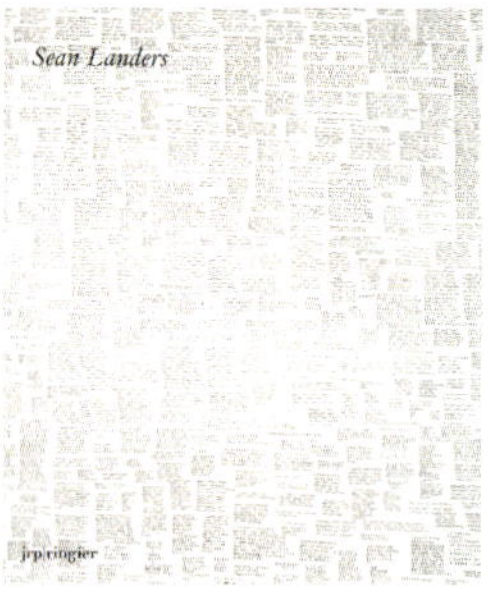

SEAN LANDERS
JRP/RINGIER

Paperback, 9.25 x 11.25 inches
160 pages / 80 color
$45 ISBN 2-940271-53-4

Since the early 1990s, Landers has made some of the most fascinating and repeatedly irritating art in circulation. As he puts it, "My original idea was to make conceptual art entertaining, sloppy, emotional, human, and funny. . . . I tried to be ironic about it but eventually became sincere. Now I'm a happy victim of my own charade".

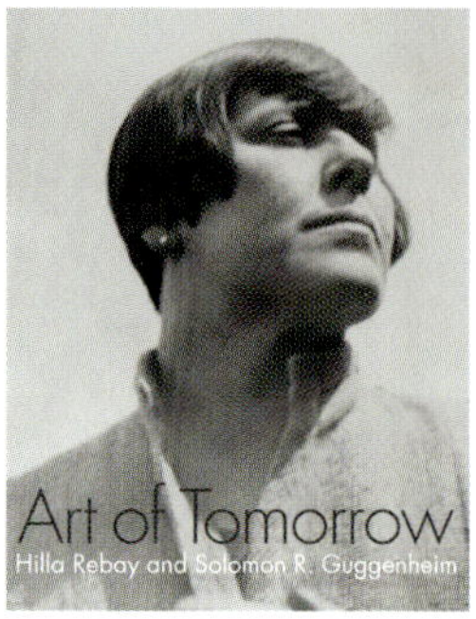

ART OF TOMORROW: HILLA REBAY AND SOLOMON R. GUGGENHEIM
GUGGENHEIM MUSEUM

Hardcover, 8.5 x 11 inches
300 pages
$60 ISBN 0-89207-327-6

A fascinating look at the painter, curator, and director who introduced Solomon R. Guggenheim to artists such as Chagall, Kandinsky, and Klee. In 1939 the two started the Museum of Non-objective painting, which in 1959 became today's Guggenheim Museum in New York City.

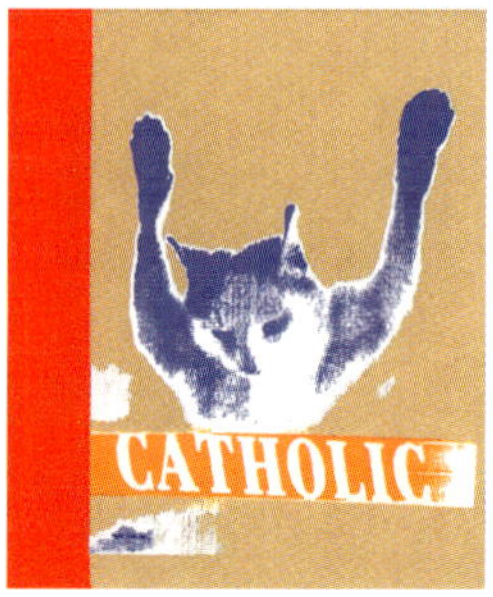

CATHOLIC NO. 1: CATS
D.A.P./EVIL TWIN PUBLICATIONS

Hardcover, 7.5 x 8.5 inches
112 pages / 104 color
$25 ISBN 1-933045-15-9

Catholic editors Jesse Pearson and Glynnis McDaris asked up-and-coming and established artists to contribute "something about cats." The results illustrate the neglected definition of "Catholic:" having varied tastes. Features visual art by Ryan McGinley and Terry Richardson; projects from Le Tigre's JD Samson and United Bamboo; and writing from Steve Lafreniere, Amy Kellner, and Eileen Myles – among many others.

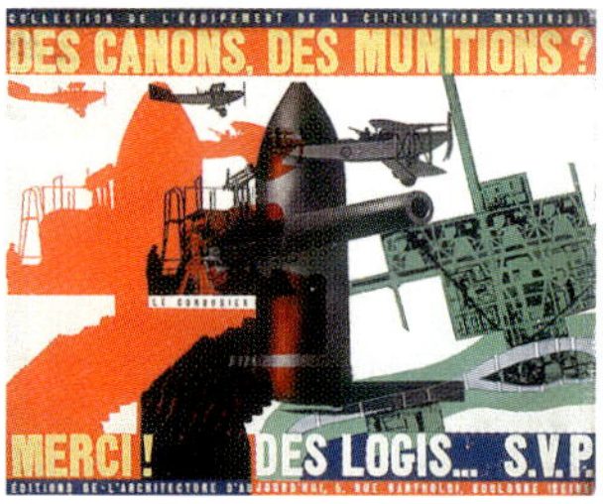

LE CORBUSIER: ARCHITECT OF BOOKS 1912-1965
LARS MÜLLER PUBLISHERS

Hardcover, 6.5 x 9.5 inches
250 pages / 200 color
$50 ISBN 3-03778-034-7

Le Corbusier is so loved, disliked, or revered for his architecture that his work as a book designer and author is scarcely known and even-more-scarcely documented. Yet, in his lifetime (1887-1965) he meticulously planned and realized over 40 books. In this publication, these works are comprehensively presented in order to familiarize viewers with the lesser-known book designer.

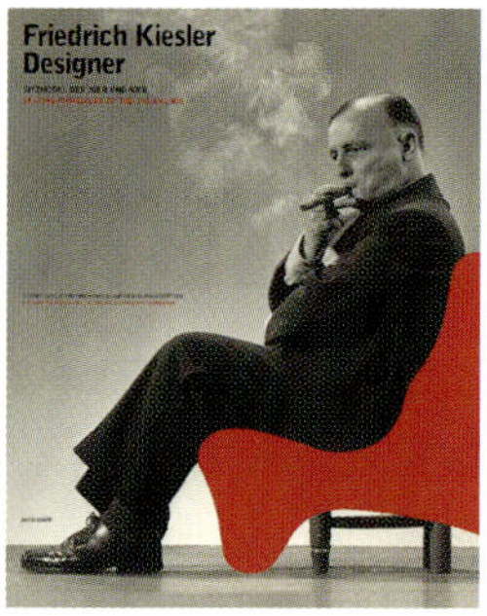

FRIEDRICH KIESLER: DESIGNER: SEATING FURNITURE OF THE 30S AND 40S
HATJE CANTZ

Hardcover, 8.25 x 11 inches
128 pages / 32 color and 68 b&w
$35 ISBN 3-7757-1544-4

Previously unpublished material relating to Kiesler's innovative furniture designs and prototypes from the 30s and 40s. Includes letters, diary entries, and photographs that chronicle the New York cultural enviorment where he lived and worked, and provide rarely documented insight into the role he played in the contemporary design scene.

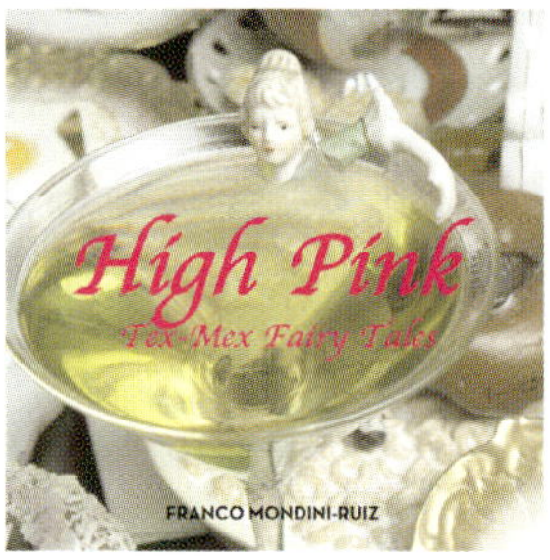

FRANCO MONDINI-RUIZ: HIGH PINK: TEX-MEX FAIRY TALES
D.A.P./DISTRIBUTED ART PUBLISHERS, INC.

Hardcover, 7 x 7 inches
126 pages / 58 color
$20 ISBN 1-933045-12-4

Fifty-six very short but hauntingly impactful stories by the Tejano artist/raconteur Franco Mondini-Ruiz touch on what it's like to grow up Mexican, gay, cultured, middle-class, and wildly fabulous and experimental in southern Texas. A true gem, with a very personal introduction by Sandra Cisneros.

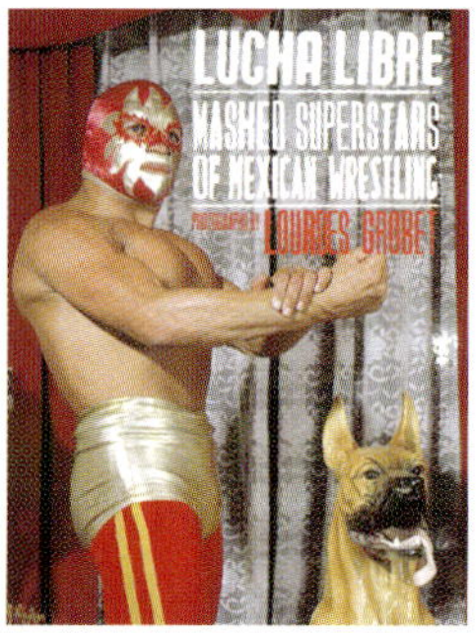

LOURDES GROBET: LUCHA LIBRE: MASKED SUPERSTARS OF MEXICAN WRESTLING
D.A.P./DISTRIBUTED ART PUBLISHERS, INC.

Paperback, 8.25 x 11 inches
296 pages / illustrated throughout
$25 ISBN 1-933045-05-1

Sexo y violencia! *A penetrating study of Mexican Professional Wrestling culture featuring over 500 photographs of* luchadores *like Blue Demon, Santo, and El Solitario, with pictures of their families, friends, and fans—onstage, backstage, and even at home. This 20-year study is the ultimate look at Mexico's masked superstars.*

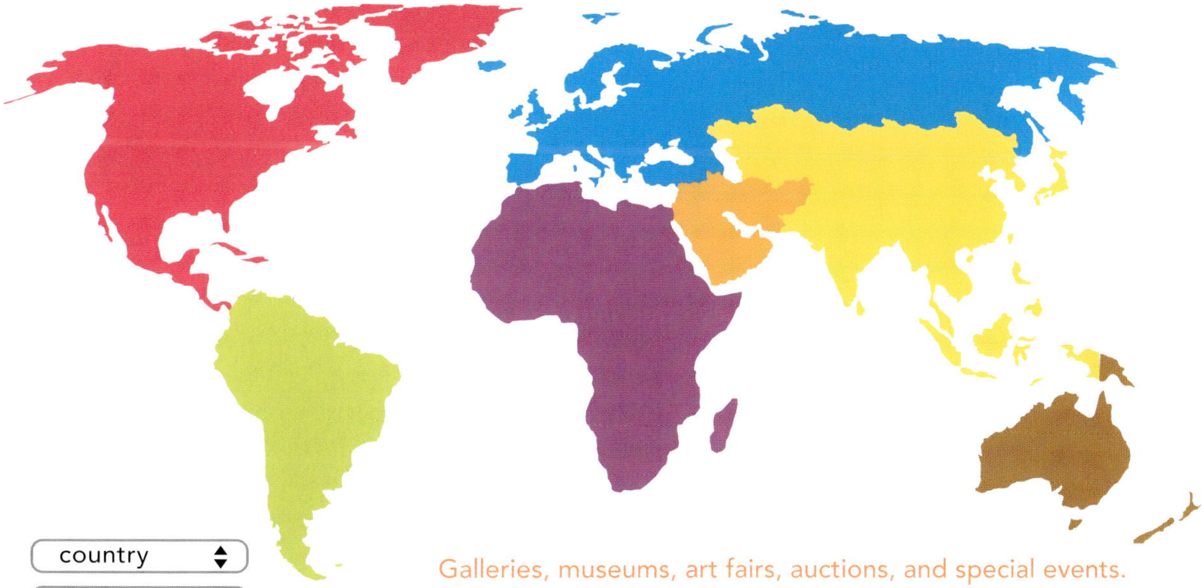

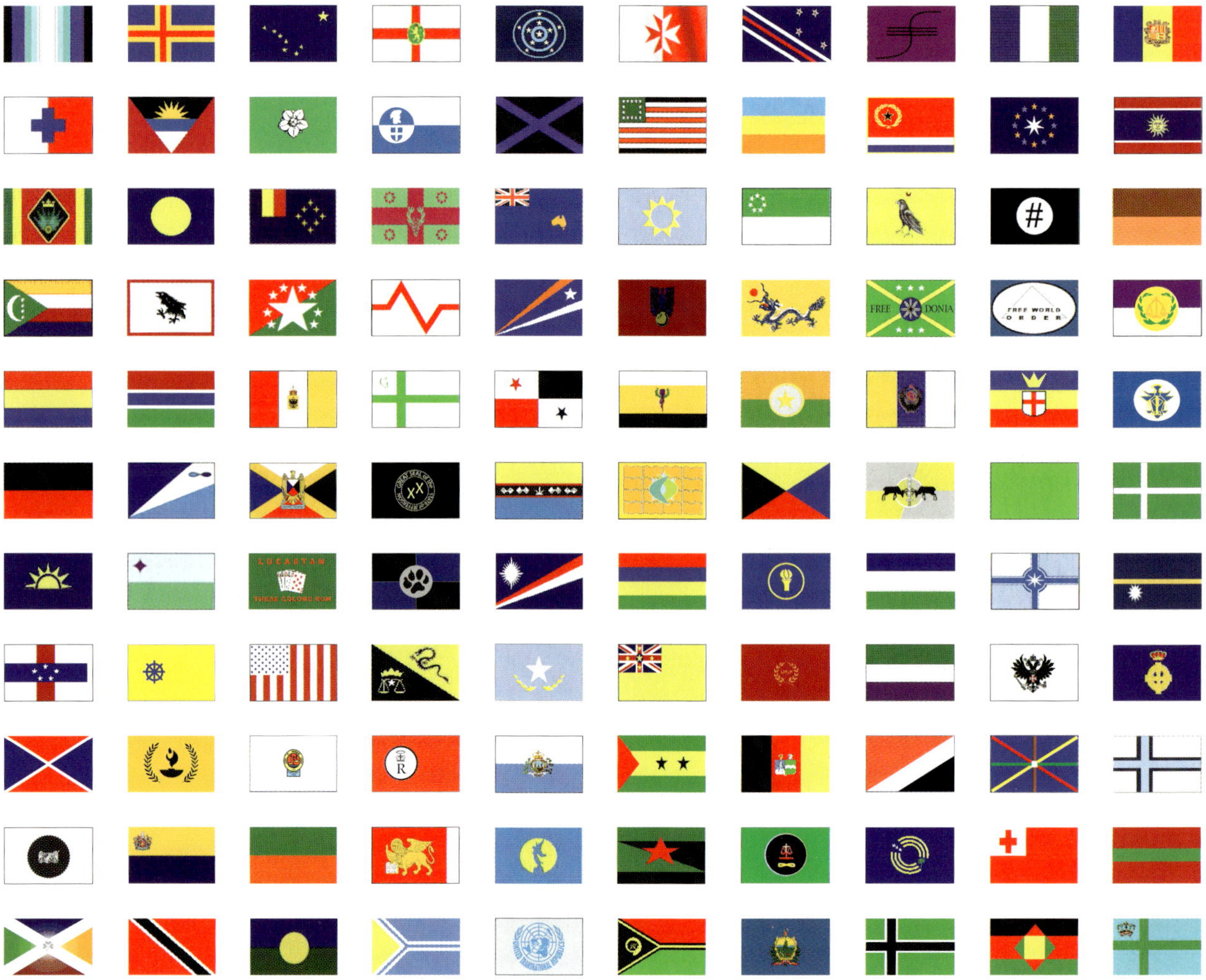
FREE
DONIA

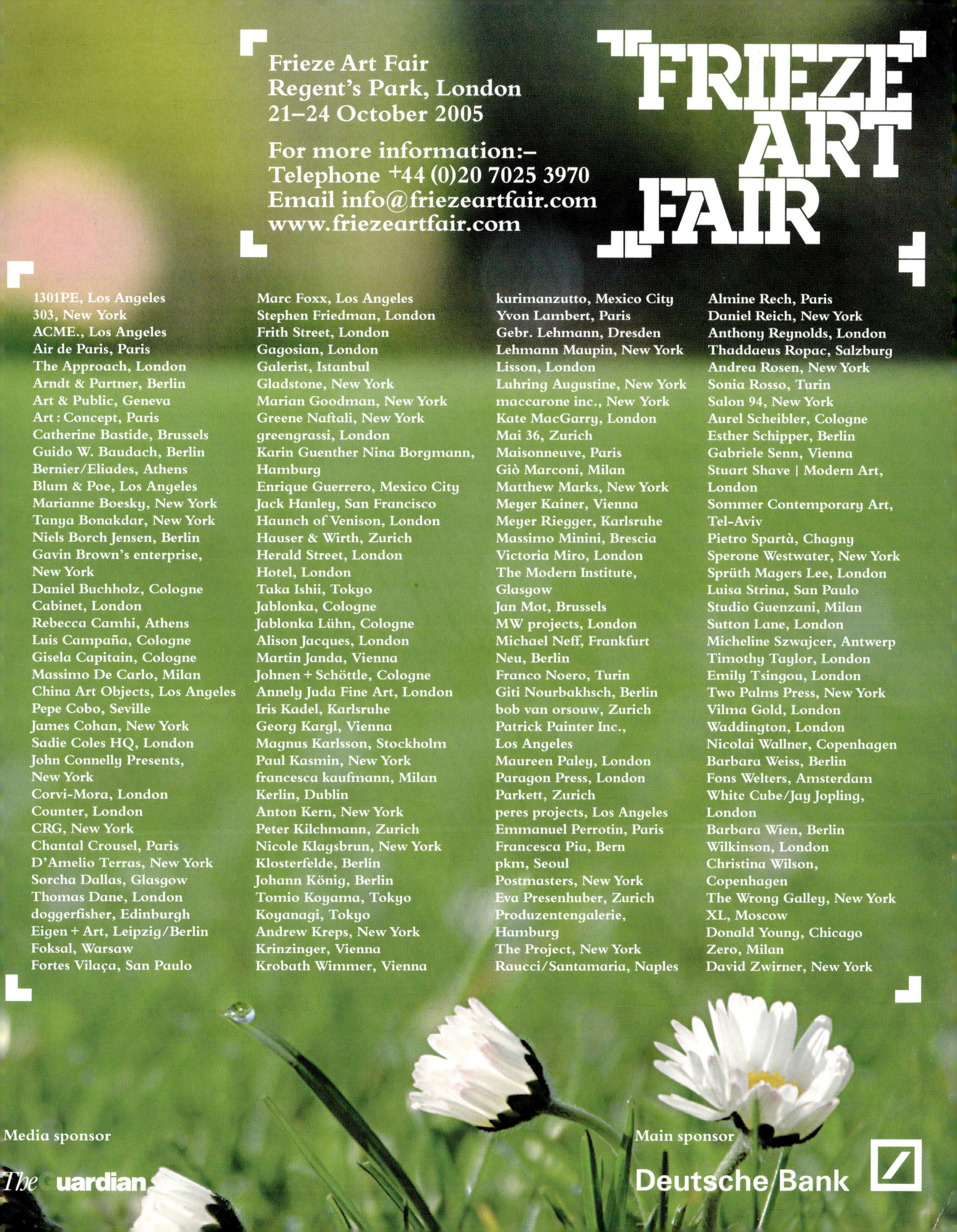

Frieze Art Fair
Regent's Park, London
21–24 October 2005
For more information:–
Telephone +44 (0)20 7025 3970
Email info@friezeartfair.com
www.friezeartfair.com
FRIEZE ART FAIR
1301PE, Los Angeles
303, New York
ACME., Los Angeles
Air de Paris, Paris
The Approach, London
Arndt & Partner, Berlin
Art & Public, Geneva
Art : Concept, Paris
Catherine Bastide, Brussels
Guido W. Baudach, Berlin
Bernier/Eliades, Athens
Blum & Poe, Los Angeles
Marianne Boesky, New York
Tanya Bonakdar, New York
Niels Borch Jensen, Berlin
Gavin Brown's enterprise, New York
Daniel Buchholz, Cologne
Cabinet, London
Rebecca Camhi, Athens
Luis Campaña, Cologne
Gisela Capitain, Cologne
Massimo De Carlo, Milan
China Art Objects, Los Angeles
Pepe Cobo, Seville
James Cohan, New York
Sadie Coles HQ, London
John Connelly Presents, New York
Corvi-Mora, London
Counter, London
CRG, New York
Chantal Crousel, Paris
D'Amelio Terras, New York
Sorcha Dallas, Glasgow
Thomas Dane, London
doggerfisher, Edinburgh
Eigen + Art, Leipzig/Berlin
Foksal, Warsaw
Fortes Vilaça, San Paulo
Marc Foxx, Los Angeles
Stephen Friedman, London
Frith Street, London
Gagosian, London
Galerist, Istanbul
Gladstone, New York
Marian Goodman, New York
Greene Naftali, New York
greengrassi, London
Karin Guenther Nina Borgmann, Hamburg
Enrique Guerrero, Mexico City
Jack Hanley, San Francisco
Haunch of Venison, London
Hauser & Wirth, Zurich
Herald Street, London
Hotel, London
Taka Ishii, Tokyo
Jablonka, Cologne
Jablonka Lühn, Cologne
Alison Jacques, London
Martin Janda, Vienna
Johnen + Schöttle, Cologne
Annely Juda Fine Art, London
Iris Kadel, Karlsruhe
Georg Kargl, Vienna
Magnus Karlsson, Stockholm
Paul Kasmin, New York
francesca kaufmann, Milan
Kerlin, Dublin
Anton Kern, New York
Peter Kilchmann, Zurich
Nicole Klagsbrun, New York
Klosterfelde, Berlin
Johann König, Berlin
Tomio Koyama, Tokyo
Koyanagi, Tokyo
Andrew Kreps, New York
Krinzinger, Vienna
Krobath Wimmer, Vienna
kurimanzutto, Mexico City
Yvon Lambert, Paris
Gebr. Lehmann, Dresden
Lehmann Maupin, New York
Lisson, London
Luhring Augustine, New York
maccarone inc., New York
Kate MacGarry, London
Mai 36, Zurich
Maisonneuve, Paris
Giò Marconi, Milan
Matthew Marks, New York
Meyer Kainer, Vienna
Meyer Riegger, Karlsruhe
Massimo Minini, Brescia
Victoria Miro, London
The Modern Institute, Glasgow
Jan Mot, Brussels
MW projects, London
Michael Neff, Frankfurt
Neu, Berlin
Franco Noero, Turin
Giti Nourbakhsch, Berlin
bob van orsouw, Zurich
Patrick Painter Inc., Los Angeles
Maureen Paley, London
Paragon Press, London
Parkett, Zurich
peres projects, Los Angeles
Emmanuel Perrotin, Paris
Francesca Pia, Bern
pkm, Seoul
Postmasters, New York
Eva Presenhuber, Zurich
Produzentengalerie, Hamburg
The Project, New York
Raucci/Santamaria, Naples
Almine Rech, Paris
Daniel Reich, New York
Anthony Reynolds, London
Thaddaeus Ropac, Salzburg
Andrea Rosen, New York
Sonia Rosso, Turin
Salon 94, New York
Aurel Scheibler, Cologne
Esther Schipper, Berlin
Gabriele Senn, Vienna
Stuart Shave | Modern Art, London
Sommer Contemporary Art, Tel-Aviv
Pietro Spartà, Chagny
Sperone Westwater, New York
Sprüth Magers Lee, London
Luisa Strina, San Paulo
Studio Guenzani, Milan
Sutton Lane, London
Micheline Szwajcer, Antwerp
Timothy Taylor, London
Emily Tsingou, London
Two Palms Press, New York
Vilma Gold, London
Waddington, London
Nicolai Wallner, Copenhagen
Barbara Weiss, Berlin
Fons Welters, Amsterdam
White Cube/Jay Jopling, London
Barbara Wien, Berlin
Wilkinson, London
Christina Wilson, Copenhagen
The Wrong Galley, New York
XL, Moscow
Donald Young, Chicago
Zero, Milan
David Zwirner, New York
Media sponsor
The Guardian
Main sponsor
Deutsche Bank

CABINET BACK ISSUES

Available back issues (pictured here) are $10 each + shipping.
Shipping rates: US $2 per issue; Can & Mex $7 for 1, 2, or 3 issues; Eur, Au, & NZ $9 for 1, 2, or 3 issues.
Note: tax-deductible donations of $250 or more will be thanked with a sold-out issue (2, 3, 4, 5, 7, 9, 10, or 11) of the donor's choice. Supplies limited.

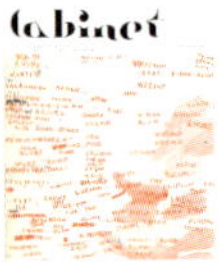

Issue 1
Invented Languages + CD

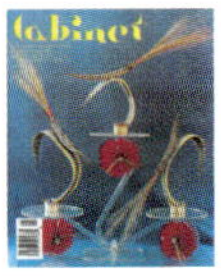

Issue 6
Horticulture + Lisa Young Poster

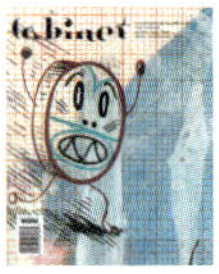

Issue 8
Pharmacopia + Postage Stamps + Vadim Fishkin Globe

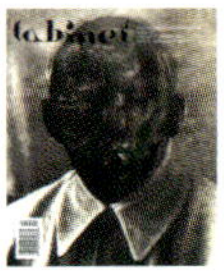

Issue 12
The Enemy

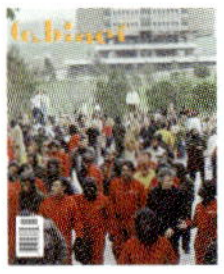

Issue 13
Futures + CD

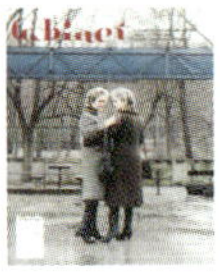

Issue 14
Doubles

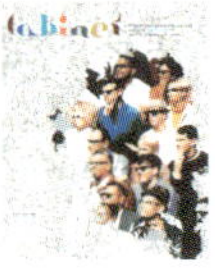

Issue 15
The Average + Rutherford Chang Poster

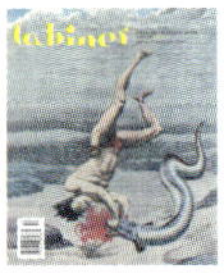

Issue 16
The Sea

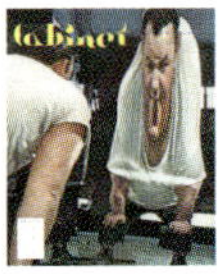

Issue 17
Laughter

CABINET LIMITED EDITIONS

Priced postpaid to US destinations
For international rates, email orders@cabinetmagazine.org

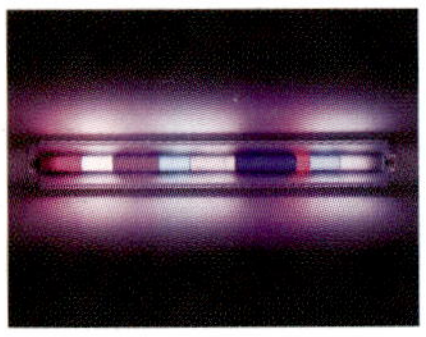

Moonlight (Luna County, New Mexico, July 13, 2003), 2003
by Spencer Finch
fluorescent light with colored filters (24 x 3 x 3 in.)
100 signed, numbered pieces; built by the artist
SOLD OUT

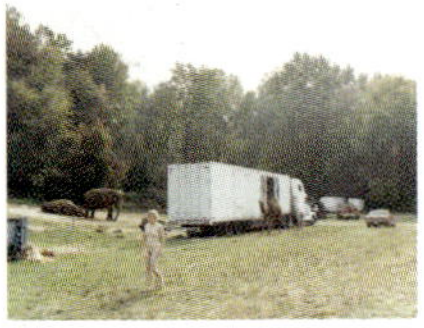

Circus Scene, 2002
by Justine Kurland
C-print (16 x 20 in.)
100 signed, numbered pieces; printed by the artist
$600

CABINET BOOKS

Special postpaid price to US & international destinations

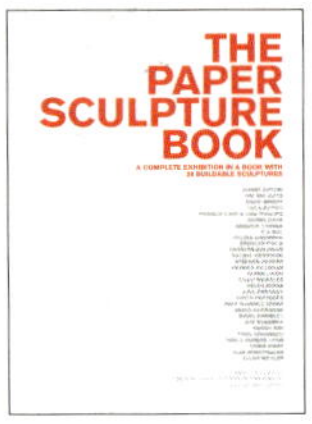

The Paper Sculpture Book
Do-It-Yourself paper sculptures by 29 artists,
all commissioned especially for this volume
160 pages, most removable
13.25" x 9.75"
Price: $27 (US); $35 (Can & Mex); $45 (Other)
Subscribers: Subtract an additional $5

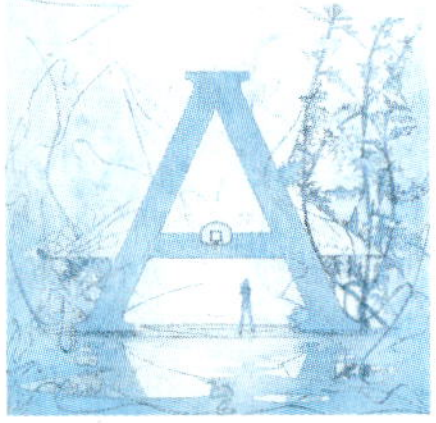

Letters from Mayhem
Illustrations by Roger Andersson, text by Albert Mobilio.
P is for *Pot* and *L* for *Loser* in this book, which depicts adolescence hovering between innocence and experience.
64-page boardbook abecedarium
10" x 10"
Price: $27 (US); $35 (Can & Mex); $45 (Other)
Subscribers: Subtract an additional $5

CABINET UNLIMITED EDITIONS

Priced postpaid to US destinations
For international rates, email orders@cabinetmagazine.org

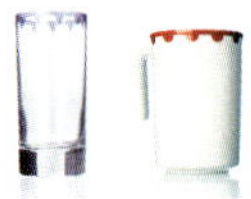

Weather Mugs and Glasses
by Bigert & Bergström (from Issue 3, *Weather*)
$15 each

Glow-in-the-dark Evil/Exit vinyl sign
by Vincent Mazeau (from Issue 5, *Evil*)
$25

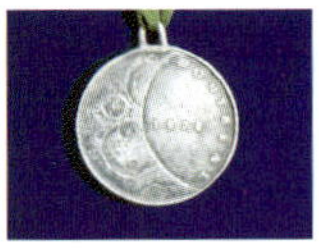

Olympic consolation medal
by Kris Lee (from Issue 7, *Failure*)
$50

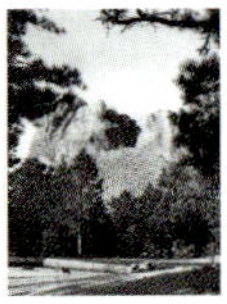

A view of Mount Rushmore in 500,000 years
poster by Matthew Buckingham
(from Issue 7, *Failure*)
$15 — ships rolled

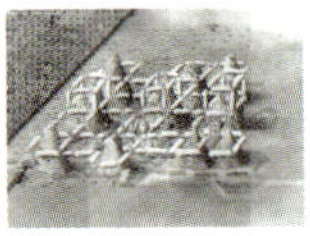

Acumulus Nobilitatus poster
poster by Paul Noble (from Issue 10, *Property*)
$15 — ships rolled

HOW TO ORDER

1 Mail a check to "Cabinet" 181 Wyckoff St Brooklyn NY 11217
2 Shop online at www.cabinetmagazine.org/shop
3 Fax Cabinet at +1 718 222 3700.
4 Call Cabinet at +1 718 222 8434.

Checks must be in US dollars and drawn on a US bank.
Cabinet accepts Visa, MC, AmEx, and Discover. The website also accepts PayPal.